The 8-Week Startup
How to Start Your Business in Just 8 Weeks

EDDY HOOD

Published in Layton, UT by The 8-Week Startup, LLC.

This title may be purchased in bulk for educational, business, fund-raising, or sales promotional use. For information, please e-mail support@the8weekstartup.com

ISBN: 978-0615721309
Printed in the United States of America

DEDICATION

For Tiffany. You are my best friend and my motivation in life. I love you.

CONTENTS

WORKSHOP 1: WHAT IS AN 8-WEEK STARTUP?

"I Want to Celebrate and Live My Life"

Taio Cruz, Rokstarr - Dynamite

That's it. You've had it. The cubicle is feeling smaller than ever before and your boss is being a real douche bag today. How much longer can you take this before you walk away from it all and lock yourself up in a tight little cell?

After all, you were meant for so much more. You know that working for your current company will never make you rich. Let's face it... Do you know anyone with a day job that is even close to the road of plenty? I'm not talking about your neighbors that are making a six-figure income at a high-paying desk job. Even if you were like them, would you really feel rich? They probably work hours on end for little fulfillment... Ah, there is the magic word. Fulfillment. Also, did you notice that I said "day job"? If you're reading this book, then you're probably like me in saying that "day job" is such an ugly term; nay, a swear word for the masses. It's got goo dripping all over it.

Yes, owning a business is the fastest and, in my humble opinion, surest way to make a lot of money. However, that's not the only reason we jump the corporate ship. We jump because we're in search of so much more than having some boss tell us what to do all the time. We are humans. We have the undeniable need to make a difference. We can hear it calling inside of us every day. We hear it in rush hour traffic as we look over and see all the other miserable drivers trying to get home after a particularly long day. We hear it when we look at our kids, our time, and ourselves in the mirror.

It's brutal. Trust me... I know. I've been there. The worst part is that you often feel like there's nothing you can do about it. You have too many things to do, not enough money, a petrified spouse, a slew of kids that poke at your insanity, and blah, blah, blah. You feel like the world has caved in around you and life's choices up to this point have buried you in deep. So here you are, up to your neck in a pile of crap... right? I'm here today to say that your assumption is completely wrong.

You have started on a course that within eight weeks will forever change who you are and what you will accomplish. I am honored to be on this journey with you for many reasons. First and foremost, I love to see people succeed, and I can't wait to see you take your turn. There is absolutely nothing better than realizing you have nothing to lose, stepping out onto that invisible ledge, and finding that there is indeed a footing... however unsure you may be about it.

Starting a business can scare you to death. But isn't that the joy of it? If you die tomorrow, will you honestly be happy with your life as you have lived it up to this point? I am guessing that you would probably wish you had more time. Most people would. In fact, I would too. Now you're saying, "Eddy, you're supposed to be the coach here! Aren't you supposed to be the one that's got it figured out?" Before you get your underwear all tied up, let me say that those who have stepped out onto that invisible ledge and lived to tell the tale learn a simple truth: **that it was the greatest experience of their lives**. Even though I have done it time and again, if I died right now I would still want more time so that I could step off more cliffs to feel the thrill of flying again and again.

So, let's get back to you, and why you're here. If you are like most Americans, the thought of owning your own business is sexy. It's rogue. It inspires images of superheroes and Greek Gods doing what the masses fear doing for themselves. It means freedom. It means money. It means responsibility for creating a better economy within your community.

All of that is possible and more unless you set up a business incorrectly. I've gone down that road before, and it's not pretty. There will be more on this business in workshop 10 when we get to scalability. Don't worry; it didn't take me for all I was worth. Let's just say that it was a good learning experience. Wink, wink.

Being an entrepreneur means great responsibility. You will have freedom and yes, you'll make a lot more money than you are right now if you use your head, along with some of the tips and tricks I teach you in this workshop. The point I want to address is that people conjure up images of entrepreneurs as folks with no responsibility. They see them as the ones who come up with great ideas and then profit by sitting on a beach. Don't get me wrong. I want you sitting on a beach while your business hums and churns. I just don't want you sitting there if your business is irresponsible.

So what is an eight-week startup? I came up with the idea one night after consulting with Brandt Page, CEO of Launch Leads – an amazing company that acts as an outsourced sales department for businesses nationwide. I was working with Brandt on developing a business strategy to help the company set proper investment levels for payroll costs given the output of the business.

Brandt and I had both competed in an entrepreneurial contest called Junto in 2008. Junto was a bit like being on The Apprentice and Survivor all at the same time. Hundreds of entrepreneurs entered the contest and 20 were picked, of which Brandt and I were two. Those 20 then went on an eight-week adventure that tested every nerve in our entrepreneurial hearts. We were put through several entrepreneurial challenges and then would have to report back each week in front of a huge community audience as to how we did.

The hardest challenge in my mind was approaching random strangers in the grocery store to raise capital for a business idea. I remember feeling like a total idiot as I asked some lady in the produce aisle if I could have $5,000 for a new business I was working on. Needless to say, she didn't cough up the dough but it was a learning experience for sure. Greg Warnock, the founder of Junto and a man that deserves my upmost respect, was trying to teach me a simple lesson. One of the key tools in an entrepreneur's box is the ability to ask. Not just for money, but for time, faith, emersion, hope, energy, resources, commitment, and success. From that moment on, I learned that if I didn't ask…I wouldn't receive.

In the end, 5 of the 20 entrepreneurs were selected as winners. Brandt and I stood on that podium together and felt truly alive. I was on a high.

As Brandt and I reflected on those eight weeks, I sat back in my chair and realized that with the right training, tools, and recipe, *anyone* could start a great business in the same amount of time. My brain started spinning as I reviewed my entrepreneurial career. I began to think of where I had succeeded and where I hadn't. When I did succeed, what did I do right? I then started thinking about all of the CEOs with whom I have consulted around the world, from manufacturing companies in Germany to medical institutes in Florida and even multi-million dollar property management firms in New York City. Here is the cool thing… They all started in their garages. Just like you. At one point, they got sick of the rat race and took a chance on themselves. You are about to do the same. Now don't worry… You won't be asked to raise $5,000 in the produce aisle. If you do manage to muster up the courage to do it, though, I want to hear about it. Send your amazing stories to stories@the8weekstartup.com. I will be checking that email personally and will respond to every entrepreneur's story I get. Even if you don't hit the produce aisle, know this: You will have homework. It won't be the kind that requires lots of text book reading. Instead, I am going to have you out on the streets, making it happen.

WARNING: If that last sentence scared you, put down this book and run away screaming.

Are you still here??? I sure hope so. I was just starting to like you. It would be a shame to see you go so soon. Well, high fives all around for sticking it out. If we were together in person, I'd give you a chest bump, like we do in one of my businesses.

Criteria for an 8-Week Startup

An 8 week startup, in my mind, is an ideal platform for a great business. If I were to bullet out what such a business would look like, here is what I would say:

- Costs less than $500 to test
- Costs less than $5,000 to start
- Has a clear and direct use to a specific group of people (no broad spectrum businesses here please)
- Allows you as the owner to remove yourself and oversee operations
- Is scalable (more on this later)
- Is automated where possible
- Is amazingly interesting to the entrepreneur
- Has high profit margins

Here is my question to you. If you could have a business that met these criteria, would you put in the time over the next eight weeks to get it done? If so, keep reading. If not then stop. Go back to the cubicle and keep dreaming of your life-to-be. I don't mean to be forceful, but it's necessary. If entrepreneurs have one quality in common that makes them the ultra-successful, it's the ability to get off the couch and act.

There is a secret in acting though. I just gave it to you. Did you catch it? To act as an entrepreneur is really just acting like you know what you're doing. Most of the time, we truly don't have a clue what we are doing. We fail, and in failing we learn. If you are scared of failing, you may not be the entrepreneur you hoped you would be. When you start your business you are going to make some really stupid mistakes. The truth is that that's how you make money. You find out what doesn't work and you do the opposite.

If you know upfront that you're going to make mistakes and you embrace that then we are going to have a great time. This workshop is designed to help you navigate through a lot of the mistakes entrepreneurs make. So rest assured that you are on the right path. However, you'll find you own ways to venture off the beaten path and when that happens, just get back on.

How to use this program

The 8 Week Startup is organized into 40 workshops. I wrote the system with the thought that you would take time each weekday to complete one of the workshops. It should take you about an hour in total. Monday through Friday, take the time to invest in this commitment to yourself by dedicating time, preferably in the morning, to sculpting your new business and future.

Here is how each workshop is set up:

1. **Tips & Tricks:** This is the "how-to" section in both written and MP3 format. I suggest that you dedicate time to printing off the workshop, reading it, and taking the time to truly ponder what is being taught.
2. **Watch and Learn:** There is a 5-10 minute video in each workshop that covers the tips & tricks in action. Watch these videos as many times as you need. Note that this section is only available to online subscribers at http://www.the8weekstartup.com

3. **Action Work**: Here is the fun part. At the end of each workshop, you will have homework. This is where you win or lose. If you do the tasks, you'll end up with a business at the end of 8 weeks that will generate income. If you don't do the homework, you'll just be another statistic. Just in case you didn't know... being a statistic really sucks.

Why Should I Listen to You?

You may be asking yourself what a 31-year-old could possible teach you about starting and growing a business. It's a fair question. Let me start off by saying that my system is not the only way to go about starting a business. There are a million people out there who have started and run their own companies. You can reach out to them to get help if you would like. In fact, I suggest that you do. My perspective comes from getting my knees bloody, writing down what works and what doesn't, and sharing it.

Let me tell you a little bit about myself before we move on so that you can understand my point of view. And trust me, I've seen the gamut.

I grew up in a trailer park raised by the best mother I could possibly hope for. When I was two years old, my parents got a divorce and I was allowed to see my dad every other weekend. Neither of my parents went to college, and I was an only child. This meant that when mom went to work to support us, I was often home alone. That gave me a lot of time to think, learn independence, and talk to myself – a bad habit that an only child can pick up. My wife still looks at me weird when she catches me talking to myself. You would think that after 10 years of marriage she would get used to it, but, hey... Who's complaining?

As I got older, my dad and step-mother got into substance abuse. I'm not talking about alcohol and cigarettes, although there was plenty of that, too. They got into some pretty heavy stuff. As a boy, I grew up watching many of their friends come to the house in a dazed rage of drug-induced mania. I remember seeing one of them collapse on the floor smashing her head on the coffee table and lying in a pool of blood. It scared the tar out of me. Really. After watching them, I decided that I was never going to go down that road. I spent many a night hiding in my bedroom with my door locked afraid of who was on the other side. I am proud to say that after many years of recuperation, my father and step-mother are clean and have gotten their lives in order. I couldn't be more proud of them.

As high school passed, I was never a popular or ultra-cool kid. I just made it through by jamming in my rock band and trying to pick good friends.

Since both of my parents never attended college, entering that world was both uncertain and impossible. How was a trailer park kid going to pay for all of this? Deep down, I knew that I always wanted to start a business, but I had no idea of how to do that. It seemed like such a monumental task that was reserved for only the best and brightest that Harvard had to offer.

I was married at 21. My wife told me one day that if I got a Master's Degree in Business, she would stand by me when I started a company. That was all I needed. Once the spouse was on board, I had steam. For the next five years, I worked my tail off and received a Bachelor's Degree in Accounting from The University of Utah. I then spent another two years finishing up an MBA from Weber State University.

During the entire stint, I only took two semesters off: one to have my first son Ethan, and the second to build my first house. Needless to say, college was a whirlwind of insanity and late nights, with nothing more than business dreams feeding me.

I remember my graduation vividly. It was a bright sunny day and there I was in my cap and gown with my beautiful wife. Her mother asked us to pose for a picture and right before she clicked the button, I leaned over and whispered "Are you ready to start that business?" in her ear. The look on her face was priceless. Maybe she never remembered making the promise so many years ago, or maybe she had hoped that I had forgotten. Well, I didn't forget.

Let me just say that spouses are often pretty tentative of marrying entrepreneurs, and rightfully so. I am so lucky to have married my wife. She is patient and supportive of even my dumbest ideas. Yes, I too have dumb ideas. Just as Babe Ruth swung more than any other player in the game to get the most home runs, a good entrepreneur never stops dreaming.

The next day, I began planning my company. At the time I was working as an auditor for a local CPA firm. I know… It was truly a sexy job. Blah. To be honest, I hated it with such a passion. The firm was great, but I was working 60 to 70 hours a week and getting paid peanuts to do it. I was making $30,000 a year, which is around $9.00 to $10.00 an hour for the time I was putting in. Not a great rate for someone with a Master's Degree. I remember sitting at my desk and thinking, I'm made for so much more than this. And I was.

How awesome it is to look back and know that I walked into my boss's office two weeks later and quit. Talk about a feeling of wild power. I remember walking to his office thinking to myself, "Holy crap… Holy crap… Holy crap… Holy crap". I stepped off of that ledge and had no idea of what I might find. Yes I had a plan, but plans are just that - plans. Once you put a plan into action, that stomach acid thing starts to happen and your butt cheeks tighten up a little. Sometimes so much that it hurts. I know mine did.

Here I am now, three and half years later at 31 years old and guess what? I'm still kicking. As a matter of fact, I am earning an income I never though was possible, I have five offices around the country from Spokane, Washington to Cedar Rapids, Iowa. I am a public speaker, author, entrepreneur, Jeeper, Junto Partner, Grow America Springboard finalist, song writer and lead guitarist, gym addict, chef in training and best of all… father and husband to the greatest kids and wife this world has ever seen. In my travels, I have consulted with hundreds of CEOs around the world, helped them to grow their companies, and had a blast doing it.

I can guarantee you this – If I hadn't stepped off that cliff three and a half years ago I can tell you exactly where I would be right now. I would be sitting at my desk, making $40,000 a year gunning for a partner position to come my way if I were to sweat, kiss butt, and give it all I had for the next 20 years of my imprisoned life. Even then, I think about what it would have been like to become a partner. Sure I would have made a good wage, but I would have been miserable. I would have been tied to that desk on holidays, during baseball games, and grid locked from 9 a.m. to 5 p.m. I would not have been free to create. To build my world as I see it. To own my life.

So, what life will you create for yourself?

Stop.

Read that question again. It is the most important part of this workshop. Let's make this easier. Fill in the homework space below and be unreasonable. That's right. Be outlandish. I hate the goal setting techniques that say "set goals that are reasonable and reachable. Reasonable is boring. Reasonable is for the cubicle crew who think reasonable thoughts and then go on to live reasonable lives so that other reasonable people will approve of their reasonableness. "Better not step out of line and be great," they say.

The fact that you're here means that you have a little bit of unreasonableness in you. That's good. Let it out. Let it fester. Turn on some music, make it loud, do your homework and start down the path of changing your life. Get ready for a ride. You're starting a company and you'll be open for business in just eight weeks.

End of Workshop Surprise

To show you how important it is for an entrepreneur to act, I will be running the program myself at the same time so that you can watch. That's right – I will be starting a new business. All of the video that I will be producing for each workshop will walk you through the tips and tricks as I apply them to starting a real life business.

In all honesty, I have no idea what the business is going to be. It's going to be a lot of fun building it in front of you though. It's funny, as I type this I can feel that buzz in my stomach. It's the unknown that is ahead of me. I think it's also intensified knowing that I will be documenting it all and filming each stage so that you can follow along.

Know this: As I build this company I will undoubtedly make mistakes with it. I fully embrace that right now, knowing that it will help me to build a better company.

Action work: What life will you create?

Today's homework is about getting your mindset in the right place. You need to understand what you want from this whole thing. It's fine to say that you want to start a business, but unless you know what drives you, then you may end up like the many who dream and the few who do. I know I sound like a broken record, but I don't care. Entrepreneurs act. They do. They learn. They do again. In that process, you'll get discouraged occasionally, which is why you need to dig deep here and really understand why you want to do this. In the end, even though starting a business can be challenging, you'll step back once it's built and it will be yours. You will have built your kingdom. It will be a kingdom that no one but yourself could have architected, so don't give up. It will be worth it. I promise.

Answer the following questions unreasonably. Think big. This is your life after all.

What life will you create for yourself?

_____

_____

_____

_____

_____

_____

_____

_____

_____

_____

Define your commitment to the next eight weeks of your life and this program:

_____

_____

_____

_____

_____

_____

_____

_____

_____

_____

_____

Today's Action: 50 Reasons for Getting Started

Action is an entrepreneur's best quality. Remember that. At the end of each workshop, don't skip the action. Do it. These are the steps that will move you closer and closer to opening your doors for business.

Write down 25 reasons for why you need to start this business right now:

1.

2.

3.

4.

5.

6.

7.

8.

9.

10.

11.

12.

13.

14.

15.

16.

17.

18.

19.

20.

21.

22.

23.

24.

25.

Tony Robbins is one of my favorite authors. If you haven't read his work, get into it after this program. It's worth the investment. At any rate, he talks about the importance of writing down how you will benefit from achieving your goals. The more reasons you write down, the more your psyche believes that you must make it happen. Think about it. You'll see more pleasure in doing it than in not doing it. If you only have one reason to start a business, then you'll probably give up after a few days or so. If you have a ton of reasons for ending the monotony and getting that business going, then you'll be unstoppable.

p.s. Today it's your turn. Today you start that which you have put off out of excuse. Today you live and celebrate the life you know is yours.

WORKSHOP 2: Finding the Right Idea for Your Business

"In Preparing for battle, I have always found that plans are useless, but planning is indispensable."

-Dwight D. Eisenhower

When you finally decide that you're going to start a business, the next and most inevitable question is always, "What the heck am I going to do?" That's when the fear starts to creep in. What if your business is a bad idea? What if nobody pays you for your product or service? Heaven forbid, what if your family and friends laugh at you? Oh, the horror of it all.

Before you beat yourself up too much, let me bolster you by saying that this workshop will address those issues. We're going to have a lot of fun in this one. By the end of the day, you are going to walk away with over 50 business ideas. You heard me. 50. Not one.

From those 50 ideas, we will move into the next workshop by selecting the five that appeal to us the most. Then we will begin testing them in the market for viability. Are you salivating yet? This isn't going to be as hard as you think, either. I can hear the complaints right now: "But Eddy, coming up with even one business idea feels impossible." I know it does, but that's because you're going about it all wrong. To help out, you'll have access to The 8-Week Idea Map, a worksheet I've developed to help you move through the thought process efficiently, generate a lot of business ideas, and have a great time doing it.

So, no complaining. You're only allowed to have fun with this. Understood?

As you move through the workshop, I want you to notice how you feel as an entrepreneur. For many people, the exercise you are about to do will be completely new to you. It will open your mind to how successful entrepreneurs think, act and move in short timeframes. I am curious to know if going through these exercises filled you with energy or completely overwhelmed you. If you are a member at The8WeekStartup.com, jump on the forums when you are done and let us know how you faired.

The wrong way to come up with a business idea

As with most things in life, there is a right way to do things, and a wrong way to do them. Coming up with business ideas is no different. Most people never get past the idea phase because they get stuck trying to find that million-dollar idea.

Let me give you an example of the wrong way. When I was in college, I had an entrepreneurial class where we were charged to come up with business ideas. Needless to say, this was a homework assignment that almost everyone was excited about. To make things easier, as well as more fruitful, I got together with three other students in the class and called a late night pizza party at my home where we would try to come up with a bunch of ideas.

At the time it sounded great. The thought of having a bunch of guys in one room brainstorming on different ideas seemed like the best way to start making our millions. After all, more brains equals more brain power… right? Well, not always.

Here is how the evening turned out: Before the night started, I couldn't turn my brain off. I was doing everything I could to try and think of ideas. Any remote possibility was written down in a small notepad that I kept in my back pocket. Easy.

The doorbell rang and in sauntered my three business-building buddies with pizzas in hand. We got to work almost immediately. If you know anything about me, it's that I cannot work without a whiteboard. I love writing ideas down, brainstorming, and visually mapping them out. So I grabbed a marker and manned the whiteboard ready for ideas. Good stuff. This was going to be a great night. I truly planned on hundreds of ideas by the end of the evening.

Once everyone got seated, I opened with the obvious question. "All right guys, we are here tonight to come up with great business ideas for our class project. What have you got?" I swear to you now, I have never heard crickets chirping so loudly. There was dead silence as everyone looked around, waiting for grand entrepreneurial inspiration.

One of the guys suggested we get up and walk around the house to see what products were around that might inspire us. Well, that was a better idea than just sitting and waiting for inspiration to strike. So we all got up and walked around. It was somewhat productive, but still not very useful. By the end of the night, we had a few ideas on the board, a missing pizza, hurt egos, and a lot of frustration.

Have you ever had a similar experience? Can you tell what we did wrong? We did what most would be entrepreneurs do. We determined that we wanted to start a business and then asked ourselves, "What idea is the perfect idea?" Let me start off by saying that that is a very stupid question. It is a question that I asked myself many times when I got started in business building. It's wrong for so many reasons, including that fact that it's vague and unattainable. There is a lot of pressure that comes along with trying to think of the perfect business.

Have no fear. There is a much better way to go about this. Let me just say that if you have ever found yourself sitting on the couch trying to think of the next big business idea, you are wasting your time. You need get organized and follow a process that will allow you to generate the largest amount of qualified ideas in the shortest amount of time possible.

Before we get into how to go about doing this, we need to take a minute to understand the true purpose of a business.

What is the purpose of a business, anyway?

A great business is not a magical pill or a fantasy in a far off land that is only attainable by the most creative of souls. In order to get the ideas flowing, you need to start with a good understanding of what a business really is. I know this sounds basic, but hang in there; it's important.

A business exists for one reason only: to solve a problem.

For some reason, we complicate this beyond all measure. We start thinking of businesses as places of social impact, cash machines, ego boosters, vehicles for giving us freedom, customer service centers, and on and on and on. Sure, many of these things come naturally from a company's growth, but at its core, a business does nothing more than to solve a problem. If it can't do that, it's useless. Is it any wonder that so many people go out of business? I would argue that too many businesses are built off the wrong premise. For example, most people think "Hey, I can build doors so I am going to start a door building business." That may be a great idea, however if your door business just builds doors and doesn't solve a problem, you'll be closing the doors on your business sooner than you planned.

Create solutions, not demand

In his book, *The Four-Hour Work Week*, author Tim Ferris addresses something that I consider to be crucial to business development: the premise of creating solutions and not demand.

When people generate business ideas the wrong way, they often come up with a few that, to them, make a great deal of sense.

Once they come up with that "wow" idea, they rush out to start building the company. The excitement of having an idea becomes so intense that they often put blinders on, and cannot see the forest through the trees. In the quest to get started, they fail to see that there is no demand for their idea. However, their excitement and the pride they feel in their idea is so strong that they dismiss the research and tell themselves that once the business is open, people will buy. Really?

That is a losing battle. Once the entrepreneur does open the doors, he or she is faced with an uphill fight of getting people interested in the product or service. Doing so costs truckloads of cash. Given that our definition of a great startup says it shouldn't cost more than $5,000 to start. Blowing truckloads of cash isn't an option.

We assume that because we like the idea, everyone else will too. Not so.

Instead of starting a business that serves nobody, and then trying to create a demand for its product or service – find a specific problem with enough people asking for a solution and build a business to help them.

Identify your groups

So how do you come up with great business ideas? It starts with looking at yourself. I personally believe that you have to be passionate about your business to be able to wake up to it every day with a drive to grow it. With that being said, if I owned a business that sold nuts and bolts, I would probably gouge my eyes out – even it was making me a billionaire. Why? Because I couldn't care less about nuts and bolts.

During my failed pizza party extravaganza, this was one of our faults. We were just looking for business ideas; essentially anything that would make money and do it quickly. I once heard someone say that you don't have to love the service or product that your business creates; you only have to love being in business to do well. I think that guy should be kicked in the shins with steel-toed boots. What a dumb thing to say. Can you imagine waking up each morning thinking to yourself, "Wahoo! I get to go to my company to make a product or service that's boring. Hot dog! I can't wait!"

So here is my question to you: Who are you? What groups are you a part of? What do you do with your time? Don't be lame and say "Nothing". A lot of people shortlist their life to nothing more than work, sleep, and raising kids. Get real. You have passions, even if you don't have gobs of time to dedicate to them every day. Maybe you're a bass fisherman, tennis player, amateur chef, secretive nose picker, body builder, dancer, arm wrestler, Kung Fu artist, poet, etc. What the heck are you? My challenge to you is to write out 25 different groups that you're involved in. Also, groups like "Dad" or "Grandma" don't count. Even though you may be a dad, it's too broad. A Kung Fu artist is much more specific and interesting. Now, if you are the dad of a child born with Down syndrome, that is more specific.

Here is where you need to list every aspect of your life. I want you to really take some time to get it all out on paper. Note that you don't have to be active in these groups to list them. Just because you don't play piano 23 hours a day doesn't mean you can't list "piano player" if you only play once a month or so. Are you ready? Let's do it!

What are the 25 groups that make you who you are? List them in this workbook below.

1.

2.

3.

4.

5.

6.

7.

8.

9.

10.

11.

12.

13.

14.

15.

16.

17.

18.

19.

20.

21.

22.

23.

24.

25.

If you didn't get all 25, go back and figure it out. This is really important. I know it's hard to come up with that many, but do it.

Why am I asking these questions? Because understanding what groups you run with is the basis for coming up with great business ideas. These are the things that you're both passionate and knowledgeable about. Being knowledgeable about something means that you are one step closer to understanding the problems that abound in that group.

In writing this, I can't help but think of a very specific group of people: elk hunters. My dad and brother are steeped in it. Every year, they go up into the mountains in search for that trophy elk. If you have ever done it, you know that it's hard work. Let's use them as an example as we move through this workshop.

Top Ten

Now that we know who you are, or rather, *you* know who you are, we can get started. Just out of curiosity, was that last exercise enlightening at all? For many, it's a lot of fun to see what they truly represent beyond just work, sleep, and kids. It's nice to know that you have an identity after all, isn't it?

From that list of 25 groups, what I want you to do is pick the ten groups that interest you the most. Don't worry; you can change your mind at any time. For now, though, it's going to be important that we start honing in on some of the data.

Guidelines for picking your top ten:

- Chose the 10 groups that interest you the most
- Ask yourself "If I had a business that addressed a need in that group, would I be motived to grow it every day?"
- Given what you know about that group, do they spend money?
- Are the problems, struggles and difficulties of that group succinct enough that you could create a business to help them?

From the perspective of our elk hunters, my father and brother have enough interest to support a business in that field if they started it. I know they would be motivated to grow it every day because they talk about elk constantly. Knowing elk hunters and watching my family members in action, I know that that group of people spends money. They spend a lot of money, actually. The real question to ask is, "Do the elk hunters of the world have enough problems that we could create a business to help them out?" Maybe.

What problems do your groups face and why?

Elk hunters do have problems when it comes to their craft. From talking with my father and brother, I know that one of the biggest problems is smell. This is where I throw in the joke that my dad and brother stink... I know. What I am really trying to say though is that elk can smell you coming from a mile away, especially if the wind is against you. So what do elk hunters do? They spray elk urine all over themselves. Sounds like fun. All kidding aside, if you want to get your elk, your human smell is a real problem. Now, I know that there are a lot of businesses out there that sell hunting gear. In doing so, part of their inventory includes elk urine spray.

Most elk hunters wanting to start a business would find themselves trying to compete directly with the major online hunting stores by selling hunting gear. What if they didn't do that, though? What if they built an online store that specialized in elk urine? The store would feature multiple brands, scents, etc. and be the one stop shop for masking smells. Instantly that store would stand out on the internet as the premier place for hunters to go to camouflage their human odor. I don't know about you, but I can't think of a store out there that specializes in elk urine. Doing a quick Google search for "Buy elk urine" brings up a few online retailers, but nothing that scares me. You could create that store and actually compete to win.

This doesn't mean that it's a good business idea though. We still need to test the market which we will do in the next workshop.

Looking at your top ten groups, we want to come up with five problems for each group that are very targeted issues.

Please understand that the elk urine store is only an example that we will use in Workshops #2 and #3. It is not the business that I will be starting as we move through these workshops. Why? I don't find elk urine fascinating enough. Go figure.

Your assignment is to come up with 5 problems for each of your groups. Here are a few questions to help stimulate your thinking as you work on this:

1. What do people in the group complain about?
2. What bottlenecks make being a part of the group difficult?
3. What makes the group challenging for newcomers?
4. What keeps people from actively participating in the group in an ongoing basis?

5. What kind of people tend to join the group?
6. What keeps people from being successful in the group?

Brainstorm solutions

Having a good understanding of a group's problem structure is half the battle. Now we just need to brainstorm some solutions to those problems. This is actually the easy part. Once you know the problem, all you need to do is think of the opposite to find the solution.

Try to find unique ways to address the issues that the group faces, but don't feel like you have to have the perfect idea. Given that you came up with 5 problems for 10 different groups, you should have 50 problems sitting in front of you. As such, you need 50 solutions.

Action work: Fill Out The 8-Week Idea Map

If you are a member of The8WeekStartup.com and have purchased "WORKSHOP 2: Finding the Right Idea for Your Business", then you can download an Excel file of The 8-Week Idea Map. I have also copied a version of it below for you to review.

The purpose of The 8-Week Idea Map is to take everything we have talked about in this workshop and organize it into a single spreadsheet.

Take time to fill it out so that you can get your thoughts organized into one single spreadsheet. Once you fill it out, you'll have 50 business ideas that we can choose from in Workshop 3.

Have fun with this one!

8WeekStartup

The 8 Week Idea Map

Step #1: Define 50 Groups

Step #2: Choose the 10 most interesting

Step #3: Define 5 Problems for the 10 groups

Step #4: Choose 5 Problems to solve

WORKSHOP 3: Testing the Idea for Stupidity

"Ideas are the beginning point of all fortunes."

- Napoleon Hill

Not all ideas are good ideas

I have a lot of stupid business ideas. Fortunately, the technique that I will share with you in this chapter is the same technique I use to weed those ideas out of my head. Having a screening process in place to check your ideas against will save you a lot of money and heartache.

It's important to remember that everyone has stupid ideas. That's what makes the good ideas so good. I'm sure that filling out The 8-Week Idea Map in the last workshop led you to some pretty dumb ideas as well as some really good ones. It's our job now to put a risk-free system in place to test those ideas to see if they are worth pursuing.

If I told you that I had such a way of gazing through the crystal ball, would you be interested in the method? Then keep reading and prepare to clear the water.

Before we get into how this works and why, let's discuss why so many ideas out there don't turn out to be profitable businesses.

First of all, many entrepreneurs get so thought-locked on an idea that they are bound and determined to make it work. Often times, it's the first real idea that they have come up with and so they stick with it, not wanting to let it out of their sight. This causes blindness to other ideas that are actually much better.

Secondly, your idea might not have a clear and useful purpose to a specific market. Those are the business ideas you hear of that fail. You know the story of the entrepreneur who emptied out his or her nest egg, bet the family farm, and then stood aside and watched it all go up in a glorious blaze of fire. I hate to say it, but it happens all of the time.

I think it's interesting that all of us can look back in hindsight and say, "Well, yeah... That was a stupid idea. Of course nobody bought it." At the time, though, the entrepreneur couldn't see that because he was distracted by the excitement of finally doing his own thing. I hate it when that happens.

Thirdly, most entrepreneurs build their businesses at a desk instead of in the real world. What do I mean by this? Most people never leave their house when they start on the adventure of building a company. Instead, they sit inside and plan for weeks and weeks building 30 to 50 page business plans and making assumptions with regards to how the marketing will respond to their offering. In a later workshop, I will address why I hate business plans, and it's for this very reason. You don't have a clue about how the market will respond to your offering unless you get out there and talk to your market. Sitting at your desk and building ornate spreadsheets and pretty graphs will get you nowhere.

I do believe in having a business plan. Don't get me wrong. I just go about it in a different way, and yes, we cover how to build that plan in workshop #17.

Why you alone don't have a clue

So why is it so hard to tell if your idea is going to be a winner? In reality, it's not. The problem is that we go about it the wrong way. Let me give you some insight into my first business if I may. It was a great learning experience, but definitely not a good idea.

The company was called The Salty Tank. I had a love for saltwater aquariums when I was in my early 20's. I couldn't get enough of the fish and coral, and the overall beauty that they added to a home. So I spent about a year reading everything I could on how to build one and take care of it. During that time, I was saving up my money because they cost a fortune. I ended up building a 90-gallon aquarium and by the time I was done, I was into it about $4,000. Those are expensive pets.

At any rate, I was in love. As people came to my home, they oohed and ahhed every time they passed it. I couldn't help but think to myself that everyone on the planet was going to want one of these things. All I had to do was build it for them. So I started a small business while I was still in school. It only cost me about $1500 which was the only redeeming feature of the company besides the cool logo.

The purpose of the business was to design, build and maintain saltwater aquariums for people in my local and surrounding cities. It was going to be great. As far as I was concerned, I was going to make millions doing something I loved. Life couldn't get any better.

I placed a small and I got a call within the first week. Wahoo! I was on my way to becoming a bona fide business owner. The sales meeting went off with a bang and he became my first - and only - customer. Read on.

I took the order and began designing the aquarium. It was to be a 90-gallon tank that was going to be installed in his wall. Because I didn't have any buying power with suppliers, I only made about 15% on the project. Yuck. My goal, however, was to make that up on the maintenance. Almost everyone loves a saltwater aquarium until they have to care for it. The monthly maintenance seems to require a degree in chemistry, lots of physical exertion, and time. As such, most people don't take care of theirs or they hire a company to do it. My first customer signed a contract to have me do the maintenance work. I was golden… or so I thought.

Each month I would spend several hours at my customer's location, cleaning, testing chemical levels and water quality, and looking after the health of his fish and coral. It was fun the first few times. After that, I hated it. Each time I went, I made $50 after the cost of supplies and gas. Given that I was there for an average of 3 hours, I was making $17 an hour.

Each night my brain searched for ways to make the business turn more cash. At $17 an hour, I wasn't getting rich. In fact, I had started a business that would make me poor if I kept with it.

I didn't get more customers because I didn't want to work for $17 an hour. It was a lot of work to get that money and I simply couldn't see a way to automate the process. Sure, I could hire another college kid to do this on the side and clean for me. That created two new problems though:

1. I would have to pay him at least $10 an hour which would leave me with $7.
2. I would have to get someone who really knew what they were doing. Saltwater aquariums were complicated and if he messed up, I would be liable.

It was a nightmare. So I settled for one customer and tried to figure out how to get out of the contract and end my ill-fated business. I had no idea of how I was going to do it until the phone call came.

The call was from my customer. He had been very happy up to that point. Naturally, I was terrified when I heard the tone of his voice. He wasn't mad, but he was in a sheer panic. His house was flooding. I was at my day job at the time and instantly ran out the door, jumped in my car, and drove the 10.2 miles to get to his house as fast as I could. I thank my boss for not firing me that day. It was the worst day of my life. When I showed up, he was very patient with me as he showed me the aquarium.

I won't bore you with the technical details of how the flood occurred, just know that water was pouring onto the ground and going through the floor into the basement. Luckily, we caught the problem quickly and there was no lasting damage to anything other than a few ceiling tiles in the basement. I was fortunate enough to have the kindest customer ever. He let me off the hook knowing that I was young and stupid. We've all been there, right?

After that day, I showed the customer how to care for his aquarium and I left it in his hands. He was happy with his newfound responsibility of taking care of his pride and joy. I was happy to be free of the business.

Here are the lessons that I learned from that business:

1. Although I had a 50 page business plan, it was total garbage. I made so many assumptions in it that I shot myself in the foot.
2. I chose a business that forced me to do all the work if I was going to make any money.
3. I only had so much time in a day, which meant that I had a limit to how much I could earn.
4. I learned the pros and cons of a service based business.
5. I learned the value of my time.
6. I learned that a business can imprison you if it's built with a bad foundation.

In the end, I was lucky that I didn't get sued. What a disaster it was. Over the years, I have learned how to avoid some of these common pitfalls.

Here is where I failed in that business and why:

1. I assumed that it would be a great business because I was good at it and I liked the product.
2. I assumed that my time upfront was expendable and infinitely available.
3. I assumed that I could do the maintenance work faster and more efficiently than was the reality.
4. I assumed that the demand for my product was large, and that I would be making millions within just a few years...I never factored in the bottlenecks of a saltwater aquarium business.
5. I assumed that my business plan had calculated all the necessary costs of running a business.
6. I assumed, I assumed, and I assumed more.

Assuming what will happen in the future is a great way to set yourself up for a "real-world learning experience." So let's take some of the assumptions out of a business. During the latter half of this workshop, as well as in the next few, we will be testing our ideas before we jump in head first.

To truly get a good understanding of how strong your idea is, you need a tool that will help you access market data instantly and effectively without spending any money. Let's get after it.

How to see if there is interest in the market

Testing your idea is easy if you know where to look. As of this writing, Google is the mother of all information. People travel its data highways every day and they do it multiple times. How often do you turn to the all-seeing Google for help? Because people use Google for almost all of their searches, Google has important assets that we can exploit. Those assets are: knowledge, keywords, and number of searches per month.

Google may not always be the data behemoth. Who knows, five years from now there may be a new ruler in town. It doesn't matter who is the data king. All that matters is that you look under that data king's kimono as much as possible to get the inside scoop.

Here is how you do it:

1. Google the following phrase "Free Google Keyword Tool"
2. The keyword tool is most likely going to be the first non-paid search result. Click on it.

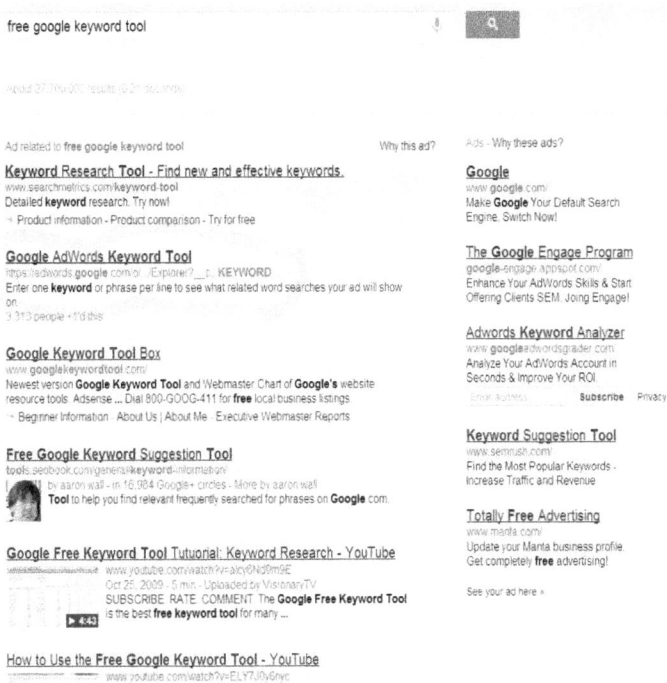

3. Click on the **[Exact]** match type in the left hand column. Leave **Broad** selected as well.

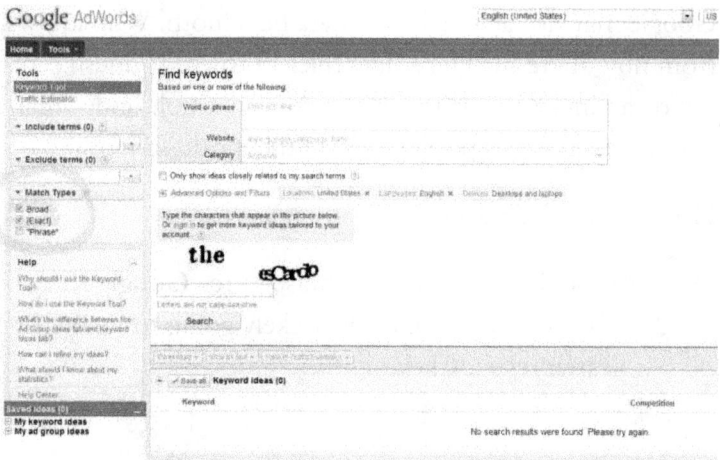

4. From the top 5 problems that you want to find a solution for, select one and start thinking like someone with that problem. Enter a search term or question in the **Word or Phrase** box. Then fill out the **captcha** and click **search**. Let's pretend that we're sticking with the elk urine company from workshop #2 as an example. I might search for "Buy Elk Urine".

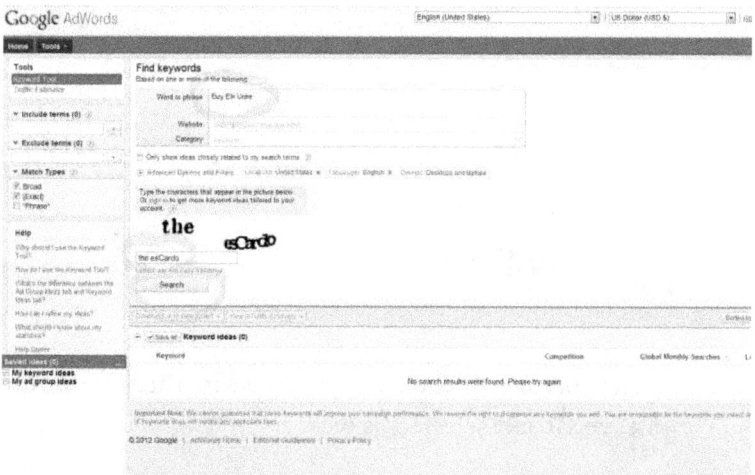

5. Analyze the results. What the tool is telling you is how many other people around the world search for that term each

month. If a lot of people are searching for it, then it's a popular topic. You have to be careful, however. Pay attention to the **competition** column as well. High competition will make it harder for you to get noticed as a new business. Here are the search results for our term, **buy elk urine**.

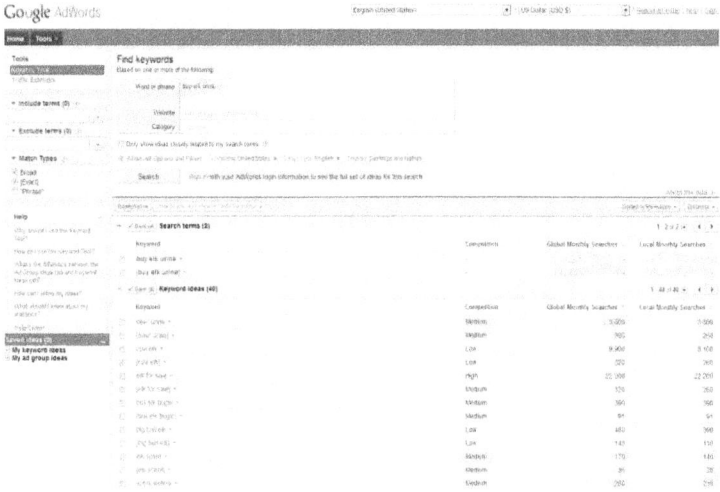

What Google is telling us about buying elk urine

So far, I am not seeing a promising business. Although we are serving a very specific need for a very specific group of people, there isn't a lot of demand for it. Here is how we can tell.

Notice the first two rows of data. One says **buy elk urine,** and the other one says **[buy elk urine]** in brackets. The one in brackets is an Exact Match. In other words, it represents the number of people that type into Google the exact words **buy elk urine**. As you look to the right, you'll notice that there isn't any data. This is because not enough people search that term for Google to be able to track it. In other words, nobody is looking online for it.

Also notice the term on the first row without the brackets. This is called a broad match type in Google lingo. What that represents are all the people that typed a search that contained the words **buy, elk** and **urine**, but that those terms were in no specific order and they may have been mixed with other words like **hunting** or **deer**.

When you look at the data from a broad match perspective, there should always be more searches per month than the exact search term in brackets. That makes sense because the board phrase match could include so many variations, while the exact phrase match only has one possibility.

Notice in row one that our broad match doesn't even have data. Apparently there aren't even people searching broadly for these terms online.

In other words, nobody cares.

Good thing you didn't rush off and start your elk urine company, huh? Be honest, you were thinking about it. But don't despair... There is more data on this page than just the first two rows. If you'll take a look the rows below, this is Google's attempt to show you similar searches, both broad and [exact], that might be of interest to you.

If you look at our search, you'll see:

Keyword	Competition	Global Monthly Searches	Local Monthly Searches
deer urine	Medium	3,600	3,600
[deer urine]	Medium	320	260

cow elk	Low	9,900	8,100
[cow elk]	Low	320	260
elk for sale	High	22,200	22,200
[elk for sale]	Medium	320	260
bull elk bugle	Medium	390	390
[bull elk bugle]	Medium	91	91
big bull elk	Low	480	390
[big bull elk]	Low	140	110
elk scent	Medium	170	140
[elk scent]	Medium	36	28
scent wafers	Medium	260	210
[scent wafers]	Medium	36	28
[deer urine smell]	Low	36	36
deer urine smell	Low	170	140
[elk urine]	Low	22	16
elk urine	Low	110	91
hunters specialities	Low	5,400	5,400
[hunters specialities]	Low	73	46

cow elk hunting	High	1,300	1,300
[cow elk hunting]	Medium	73	73
bull elk for sale	High	91	73
[bull elk for sale]	Medium	22	22
human odor	Low	5,400	3,600
[human odor]	Low	36	22
deer urine for sale	Medium	22	22
[deer urine for sale]	High	12	< 10
scent eliminators	High	1,300	1,000
[scent eliminators]	High	22	16
special ties	Low	14,800	12,100
[special ties]	High	46	16
rutting elk	Low	880	590
[rutting elk]	Low	28	16
[elk hunters]	High	16	16

elk hunters	Low	1,600	1,300
[elk rut season]	Low	12	< 10
elk rut season	Low	140	110
bear elk	Low	1,600	1,300
[bear elk]	Low	< 10	< 10

Notice that the second column is called **Competition**. This column is telling you how many websites out there are competing to be found for that given search term or keyword. The third column tells you how many people searched for that keyword last month on a global level, and the fourth column displays that same information on a local level.

We are looking for keywords that have medium or low competition with a decent number of searches monthly. If I really wanted to start a store that sells elk urine to mask a hunter's smell, I am not seeing any alternative keywords above that look remotely promising.

In the end, shoot for keywords with the following characteristics:

- Have a low or medium competition rating
- Have at least 500 searches a month

Ranking your ideas

Go through the above exercise for each of the 5 problems that you are interested in solving for a specific group of people. Don't try just one search term, though, like we did in the above example. We might have also tried **purchase elk urine** or **buy hunting scents**. Try a few, because you never know what the masses use as a search term for a given product or service. If you try several terms and none of them are producing low to medium competition with at least 500 searches a month, trash the idea and move on to the next one.

If you get through all five problems you're trying to solve and you can't find a winner, then go back to The 8-Week Idea Map, find five more problems from your bank of 50 ideas and start over.

Action work: Master the Google Keyword Tool

Take some time today to put this tool to use. Know that this isn't the only way to test market interest on a particular product or service, but it's sure a great way to do it for free. Thanks Google.

1. Grab your list from Workshop #2 that defines the five problems you want to solve
2. Open up the Google Adwords tool, crack your knuckles, and get started
3. Think of at least 10 different searches a customer might perform for each business
4. Run those searches and do your analysis to find strong interest and manageable competition
5. Pick a winner as your most prominent business idea or start over with new ideas if nothing turned out to be promising

As an entrepreneur, you always want to be aware of little tricks like this one. Free information is mana from heaven. Partake of its goodness and use it to grow a better company.

WORKSHOP 4: The S-D-B Formula and why it Works

"If You Build It, They Will Come"

- Field of Dreams

Marching into battle blindly

Who will come? If you go out and start that business who is going to buy from you besides your mom and your Uncle Harry? If you took workshop #3 seriously, then you're further along the path than most in knowing that there's at least some interest in your potential business.

Don't you find it funny that people talk about how risky owning a business is? As Warren Buffet once said, "Risk comes from not knowing what you're doing." How many entrepreneurs out there get an idea, put a lot of money into it, and then wish for the best without ever testing the market or talking to a future customer first? A lot of people have gone down this road, sadly.

Why do people do it? They do it because it's easier to just start the business and hope for the best. Think about it. Once you get an idea, that's the end of the "thinking phase". If you're going to do this correctly, now you actually have to go outside of your comfort zone.

Doesn't it make sense to take your idea to your target market and see if they'll buy first instead of investing everything you have and then hoping that people will magically show up? *Field of Dreams* was a great movie, but let's be honest... They won't come just because you built it. Then again, if you can get Kevin Costner to help you build your business… maybe they will.

If you think about it, starting a business without speaking to your customers first is like marching into battle blindly. Can you imagine being in charge of a vast army of faithful soldiers who would follow you into the depths of insanity if you ordered it?

Pretend, if you will, that you are a General preparing for war. Would you honestly gather all of your men around you and say, "Men, I have no idea who we are fighting or what their capabilities are. I don't know if there are a hundred or a billion of them, and to be honest, I don't care. Why? Because I'm feeling lucky today. Let's be honest here. I believe in us so much that once we walk over that hill, they'll see our colors flying and they'll lie down like dogs! We will be the victors. I just know it! Who's with me?!"

I suspect that few of us would step forward in that instance. I know I wouldn't. Isn't that what we do to our families, though? As entrepreneurs we often ask those who trust us the most, our spouses and children, to follow us over that hill and meet our enemy will nothing more than sheer hope to get us to the other side.

Wouldn't you rather send out scouts first? Wouldn't it be nice for them to come back and tell you everything you needed to know to win? After all, knowing where the enemy is camped, how large they are in number, what weapons they have, and what their intentions are can be some useful information on the battle field.

So don't a lazy General. Do your homework and lead your troops into a successful campaign. I gotta say, I'm feeling pretty patriotic right now.

The S-D-B formula and why it works

What I am about to share with you isn't a top-secret government formula, kept within the confines of Area 51. As a matter of fact, many people already know it – they just don't apply it. S-D-B stands for Sell, Design and Build. And yes, I came up with the name. Catchy, isn't it?

Most entrepreneurs get this formula mixed up. They turn it into the D-B-S formula. As such, they design their product or service, and then they build it and finally sell it. This flawed formula assumes that the entrepreneur has a perfect understanding of what the market wants. Well here's a revelation…the entrepreneur doesn't have a clue of what the market wants. How could you possibly know what thousands of people want? When you design first, you end up creating a solution that most likely won't be understood.

Once built, the entrepreneur takes the business and tries to sell his or her wares and is left to wonder why nobody is buying. He might think to himself, "But I did my homework in workshop #3, and found that there was interest in my market. I used the Google AdWords tool and there were a lot of searches and low competition."

Well that may be true. However, there is more than one way to solve a problem. If your solution leaves your market scratching their heads, you'll be left in the dust scratching your backside.

Not all solutions make sense. I will often look at a product and cringe. I know what the entrepreneur was trying to accomplish when she developed it, but it's painfully obvious that she didn't consult with her potential users as she developed the solution. In the end, she missed the mark.

The S-D-B formula on the other hand is like a beautiful symphony of efficiency. Here is how it works.

   Step #1 Sell: Sell your product or service before you have even started your business.

Step #2 Design: Take what you learned and design the proper solution.

Step #3 Build: Build the solution and sell it to the market!

Isn't that beautiful? Instead of sitting at your desk all day long trying to figure out how to solve a group's problems, you actually work with the group to get the right solution. Then you build it and they'll buy it, because they asked for it. I know… It's like drinking sweet nectar.

One of my favorite businesses is a company called Threadless. I love this company for two reasons:

1. They are S-D-B Masters
2. I am a sucker for graphical t-shirts

A lot of online t-shirt companies approach the market in a similar fashion. They start a business, open up their online web store, find a bunch of companies to buy shirts from at a discount, and then resell them for a profit. It's pretty old fashioned, but if you want to get lost in a sea of competition, it's really effective. Notice how this model uses the D-B-S formula. The business owner designs what he believes will be the best and most sought after inventory. He chooses the t-shirts that he thinks everyone will want. Then he builds his business, and starts selling; however the selling portion is usually pretty abysmal.

Threadless, on the other hand, has it figured out. They hold contests for artists wanting to get their name out. These artists submit their art online and Threadless then displays that art to visitors of the site. Each visitor can vote on his or her favorite artwork. They winning piece of art is then turned into a t-shirt!

Once the t-shirt is made, everyone that really liked the art can now buy it and wear it as clothing. It's genius! Threadless essentially takes much of the risk out of carrying inventory by ensuring that if they produce a shirt, there will be a built-in base of people that will love it. They first sell the product by holding a contest and getting people to say, "Hey, that would be a sweet t-shirt!" Then they pay the artist for the rights, design the shirt, and build it.

With this strategy, how much more sales do you think a t-shirt company would experience? A lot more. The t-shirt market is very saturated which means that there are a lot of t-shirt stores out there. The founders of Threadless found a way to beat them all and get to the head of the pack overnight.

I love it.

As an avid customer, I constantly buy shirts from Threadless. Not just because I love the artwork, but because I love the business. It's just fun to be a part of the process.

The question I always get

Here comes the question I always get: "How can you possible go out into the market and sell a product or service that you currently don't have?" It's a fair question, and one that has many answers.

As new entrepreneurs, we're so brainwashed with the D-B-S way of doing things that we honestly don't see how it's possible to sell a product or service before we have it to sell. My challenge to you is this: Find a way. It will be crucial to your success and well worth the brain power that you put into it.

Before you tell yourself that your particular product or service is so unique that there is no possible way to sell it before you build it, know this – there is. Telling yourself otherwise is just a copout. It's an escape in the otherwise necessary steps that you need to take to become a good business owner.

You will need to find a way to penetrate your market with little or no cost to you. If you remember, a requirement of a good 8-week startup is that it should cost less than $500 to test. So that is your budget. No more.

Applying the S-D-B formula to your business will be a unique process. Why? Because your business will be unique. A business has a mind of its own, you know. Your customers will have different needs, wants, and tastes. Your cost structure will be one-of-a-kind.

Here are just a few different ways that you could apply the S-D-B formula.

You could do any of the following:

- Spend an afternoon with your target market. You know, the group that has the problem you're trying to solve. Ask them if they would buy your solution.
- Create an eBook on the topic and sell it for $5 online. Place an ad in the e-book for your upcoming solution.
- Join an online forum where members of your target market hang out. Ask key questions, and listen.
- Take pre-opening orders.
- Hold a contest like Threadless and let the community design and vote for the future product or service.
- Start an EBay store for your product.
- Spend the afternoon cold calling to see what kind of interest you can stir up.
- Have a demonstration party with your target market. Invite 20-50 people to your home and demonstrate what your product or service will do.
- Place an ad on the radio for 1 week and see what kind of response you get.
- Create a website and drive people to a landing page via Google Adwords asking them to download something.

However you do it, the goal here is to not march into a product or service blindly. You want to make sure you understand several things before you go investing more time and money in this.

Here is what you need to know:

1. Is there a strong demand for my proposed business?
2. Do the people I am trying to service actually have money that they are willing to part with?
3. Are there questions or features you hadn't thought of that came to light as you spoke with your prospective audience?
4. What is the right price point for your product or service?
5. What is the sales cycle for this product or service?

Let's run a little scenario here. Pretend that you decided to hold a demonstration party in your home. You spend $250 on an advertisement to get 35 people to attend. Great! You know that you have some interest and a market that will respond.

As you hold the party, these people are going to start asking questions that never occurred to you. I guarantee it. They will see the product or service from a whole new perspective. That's good, though. New perspectives will add features and benefits to your business, as well as weed out some of the bugs.

As you talk with them, you might find that your asking price of $45 per unit is far too low. They might say "If it's done right, we would gladly pay $60 for something like that". Or maybe they would only pay $30. Who knows? One thing is for sure though – you don't know until you ask them.

You will also learn about the sales cycle of your business. The sales cycle literally is the process of how long it takes from meeting a potential customer to getting them to buy. In my accounting business called Ignite Spot, the sales cycle can be as long as two months. Why? Because getting a new accountant demands trust. However, if I were selling shoelaces, I doubt my sales cycle would take as long. Knowing your sales cycle is vital to what we will be doing later on when we forecast cash for the first 12 months.

Setting yourself up for success

As you venture forth into selling first, we need to set up a few expectations so that you come out of this still feeling good life.

Here is what I don't want to have happen: You muster up the courage to take your first step and you get a "no." Then you throw your hands in the air and cry "Uncle," at which point you write me a nasty email saying, "I told you this wouldn't work!"

Good grief. Let's set some ground rules. Let's shoot for the following to occur:

- You talk to enough people, more than just two or 3, to get a well-rounded response from your market.
- You go into this completely unmarried to your business idea. It's only an idea after all. That way you can keep an open mind as people give you feedback. Don't defend the idea against the naysayers. They're your future customers, after all. Instead, take notes and listen.
- You don't spend more than $500 on this project. If you do, you're not a true 8-weeker and therefore aren't allowed to be a part of our cool little club.
- You must be willing to let the ship sink if it stinks!

Let's talk about that last one for a minute. Besides the fact that it's fun to say, it is a real decision you must make before you start. If you get out there and talk to enough people, and everyone gives you negative feedback, then be happy and not mad. Why? Because it only cost you $500 or less to find out that your business idea stinks. Be thankful that you weren't the guy that bet the farm to find that out.

One of the best qualities of an entrepreneur is the ability to walk away from ideas in search of better ones.

This means that you may go through six ideas before you find a real winner.

Action Work: Take a day off and meet your market

Can you feel the excitement? I can! You're about to make it happen. Here is what I want you to do. Walk down the hall to your boss's office and request the day off. When she asks why, just let her know that you need a little "R & R." She'll think you mean rest and relaxation, but what you really mean is research and refine.

Did you do it? If not, I'll wait.

That's right. Put this workshop down and go talk to the boss. Don't worry, I'll still be here when you get back…

Now that you have a day off, get to work! Find a way to sell your potential product or service. You can use some of the ideas I mentioned earlier in this chapter, or you can come up with your own. However you do it, here is what you need to do to get an A on this assignment:

1. Ensure that you reach at least 30 people in your market
2. Document everything they say
3. Measure their interest in the product
4. Ask them the following question: "If I built this, would you buy it?" When they say yes, follow up with, "Great, can I get you on a pre-order list, so that when it's ready I can give you a call?" Don't skip this question, either.

5. Test different price points and see what the reaction is.

Just think about this: If you do the exercise, you'll walk away with a built-in base of fans for your business, a powerful understanding of who your target market is, and you'll have an overwhelming feeling of entrepreneurial euphoria surging through your veins.

WORKSHOP 5: Choosing a Service or Product

"If you want to conquer fear, don't sit home and think about it. Go out and get busy."

- Dale Carnegie

Wahoo! By now you've spent some time with your target market! Good for you. Having done so is a major leap forward.

The work that we did in the last few workshops will, at least in part, determine whether or not you are starting a service or a product based business. Were you able to define a particular business that made sense to you and to your target market? How did the testing go? I would venture to guess that you found out a lot about your assumptions and learned something along the way.

Now that you have a specific group of people for whom you're going to solve a problem, and you have a tested solution in place, you need to determine how you are going to deliver that solution.

So here you are, feet firmly planted at the fork in the road. As you survey the land, you realize that you must make a decision. Will you sell services or products? As you sit at this fork in the road, you find yourself wondering which one is right for you. I'm here to say that both have pros and cons. Both can bite you in the butt. Both can make you insanely rich.

Think about the last time you bought a service and the last time you bought a product. Let's review a few of the purchases I have made. I recently bought a new Jeep Rubicon. It's my baby. When I bought it,

I had the luxury of doing some research. Since I'm a Jeeper, I knew what I wanted in the vehicle. Once I found the Jeep with all the fixin's, I called up the seller and test drove it. That's the beauty of a product. The customer can test drive it. Whether it's an office chair, a Jeep, or a pen – he can try it out. Selling a product means that your customer can make the most of that "trial" experience.

Buying a service is a whole different enchilada. You can't touch a service. You can't see it, smell it, or try it out. As such, your customer is buying blindly, for the most part. This can cause a lot more stress for the customer. Since he has no idea of what he is getting into, he must trust you when he buys from you.

There are a few tools to make this easier though. Testimonials from clients, for example, makes it a bit easier. If you are going to sell a service, know that you are selling an intangible. I'm not saying service companies are bad. Nay, I own one myself and I love it. You just have to be the kind of person that can communicate the value of something that the customer cannot see.

This is a big deal. Deciding if your business will provide a service or sell a product will determine the entire structure of your company, your time, and ultimately your life. Not all people are suited to sell services, and not all people are suited to sell products. When you think about it, there are a lot of differences that you need to consider.

A product-based business has some of the following features:

- Less customer interaction
- A need to focus on quality of material, production, packaging, etc.
- Cost per unit becomes a huge key metric
- Distribution channels are vital to your success
- Carrying inventory may be necessary

- You'll most likely have shipping, tax, and other related costs to consider
- You'll be working with manufacturers or drop ship companies
- You may need to buy in bulk to get a good enough discount to make a profit which may mean more of an upfront cost
- You can put more systems in place to automate a product-based business
- The accounting, purchasing, management, and operational needs tend to be more complicated
- You'll make money based off of building the right product mix and selling it for the right price

Here are just a few of the characteristics of a service-based business:

- You'll have a lot of customer interaction which takes time and is hard to automate
- This type of business is much harder to scale and grow
- It is easier to start this type of business due to a lower cost of entry
- You'll be selling something intangible which can be more difficult than a product that people can test out first
- You have inherent bottlenecks in a service based business which make it hard to generate a lot of income quickly
- You can take a skill that you know well and provide that to others which takes some of the risk out of starting your company
- You can also get trapped in your service company as the only one who know how to get the job done
- You'll make money based off your time and materials

Of course there is a lot more to think about, but know this... running a product-based business is very different than running a service-based business.

Which type of business is right for you?

What kind of person are you? Do you enjoy lots of customer interaction by providing an in-person solution that makes people happy? Are you the kind of person that is looking for a lifestyle business (a company that will provide you with a good lifestyle once you get your client base up and running)? Do you like managing people, culture, and brand experience? If so, a service-based company may be a good fit for you.

On the other hand, do you like the idea of providing a tangible product that made someone's life better? Do you like the idea of figuring out how to build a low cost, high quality, production system that generates cash every time a product is sold? Do you like the idea of a growth business (a company that can grow larger and larger, since generating revenues are not directly tied to your time and your billable hours)? If so, a product-based business may be right for you.

I have heard some of the best entrepreneurs out there say that service companies are a waste of time. Not so. There is no right or wrong answer here. What we need to determine is what you want out of your business.

For example, selling a product-based business would most likely be easier than selling a service-based business since investors can quantify a tangible product, market demand, and costs much easier.

A service-based business is easier to pass on to the kids. As they grow up, they can learn the trade, and take over - thereby picking up a profitable lifestyle along the way. That's not to say that you couldn't pass on a product-based business to your kids. Of course you could. It's just more common for service-based businesses to be handed down.

Examples of product and service companies

It might help to take a minute to go over some examples here. You obviously know the difference between a product and a service. At the same time, we may learn something here as we brainstorm.

Examples of product based businesses:

- The 8-Week Startup is a product-based business. How is that you ask? I created a product, which is the content you are reading right now.
- Online web stores that sell herbal remedies to holistic healers
- Custom-made watches for surfers
- Selling MP3 music or sound clips online to movie producers and amateur film makers
- Selling how-to dance videos to middle-aged married guys who want to take their wives dancing

Be careful as you look at your business. Some businesses may look like product-based business, but are not. Selling food for example is not a product-based business. You might think that you are creating a tangible thing that people are buying. That's true. However, people don't come to your restaurant to get the tangible product. They come to your business because they are sick of cooking, and they want someone to cook for them. The true calling of a restaurant is to provide a great service.

Examples of service-based businesses include:

- Accounting and consulting firms such as my company, Ignite Spot
- Mowing lawns for senior citizens
- Teaching guitar lessons
- Providing virtual assistants to overworked CEOs

- Teaching middle-aged married guys to dance in person at your studio

Do you see the main difference between a product and service? It's your time. A service-based business requires a lot more of your time. Sure, a product-based business will soak up a lot of time, too, but once the business is built, systems can be set in place to reduce your time input.

For some people, that's a great thing. Some people really love getting absorbed in their work and want to touch people's lives. Other people want to have a little more of a hands off approach by selling products.

A lot of people will jump in here and say, "That's just not true. There's a lot of customer service that comes along with selling a product."

No there's not. When was the last time you spoke to the guy that developed your water bottle, television, or iPhone? Probably never. Sure, you may have had a complaint if the product was flawed, but you probably spoke to a customer service representative for a few minutes.

When was the last time you spoke to the guy that provided your plumbing, legal work, or speech impediment service? You speak to them constantly. Every time they earn money from you, you interact with them.

Can a business be a hybrid?

Of course. Many businesses provide both a product and a service. There is nothing wrong with this approach, but my argument would be to start out as either a product or a service company and move into a hybrid down the road if it suits you. Don't try to be both out of the gate. Get good at one or the other first.

Given that they are so different from each other, you don't want to start off by trying to nail both. Your marketing message will be muddy and your solutions to your markets problems will be flimsy at best.

If the time does come for you to consider becoming a hybrid, make sure it's worth it.

Homework for the product-based business crew

I'm going to assume that you are starting a product-based business for a moment. First you need to understand that your product has to reach out to your target market in a very direct way. In our examples of product-based businesses, notice that I didn't use selling watches as an example. I used selling custom-made watches to surfers.

To get started, let's get you doing the following homework:

1. Find a pony to ride on. Is there another company, marketplace, or area that is catering to your market that would allow you to sell your product to their customer base? Who can you partner with in the beginning to start moving product? What you don't want to do is try and create your own sales platform in the beginning. Find someone that is already reaching customers efficiently and try to work with them to get your product into the mix. Take some time to list below whom you will contact about a possible partnership.

   _____

   _____

   _____

   _____

   _____

   _____

2. If you need to manufacture your product, do a quick Google search to find manufacturers that make similar products. For example, if you want to develop watches for surfers, Google watch manufactures and list at least 10 of them here.

_____

_____

_____

_____

_____

_____

_____

_____

_____

_____

_____

_____

_____

3. Find the email for each manufacturer and send an email asking them the following questions:
   a. What types of products do you typically manufacturer and what materials do you use?
   b. What is the minimum production run?
   c. What will be my cost per unit on average?
   d. What are your payment terms?
   e. Do you also produce the packaging for the product?
   f. By what safety regulations do you abide?
4. If you're going to resell a product versus manufacture one, determine which companies you can sell for, call them, and ask if they drop ship. We will talk more about drop shipping in a later workshop. For now, if it's a new term to you, just

know that the customer buys the product from you, and the drop shipper pulls the product off their shelf and mails it to the customer as you. It essentially eliminates your need to carry inventory, but you can lose a good amount of profit in exchange for the convenience. Google search drop shippers in your industry and list them below.

_____

_____

_____

_____

_____

_____

5. If you do need to carry inventory, where are you going to keep it and how will you stay organized?

_____

_____

_____

_____

_____

_____

Carrying inventory should be avoided if possible as a new business owner. It costs too much to acquire and hold. If you can set your business up so that you can avoid holding and managing inventory, you may want to seriously consider that option.

Homework for the service-based business crew

Now let's assume that you are venturing down the road of services. For many of you, starting a service-based business, while trying to maintain a day job, is the trickiest part. After all, providing a service requires you to go to your customer and that can be difficult if you are chained to a desk.

1. Find a way to schedule your week so that you can dedicate a blocked amount of time to servicing clients. You may need to ask your boss if you can rearrange your schedule to work different hours, or even different days of the week.

2. Begin thinking of your time as valuable. You need to start tracking what you do and why. When you invoice your customers, you'll need to be able to show how your spent your time. Do a quick online search for "time tracking software" and find an online time clock that you can use. Many of the time tracking software packages will have a free or lite version which should get you started. I would also suggest finding one that has an app that you can use on your smart phone. Being able to log time in the field is extremely helpful.

3. Calculate how much you could earn as a service-based business. To do so, take what you will charge per hour and multiply it by 160 hours a month. Now I know that you won't work and bill all 160 working hours in a month. What we are trying to do here is determine what your absolute ceiling is. You see, with a service-based business, the amount of revenue you make is directly proportional to the amount of time you and your staff has.

4. Ask yourself if the figure you calculated in step 3 is worth it. If not, the ship stinks and you need to let it sink. At this point, simply go back to your 8-Week Idea Map and keep testing business ideas.

Hopefully you have a good grasp on which direction you'll be taking. It's hard to pick, though. For me personally, I like service based businesses because I get to be with my customers. On the other hand, I like product-based businesses, too, because you can grow them without as many bottlenecks.

:Once you get your business set up, you can always start more companies. And I suggest you do.

WORKSHOP 6: Building Your Business Strategy

"I seem to be some sort of lightning rod. I just really irritate people, you know? I really do."

- Howard Stern

Radio DJs amaze me. Have you ever noticed that the ones who are the most outlandish are the ones that keep their jobs? It's the extreme left or right-winged radio personalities that have listeners. It's the ones that say what's on their minds that stick around. Yes they offend many, but they keep their jobs and make a lot of money. Why is that?

It's because we're starved for the unique. Our lives are pretty much repetitive if you think about it. You have a schedule that you stick to day in and day out unless a major event knocks you off of track.

Because of this, we tend to notice what's different and ignore everything else.

This is an important rule of business strategy. Essentially, you need to figure out how you're going to stick out. Historically speaking, most businesses have found that there are two good ways to do that.

1. You can be the business that sells for the cheapest amount possible
2. You can be the business that sells the service or product with all the bells and whistles

Think about it. Companies that pick one of these two strategies and stick with it are the ones that truly win.

Can you think of any businesses that fall into category #1? Wal-Mart comes to mind for me. They fully embrace the low-cost leader position for their industry. Taking that route, they focus all of their branding, culture, and energy on having the lowest prices possible. Does it work for them? Absolutely.

On the other end of the strategy spectrum, what companies can you think of that are proud of their price tag and flaunt it? How about Ferarri or Gucci or Serendipity's Ice Cream Dessert? Did you know that people are paying Serendipity $25,000 for their Chocolate Sundae?! It's called the Frrozen Haute Chocolate. I'm not kidding. It's made from a mixture of 28 cocoas from all over the globe, it's laced with 5 grams of edible gold, and served in a goblet made for Kings. On the top sits whipped cream and a side of La Madeline au Truffle which costs a mere $2,600 a pound! The thing does come with a gold and diamond bracelet as a souvenir. Holy Crap! That's some expensive ice cream. Here is the great thing though…people are buying them! Why? Because people want to be able to say they bought it I guess. Also, Serendipity has gotten an insane amount of free publicity for it. Being bold has paid off.

Unless the company is the low-cost leader or the high-end differentiator, do you usually buy from them? No. The businesses in the middle usually get trampled on. Unfortunately, most businesses reside in the middle. It's a death trap.

Here's where the problem lies. Most business owners don't want to stick out. They fear that being different is too risky. As such, they often try to be a little of both. In the end, they provide a product or service that has average benefits for an average price.

What have they done to themselves? They've made themselves boring. If your company is average, is it really going to get recognized when you place that ad in the paper that says,

"Buy from us. We provide an all right product for a price that's decent"?

I declare to you here and now that nobody will notice you. So what do you do?

Pick a strategy, kick butt, and take names

You need to determine if you're going to be the low-cost leader in your industry or if you are going to be the high-end differentiator. Here's the tricky part, once you pick, you can't go back.

Imagine if Wal-Mart put out a press release tomorrow that said, "From now on, we're going to be the most expensive guys on the block. We're going to sell the best brands and give you amazing service the moment you walk into our stores".

What would happen to Wal-Mart? They would go out of business. That's what would happen.

That's because you can't easily convince your market that you are one thing, and then switch the next year because you feel like it. If Ferarri started producing a $10,000 sports car, their brand would be ruined forever.

A lot of business owners fail here because they don't make the decision up front as to which strategy they will follow. They just open their doors and go with the flow. As such, they're always driven to the middle and eventually go out of business. It's a veritable killer.

So today, you get to pick what you want to be to the world. Do you want to be the cheap solution or the company that makes people drool?

Before you pick though, you need to understand the implications of being a low-cost leader and the high-end differentiator.

The life of a low-cost leader

Being the cheapest guy on the block has some draw to it. Why? Because when you go shopping, you often look for the cheapest solution. We're taught that, if all things are equal, go with the cheapest one.

There is some pain involved here though. First, the competition is intense. Everyone likes being the low-cost solution, which means that almost nobody wins. As companies start advertising 50% off, price wars ensue, and profits continue to decrease.

If you choose this path, you have a lot to think about. You will need to get a good understanding of who else in your space is pushing this strategy. I guarantee that there are at least a few companies already trying for the #1 spot.

Don't kid yourself either. I've heard many an entrepreneur say, "My idea is so unique that nobody is doing it." To them, I often say "Have you done a Google search to prove it?" They almost always say "No." When an entrepreneur comes up with a new idea, the idea is usually just new to them. Because they have never heard of it before, they assume that nobody else has either. There are billions of people in the world, and I seriously doubt that you're the only person that has had this idea. Since you can pretty much plan on someone else already doing your business somewhere in the world, you can also plan on someone trying to be the low-cost leader.

In all honesty, it's not my favorite strategy. The only way to win is to be cheaper than the cheapest solution. Once you finally do get to that coveted "Low-Cost Leader" position, you're not making money anyway because you're not charging anything.

Makes you wonder why so many people go down this road.

I'm not saying you shouldn't go this route. It depends on you, your connections, and quite honestly your product or service. Let's look at the alternative though first.

Being the high-end differentiator

At the other side of the rainbow is the high-end differentiator. This type of business has a lot of options. In my opinion, the best part about being the high-end differentiator is that you don't have to fight your competition based on price alone. If you set up your company the right way, you'll be bringing something unique to the table, which makes cost less of an issue.

Think about our $25,000 cup of ice cream. Nobody else in the market has the guts to create it. Serendipity wins.

There are a lot advantages to this strategy including:

- People are more likely to talk about what you are doing
- Your marketing can speak about what makes you great versus just the price
- You make more money on each transaction
- You get more satisfaction, in my opinion, by providing something great that people like
- You can create a culture in your company around being the best
- As you grow and develop, you get to think about how to add more value and features versus how to keep cutting costs

The biggest complaint I hear when I discuss business strategy is, "What if there's a recession? If people don't have money, I don't want to be the expensive guy!" That's a great point to consider. My rebuttal to that is that I would rather own a business that makes great profits during the good times and therefore has some fat to weather the storms when recessions come. I'm not particularly interested in running a business that has razor thin margins regardless of what the economic forecast looks like.

To be a winner in this realm, you need to have a USP. USP stands for "Unique Selling Proposition" or "Unique Service Proposition."

In essence, it's the unique thing about your service or product that gets people to pay a higher price.

Take what you learned from your target market and try to figure out a way to use that information to your advantage.

Even though I'm biased towards being the high-end differentiator, that doesn't mean it's the right strategy for every company. Some products or services have to be the cheapest in the market to win.

How to tell if your product or service is destined to be a low-cost leader

If you are starting a business that is selling a commodity, you may have an issue on your hands. A commodity is anything that has no discernible features, and therefore is bought by the consumer based on price alone.

Take corn for example. To me, corn is corn no matter how you shuck it. If a farmer developed an ear of corn that would instantly add 2 inches to my biceps, I would think otherwise. I don't see that though when I go to the store. All I see is corn. It's yellow with a green husk. When I buy corn, I look at price, and so do you, I suspect.

I highly doubt you have cornered yourself into selling a commodity if you have taken the time to do the first five workshops in this series. That's because we've forced ourselves to find targeted solutions for a specific group of people. It's possible though. It you are selling a commodity, you really can't take on the strategy of a high-end differentiator.

For the most part, people have spent their lives spending as little as possible for corn. If you create a new breed of corn and try to charge three times as much, the market probably won't respond. Humans are creatures of habit and that's why building a commodity business can be dangerous.

If you're facing a commodity business, you may want to start over at workshop #1 and look for a product or service that will allow you to stand out.

So, how do you go about finding your USP?

I'm not going to lie… Finding a USP can be difficult. Essentially you are looking for a way to stick out that is unique and hard to copy.

Take computer monitors, for example. The monitor makers of the world are all competing on size and clarity. If you walk into the local office supply store and hit the monitor aisle, they are all the same. Most advertise their screen size, color, and clarity. Boring. Because they do this, everyone is essentially reduced to price as the final unique proposal. You as the consumer find yourself getting lost in pixels, ratios, and refresh rates. In the end, you just go with the one that fits your budget.

There is no real USP in the computer monitor aisle.

What if we started a company that sold computer monitors to teenage girls? I'm making this up on the spot, so give me some leniency, here.

What if we made pink monitors, covered them in glitter, and put a killer sound system in them loaded with the latest Justin Bieber tracks? You could even add a feature using the camera in the monitor that would allow the girls to check their makeup, chat with friends, and on and on.

Now we are differentiating.

Take that, computer monitor makers! In one fail swoop, we stood out and made a difference to a group of people. Awesome.

Here are a few things you can do as you start developing your USP:

1. Look at your notes from Workshop 4. What comments did your target market make as you interacted with them? What did they ask for that you hadn't thought about?
2. What could you add to your product or service that would make your target market worship your company? I would argue that adding a little glitter to a monitor would make teen girls far more giddy over the standard black that all monitors come in. What is your glitter?
3. Looking at the specific group that you're trying to help. What type of people are they? Are they nerdy? Glamorous? Fastidious? Freaky? Fat? Skinny? Grumpy? In general, how do they act? If your group is anal, give them a unique feature that allows their analness to shine. Sorry, I actually laughed when I wrote that.

A word to the wise, here: I'm not suggesting you be different just to be different. That will get you nowhere. Your uniqueness needs to be valuable. Don't get lost in this exercise trying to come up with the most outrageous stunt or feature. The purpose is to give your target market a solution that makes them swoon. Simply dressing up like the Statue of Liberty while you provide your service won't do it. In fact, that would be a really stupid idea. Can you imagine your plumber showing up dressed like the Statue of Liberty? Sure, you would tell your friends about him, but you wouldn't be giving him referrals. You would just be making fun of him.

Action work: Develop your USP here and now

All right. Let's dance. We need to get some homework done before we end this workshop. By the end of the day, I want you to have a USP that you can really get excited about. After all, this is what makes you special. It's what makes people share your stuff on Facebook.

1. List out the standard features and benefits that usually come with a product or service like yours.

_____
_____
_____
_____
_____
_____
_____
_____

2. Define the characteristics of the group you are serving. What are they like? What are their personalities? Where do they hang out? What do they truly care about when they use your product or service?

_____
_____
_____
_____
_____
_____
_____
_____

3. What did you learn from workshop four that will help you? What requests did your target market make as you talked with them?

---

4. What is your USP going to be and why?

There you have it. If you did your homework, you should now be armed with a USP or unique selling proposition. That's something to be proud of! Most people don't have one. Covet it. Feed it. Make it your be all and end all. Put it on a t-shirt and wear it proudly. It's your way of sticking out. If you have to, climb up on top of your roof and yell it out to the world!

WORKSHOP 7: The 3 Most Important Resources to a Startup

"Luck is a dividend of sweat. The more you sweat, the luckier you get."

- Ray Kroc, Founder of McDonalds

Imagine signing up for a marathon. You've committed yourself to over 26 grueling miles of running. Now imagine that you did nothing to prepare. You didn't exercise, find a running buddy for support, or even invest in a good pair of running shoes. In fact, imagine that you showed up to run your marathon 100 pounds overweight and wearing a mini skirt and high heels. How well are you going to do in the race? I would bet that you wouldn't get much farther than 100 yards before you either twisted your ankle or fainted from exhaustion.

Why would you do that to yourself? Why would you commit yourself to something so monumental without having the right tools, resources, and support team in place? You wouldn't. I've gotta say though, if everyone showed up to a marathon overweight and dressed like that, I might just take the day off to watch the race.

Business is no different. Don't show up to the race without your gear, people, and resources. In this workshop, we'll be discussing the three most important resources to an 8-week startup company.

Resource #1: People are the bread and butter of business

I know that there are a lot of books out there that teach you to do whatever you can to limit the number of people in your business. The theory is that people cause complications, headaches, and emotional tidal waves. I won't lie; I've surfed a few of them myself with some employees, but that's not the point.

The point is that a good business is about people. Good people make all the difference. I don't propose trying to build a business that is people heavy, though. A company that is laden with payroll becomes stiff, bureaucratic, and unaccountable.

What I am calling for are gurus. Every good business has a nucleus of gurus; people that love you, your idea, that passion behind it, and want nothing more than to be a part of the mission. Oh yeah, and they have some pretty stellar skillsets, too.

Your goal should be to get the right group of people working within and outside of your business so that you can extract yourself and be a business owner. If you fail to do this, you'll end up a slave to your company. I promise you now that you'll work more hours and face mountains of stress if you try to do it all yourself or if you hire a bunch of duds.

So what type of people do you need?

First and foremost are mentors

You can do this one of two ways. You can either go out there and try to figure this out on your own which will take months if not years to discern, not to mention that it will cost you an arm and a leg due to messing up – or you can get a mentor. Getting a mentor will speed up your learning process a million fold, literally. My mentors are gold.

To me, they are the most important people I know, next to my wife and kids. They have saved me hundreds of thousands of dollars, years of experimenting and failing, and they have been my cheering section when nobody else was cheering.

Get three mentors. One is not enough. When you do get a mentor, you want to look for entrepreneurs who have gone out in the world and succeeded. The best part about entrepreneurs that have done well is that they love supporting others on the pathway to business. It's like there's a code that all entrepreneurs live by. Why do so many entrepreneurs support becoming a mentor to up-and-coming superstars like you? Because they were you once. They felt that loneliness that comes with starting a business. They felt that awe struck surge of excitement coursing through their veins. They also needed a mentor at one time, and most likely they found one.

So how do you get a mentor? You ask. As part of your homework later on, I will have you discover the possible mentors in your life and then you're going to take each one of them to breakfast or lunch and ask them to mentor you and your new business. Note this: mentors won't ask for payment or equity in your company. If they do, they're not for you. Thank them for their time and politely decline.

When you do get a potential mentor to a meal, tell them about your business. Be open with them and willing to learn. They aren't going to steal your idea. Trust me. Then ask them the following question, "I have a lot of respect for you and what you have accomplished. This is my first business and I was hoping to be able to share my progress with you as I build it and see if I could get some feedback. I really think your background would help me foresee some of the pitfalls before I hit them. Would it be all right with you if I sent you an email or called every few months if I had questions?"

He or she will probably grin from ear to ear out of sheer pride for you. As a fellow entrepreneur, they'll know exactly what you're doing and they'll want to hug you for it. That's because you're trying to do it right.

Second are groupies

Every business needs groupies. Just like rock bands that have raving fans that following them around the country, you need 10-20 people that will spread your gospel. Here is the best part: People like being on the trendy side of things which means they need little persuasion if you set up the relationship right.

It's amazing what people will do for free or for some recognition. Seriously. What you need to do is identify 10-20 people that are your closest friends, family, and colleagues and get them a t-shirt. Let them be the first ones that heard about you.

If your business is of the kind where you can give some product or service away to them, do it. Then ask them to use it, love it, blog about it, Facebook it, and make it magical.

Here's what you do. Call a pizza party and let them know what's going on. When you invite them, tell them that you are starting a new business and that, as someone close to you, you want to give them a preview along with some free stuff. When they come to the pizza party, you need to ask them to actually be a groupie.

The conversation might sound like this, "Sara, I've started a company that sells glittery pink monitors to teenage girls. We're opening in about 7 weeks now and I could really use your help. I was hoping to find some people that I could give monitors to as a free gift. In the end, I would love it if you could spread the word about my business assuming you like the monitor."

Then, when everyone has heard the spiel, give them instructions. For example, you might ask them to take their monitors home, use them for a week, and then start blogging about them, posting on Facebook, and letting others know what's going on.

If you can find a way to make these 10-20 people the "in" crowd, you'll be handsomely rewarded.

Third is a management team

Here is where your business flourishes. Talent is so important. Don't just hire an accountant or an office manager. Get the best possible people and train them very well. Knowing when it's time to bring on a management team is crucial. You won't be doing this during your 8-week program. Getting your management team in place will most likely take much longer. However, when it's time, here is what you want to look for in your team:

- Hire people who are passionate about life and the thought of working in an entrepreneurial environment.
- Get people with skills. This is a no-brainer, but you would be surprised at how easy it is to hire someone because you like them regardless of their skillset.
- Get people that replace you. In the end, your management team needs to take care of the bookkeeping, staffing, customer service, maintenance, sales, and everything else. Your job in the future needs to be to get reports from these people, spread a vision, and help out where needed.
- Hire people that are smarter than you. I know when I have achieved this, because the position and company actually improve when that person is hired. If I have to watch the person like a hawk, fix mistakes, and double my effort...I hired someone dumber than myself. Let those people go, and try again.

Bringing the right people into your business allows you to exponentially grow the skills of the company. To do this correctly, you need to have a good and honest understanding of yourself. If you're not a detail-oriented person, don't pretend that you are. Get someone that is and let them check the boxes.

Resource #2: Cash

You probably have been asking yourself how you are going to get the money to start this business. If you'll journey back to the first workshop with me, you'll remember that we don't want this business to cost more than $5,000 to start. There are a lot of businesses out there that would cost more than that to get off the ground. Make those kinds of businesses be your second, third, and fourth companies if you like. You'll be able to afford them at that point as well as stomach the risk.

Let's clear the air. Having lots of money to start your business is not necessary. In fact, I have seen it cripple a lot of entrepreneurs. They get lazy when there is a lot of money in the pot to play with. You won't have that option. As such, every dollar invested has to have a return on it. No funds will be wasted.

I don't care how you get your hands on $5,000, just find a way… as long as it's legal, of course! Here are a few suggestions:

- If you've got excess cash in the bank, pony it up
- Ask mom and dad or other family members
- Use your tax return
- Have a huge yard sale and get rid of all that crap in the basement
- Find a one-off project that you could complete for a business using a skillset that you're good at
- Ask your mentors for possible solutions
- Ask the lady in the produce aisle for $5,000 to support you – she might just say yes!

Whatever option you choose, know this: If you use your own money you'll be more successful. If you borrow, you'll be less responsible with how you invest it. Trust me on this one. As an accountant and consultant to businesses worldwide, I have seen entrepreneur after entrepreneur blow through someone's money, but when they spend their own they only do it when it makes sense. Go figure.

Resource #3: Daily Know-how

I was recently asked by a colleague what she could do to grow as fast as possible as an entrepreneur. I thought it was an interesting question. My response to her was, "Who is your favorite author?" She started listing off some great fictional books that she loved. I told her that if she wanted to grow as fast as possible, she would need to change up her library experience. I put her on a crash course of intense reading for six months.

There are so many good books out there that will teach you exactly what you need to know to get your business moving. Read them. If I were to give you a list of the top ten business books according to Eddy Hood as of this writing, here is what I would say:

1. The E-Myth Revisited by Michael Gerber
2. The Art of Closing the Sale by Brian Tracy
3. Tribes by Seth Godin
4. Purple Cow by Seth Godin
5. The Art of the Start by Guy Kawasaki
6. Duct Tape Marketing by John Jantsch
7. Mastering the Rockefeller Habits by Vern Harnish
8. Brains on Fire by Robbin Phillips, Greg Cordell, Geno Church, and Spike Jones
9. Eat that Frog by Brian Tracy
10. Inbound Marketing by Brian Halligan

If you went out and bought all of these books, you would be $200 - $300 into the best education possible. I received an MBA which was a great degree to get, but I've got to be honest…. I have learned way more practical how-to knowledge from these ten books that I ever did in the MBA program. Don't get me wrong; the MBA program taught me about things like the Fisher Effect. But the books above taught me how to get a customer and keep him happy. Awesome.

One of the best things you can do for yourself is build the right kind of library and absorb it. Relish and put into practice what you learn. You'll be grateful that you did.

Action Work: Get Some Mentors, $5K, and a Library

As you can probably guess, I want you out on the street again today. By the end of the day, I want you to have prospects for 3 mentors, $5k in your pocket, and a true business library.

1. Go through your Facebook, Linkedin, and other social media accounts to find three people that you feel would make great mentors for you and your new business. Contact them and ask them if you could take them to lunch. Then ask them to be your mentor.
2. Determine how you are going to get your $5k and then go get it.
3. Get the above stated books ASAP. I prefer them in audio format so that I can listen to them anywhere I go. I also have an E-Reader (Nook) that I keep mine on.

Once you complete the above homework, you'll be armed with a support team, funds, and some of the best advice on the market. Go get 'em, tiger.

WORKSHOP 8: Calculating Your Gross Margin

"I finally know what distinguishes man from the other beasts: financial worries"

- Jules Renard

Money isn't the basis for all happiness, but it's sure hard to be happy when you don't have enough of it. With that being said, there is one number I want you to learn inside and out as it pertains to your new business. It's called gross margin, and it's one of the most important drivers of your success.

Gross margin influences a lot of different things in your company including how profitable you are, how much cash you have moving through the company, the level of quality you can deliver to your customers, and ultimately how well you sleep at night.

When I meet with business owners, I drill this number into them. It's surprising to me just how many entrepreneurs don't know their gross margin. I also find it surprising that the ones who do are the ones that are doing well. There must be a correlation in there somewhere...

What is gross margin?

Gross margin is a percentage. We're not talking about gross profit here. Let's clarify what both are to make this workshop more useful.

> **Gross Profit:** This is the dollar figure that represents the amount of money you keep when you sell your product or service after your pay for the direct costs it took to make or

sell it. For example, if you sell a lamp for $50 but the cost of parts to build the lamp were $30, then you have $20 left over. That $20 is gross profit.

Gross Margin: As mentioned before, this is a percentage. It is calculated by dividing your gross profit by your revenue. In the case of the lamp, we would divide the $20 gross profit by the $50 sales price to get a gross margin of 40%.

Do you feel all geeked up yet? If not, get your nerd glasses on. Keep in mind though that the geeky stuff is what makes you money. Therefore, it's worth learning. Read on, fellow geek. Read on.

Now that you know what your gross margin is, what that heck does it mean? Well, the gross margin is often called the contribution margin because it represents what you have left to contribute towards the other costs that come with running a business. We call these costs overhead.

Think of it this way, if you sold $100 of stuff and your gross margin was 40%, then you would have $40 to contribute towards paying for overhead.

Why you need to know all of this

Knowing your gross margin will help you to accomplish a few very important tasks in your business.

1. Calculate your break-even point, which we will do in the next workshop
2. Improve the profitability of your company in a sustainable manner
3. Set up warning signs to warn you of when your company is headed downhill

Once your business is up and running, you'll want to calculate your gross margin every time your accountant gives you your financial statements. If the percentage is getting bigger, that's good. If is getting smaller, you're doing something wrong.

Learn to speak accountant lingo

When I got my Bachelor's Degree in Accounting, I did so because money is the language of business and I wanted to be able to speak that language. I wanted to be fluent. I didn't do it because I loved debits and credits. As exciting as that stuff is, I studied my accounting text books from the perspective of an entrepreneur. While all of the other students had grand accounting visions, I had other plans.

Next to selling, accounting is the important skill you're going to need. Don't skip it. Now that you know a little bit about gross margin, let's take some more time to define a few more key terms and work through some examples for you.

> Revenue: The total sales your company has generated over a set amount of time.

> Cost of goods sold: These are the costs you incurred to produce your product or service. They include materials, direct labor, machine time, etc. If you had to incur the cost to make the sale, then it's a cost of goods sold. In the accounting world, we often call them COGS as in the cogs of a gear.

Example: A lawn mowing company

Let's pretend that you own a lawn mowing company. It's the summer months so things are really pumping for you. As such, you've hired a bunch of guys to help push lawn mowers. Things feel like they're going well. In fact, you have never had so much business!

At the end of the month, your accountant does his calculator thing and adds it all up. He then hands you your profit and loss statement which simply shows you the revenue you generated for the month less your costs. At the bottom of the report, you find out if you were profitable or not. Let's assume you generated $30,000 in revenue. You get excited! You've never generated that much revenue in one month! As you look further down the report, he lists your cost of goods sold at $20,000. When you ask him what in the world could have cost you $20,000 he lists the following:

- The fuel to run the lawn mowers
- The hourly rate of the laborers that cut the grass
- The trim line that was bought for the edge trimmers
- The cost of the garbage bags to put the grass in

Again, these are all costs that you incurred because you mowed lawns. If you hadn't mowed lawns, you would not have had to pay $20,000 for all that stuff.

Just below the cost of goods sold line, he lists your gross profit. Can you tell me what it is? If you said $10,000 you're right. Now, here is the pop quiz…what's this company's gross margin? It's 33.33% and you would know that because you divided the gross profit of $10,000 for the month by the company's revenue of $30,000. Whew! Now we are getting somewhere. Give yourself a hug.

Note to reader: If you actually just gave yourself a hug, give yourself a high-five.

As you sit back and calculate your gross margin, you realize that for every dollar of lawn mowing you sell, you only get to keep 33.33 cents.

Now you find yourself scrolling further down the report to the next set of numbers. What you should find next is overhead. When you read through this section, you find the following expenses:

- Marketing
- Payroll for office staff since you have to pay them regardless of mowing lawns or not
- Rent
- Insurance
- Utilities
- Cell phone
- Interest expense
- Dues and subscriptions
- Etc.

Your accountant has kindly totaled all of that up for you and your overhead comes out to $7,500. So, since your gross profit was $10,000 and you still had to pay $7,500 for overhead, what are you left with? Ding! Ding! Ding! $2,500.

That $2,500 is called net profit.

Can I just say, good Job for sticking with me through that? Did it make sense? If not, grab a piece of paper and write the numbers out until it's clear. We went through that little scenario for two reasons. First I wanted to see if you could calculate the gross margin for the month, and second, I wanted to see if you could distinguish between cost of goods sold and overhead for a service company.

You see, service companies are a little harder when it comes to cost of goods sold. That's because you're more often than not selling time, and time is hard to quantify. Did you notice that the guys pushing lawn mowers were a cost of goods sold and the office managers were overhead?

If all of this feels overwhelming, have no fear. I've created a spreadsheet tool called The 8-Week Margin Calculator as part of this workshop. It will walk you through identifying your costs and calculating your margin. In addition to that, I've included a fake profit and loss statement for a service company and a product-based company so that you can see how we determined their cost of goods sold, gross profit, and most importantly their gross margins. I pulled these reports right out of sample QuickBooks files so that you could see what a P&L (Profit and Loss Statement) looks like.

How to use gross margin to make decisions

Here is where all of your gross margin knowledge pays off.

You're probably saying, "That's great and all, but how will it help me to build a better business or get one started?"

Ah, my young padawan, you ask great questions. Here is one of the many reasons that gross margin is so important. After you do your homework today, you're going to know what your gross margin should be for your business. Let's say you're going to have a pretty healthy gross margin at 70%.

Now let's assume that you want to incur an ongoing monthly cost for your business. Maybe someone approached you wanting to be a salesman for the company. After much negotiation, you come to a monthly salary of $3,000.

Here is where many people mess up, so pay attention!

Most entrepreneurs would think to themselves that they only have to sell $3,000 of stuff each month to cover the salesman's salary. Is that what you thought? Come on...be honest. Well, it's just not true. He actually costs you $4,285.71! How is this possible you ask? Because of your gross margin. If you remember, we're pretending that your gross margin is 70% which means that for every dollar you sell of your product or service, you only get to keep 70 cents.

If you take his salary of $3,000 and divide it by your gross margin of .70 you get $4,285.71 which is the amount you would have to sell in order to get $3,000 back after paying for your cost of goods sold. Those dirty little COGS will get you every time!

Do you see now why gross margin is so valuable?

What if your gross margin was 36% in last example? Then the actual cost of your $3,000 a month salesman is really $8,333.33. Ouch!

The question you need to ask yourself is if this guy is really worth over $8,000 a month to you or not. The answer lies in whether or not he can sell **at least** $8,333.33 in new business every month. If he can't then don't hire him. You'll go out of business.

This works on other things, too. What about getting high-speed internet for $100 a month? If your gross margin is 70%, you actually need to sell $142.85 a month to cover that darn internet bill. It's false advertising at it's worst. I know!

What I want you to get from this entire workbook is this:

Know your margin well. When you want to bring on a monthly overhead cost, take that figure and divide it by your gross margin to find your true cost. Then ask yourself if it's still worth it at that point.

You see? Being a geek isn't so bad after all. I swear to you now that if entrepreneurs knew that one little trick and actually used it, we would have a lot more businesses still in operation these days. However, entrepreneurs just see the sticker price and think, "I can pay that."

Then, when cash gets tight, they can't figure out what in the world went wrong. I can tell you what went wrong… They don't know their gross margin or how to use it to make decisions!

How to improve your gross margin

Your goal as the business owner is to always try to improve your gross margin. You want that percentage to be as high as possible. So how do you pull off this fancy bit of foot work? There are only two ways to dance the jig. Here they are:

1. Increase your prices
2. Find cheaper cost of goods sold or COGS

Increasing your prices is usually not the option most businesses take. It tends to turn customers off. If you do decide to increase prices, you need to have a reason for doing so. This usually means finding new and better ways to be more beneficial and valuable to your customers so that they will pay more. Be careful though…adding value can often lead to adding more COGS. If that happens, you may not improve your gross margin at all. In fact, you might make it worse.

The route that most businesses take is to find cheaper cost of goods sold. They do this by getting material cheaper through buying in bulk, hiring cheaper laborers, and constantly negotiating rates.

Action work: Time to meet your gross margin

We need to determine what you gross margin will be so that we can manage some of the planning items in the future workshops which include calculating your break-even points and knowing which equipment to buy.

If you have purchased this workshop through the8weekstartup.com, then you will have access to all of the downloads I've prepared for you.

1. Open up the product and service company exercises in your download. Your task is to review each of these profit and loss statements, and determine what the gross margin is for each company. I've posted the correct answer at the bottom of the second page of each report.
2. Fill out The 8-Week Gross Margin Calculator in your workshop's download folder. This is an excel spreadsheet that is designed to help you track your price point, cost of goods sold, and gross profit, and of course…your gross margin.
3. Now that you know what your gross margin is targeted to be, figure out what your true cost would be for the overhead that you feel you may need.

Just think of how popular you'll be now! You can strut into that party this weekend as the guy or gal that knows gross margin. It's a great icebreaker, too. If you're on that first date with someone, just let her know that your gross margin will be 63% and she'll fall deeply in love with you.

All kidding aside, knowing your gross margin actually does make you cool because very few business owners know theirs. You're already miles ahead of the pack.

Here is a shot of The 8-Week Gross Margin Calculator that you can get in your download packet:

8WeekStartup

The 8-Week Gross Margin Calculator

Only Fill Out the Blue Squares

Step #1: List the price of your product or what you charge to service one customer

Step #2: List out all of the costs you will incur to make one product or service one customer

Direct labor	
Materials	
Fuel	
Supplies	
Machine time	
Other	
Other	
Other	
Other	
Other	

Total Cost of Goods Sold | $ - |

Step #3: Review your calculated gross profit per unit or service of one customer | $ - |

Step #4: Review your calculated gross margin per unit or service of one customer | **#DIV/0!** |

Step #5: Enter the monthly cost of planned overhead expenses to see your true costs

Planned monthly expense	Sticker Price	Your actual Price
Rent		#DIV/0!
Cell phone		#DIV/0!
Insurance		#DIV/0!
Payroll		#DIV/0!
Marketing		#DIV/0!
Other		#DIV/0!
Other		#DIV/0!
Other		#DIV/0!
Other		#DIV/0!
Totals	$ -	#DIV/0!

WORKSHOP 9: Calculating Your Break-Even Point

"I wasn't a financial pro, and I paid the price"

- Ruth Handler

There are a few things in life that will never die: rock n' roll, apple pie, and the unyielding need of every entrepreneur to know and understand their break-even point. Unfortunately, calculating your break-even point is not as simple as just adding up the costs. If you were with us in the last workshop, you'll know exactly what I'm talking about.

Let's think about the quote at the beginning of this chapter. You may not know who Ruth Handler is, but you know all about her creation known as "Barbie". Ruth and her husband Elliot Handler created the behemoth toy company we know today as Mattel. I find it amazing that such a successful person like Ruth felt the sting of financial foggery at times. It's a strong warning that all of us, no matter where we are in life, need to get better at financial management.

Here's the problem: The accounting of a business rarely gets attended to for the same reasons that most families don't keep a personal budget. It's not as much fun as talking with customers, eating ice cream, or watching a movie. That means that financial "stuff" usually hangs out on the backburner. Consequently, things that sit on the backburner tend to catch on fire.

What is the break-even point anyways?

The break-even point is a dollar figure that represents how much you have to sell every month in order to pay all of your bills and walk away unscathed. If a company breaks even, it means that it generated $30,000 in revenue and spent $30,000 on cost of goods sold and overhead. In the end, there was nothing left. Yuck.

It's a crucial number to know and I'm sure you can see why. Imagine a doctor trying to do heart surgery on someone in an operating room that's void of all light. Imagine the doctor saying, "I'll do it by feel alone!" Sorry doc, but you're not coming near me with that scalpel. I don't care how good you are.

This is what entrepreneurs do, though. They often operate in the dark with nothing more than a gut feeling to guide them through complicated decisions. You're not that kind of entrepreneur, though! Heavens, no… You're an 8-week startup kind of person. That means that you're here to do it right.

The best part about all of this is that calculating break-even only takes a few minutes when you know how to do it. That seems to be the law of life. When it comes to the most important things, they're often easy to do but we shun them anyway.

In this workshop, I want you to be able to walk away with a good understanding of what your overhead and break-even points will be. This kind of information is extremely useful when it comes to planning the future of the company. In a later workshop, we'll be forecasting the first 12 months of cash. That's pretty hard to do accurately if you don't know your break-even point as well as your gross margin.

Becoming a master of overhead

Overhead stinks. These are the costs that you have to pay for regardless of selling something. They are the fixed costs that just don't go away unless you cancel an account or a contract. The word overhead makes me squirm. It's like toxic sludge that turns the best of businesses into undead zombies.

Some overhead is necessary, but most of it is driven by ego. We often spend way more on things that we don't need to in order to feel and look important. Now that you know how to find the true cost of ongoing monthly expenses, which you learned in the last workshop, you know that paying for this stuff is often a lot harder to do than it seems.

In today's day and age, entrepreneurs are getting better at managing overhead. Companies are becoming more nimble. They can move in the market when things shift because they aren't tied down to monthly costs and long-term contracts.

That's important if you are going to create an 8-week startup. You need to be nimble. "Float like a butterfly and sting like a bee," as Ali would say. Do what you need to do to keep unnecessary costs out of your business.

How do you do this? It's easy. You learn to say "no" to yourself and to the salesman across the table. A salesman doesn't truly care about your financial success so he's not considering how the transaction will benefit you in the long-term.

I bring all of this up now because we need to plan out your overhead in a responsible fashion. As we start calculating your break-even point, make sure that you only add monthly costs that your business will absolutely need to be successful. Some of the best entrepreneurs I know are the ones that care more about their company's bottom line than their own personal agendas.

The obvious point to make here is that your break-even point goes down as you decrease your overhead. The lower the break-even point, the better, which means that you job is to figure out how to run your company with as little overhead as possible.

This means being creative in many instances. For example, many people outsource functions versus hiring in-house employees. Other entrepreneurs share rent with other businesses, etc. Keep your mind open and ask around for ways to decrease your costs.

The #1mistake when calculating break-even

The #1 mistake when calculating break-even is forgetting about yourself. I have seen so many entrepreneurs do this. I'm not kidding. I can't count the number of entrepreneurs who have started and built companies but haven't taken a paycheck in months. I honestly don't know how they survive, but I can tell you this... that's not the life we're looking for.

When entrepreneurs start planning out their business, they add up all of their costs and tell themselves that any income the business makes after the bills are paid will be their paycheck. This is budgeting to fail in its grandest fashion. If you don't make room for your paycheck as a fixed monthly cost within your business, you'll find yourself always being the sacrifice.

Budget for yourself and get a paycheck. Otherwise, why start a business? I know there are a lot of people out there that say that entrepreneurs should struggle in the beginning if they're going to get their companies off the ground. I personally don't think that has to be the case if you plan properly.

You don't need to budget a six-figure income out of the gate though. That would bleed your new business dry pretty quickly. Figure out what you need to be comfortable and add that as a monthly cost. Cut out the fat in your personal life for the first year or so, but don't cut out your paycheck.

How to calculate your break-even point

I promised you that this would be easy, so I'll keep to my word. We'll take a lot of what we learned in the last workshop and apply the same principles here.

What you need to do first is make a list of all the overhead costs you think you will need to service your customers. We're trying to calculate the break-even point of your business as of the day you open your doors. What costs will you have that you'll need to pay for monthly?

Don't be like so many novice entrepreneurs out there and say "I have no overhead". All that tells me is that you're too lazy to actually sit down and think about all of the costs you will actually incur each month. If there was a business out there that had no overhead, it would be the only business that people would ever start.

So list out your costs and take some time on this. Here are a few ideas to get your brain going:

- Your minimum monthly salary to be comfortable
- Your cell phone bill
- The internet
- Monthly rent if you can't start out of your home
- Liability insurance
- Marketing costs
- Server costs
- The monthly fee to host your website
- Those outrageous utility bills

Our goal here is to plan for your growth. Given that your sales will need to ramp up, you need to find a way to get these costs at a discount in the beginning. For example, if you get an insurance quote for $100 a month, ask your agent if you can ramp that up as you get larger. Maybe he can work out a plan where you pay $60 a month for the first 3 or 4 months.

Note that these costs are different than the $5,000 investment defined as the startup cost of your business in workshop 1. Startup costs are one-time costs that you will incur to get off the ground.

Once all of your overhead costs are listed, all you need to do is add them up and divide the total by your gross margin. Voila! Your break-even point has been born. Welcome it to the world like a proud papa.

An example of calculating a break-even point

Let's say that your gross margin is 57%. If you don't remember how to calculate this, head on back to workshop 8 and get it done.

Now, let's assume that your overhead adds up to $4,842 a month which includes your minimum monthly salary. You have done everything you can to get your costs as low as possible and you'll be rewarded with a low break-even point. All we need to do is divide the $4,842 a month in overhead by the 57% which equals $8,494.74.

What this means is that you would need to sell $8,494.74 in stuff to have enough money to pay for your overhead each month.

Let's take this one step further by figuring out how many units you would need to sell or how many customers you would need to service. What is the price of your product or service? Let's say that you sell your product or service one customer for $175 before sales tax, which we don't count because we don't get to keep sales tax. The local government has dibs on that stuff.

That would mean that you would have to sell 49 units a month in order to break even. I got to that by dividing the break-even point of

$8,494.74 by the sales price of $175 per unit. So, anything over 49 units is gravy… and we love gravy.

What to do with your new found knowledge

In the above example, you would have to sell 49 units every month just to pay the bills and your minimum monthly salary. That's some pretty valuable information if you ask me. Now you need to ask yourself if you can sell that much.

Knowing your break-even point and how many units you need to sell will allow you to take an open and honest assessment of the company. It allows you to make crucial tweaks now before you open your doors.

This is why having low overhead is so important for a business, especially a startup. Until you actually begin generating revenue, it's really hard to know how much you'll actually sell. So, don't rush out there and lock yourself into a 3-year lease for a $2,000 a month rent payment. You'll likely regret it.

Don't be a lemming with your $5,000 in startup money

Entrepreneurs can act like lemmings when it comes to starting a business. It's funny but true. Here is how the story goes.

For many entrepreneurs, starting a business means having physical proof before they start selling. This means that entrepreneurs often blow their startup cash on things that don't matter in an effort to create an image. They buy desks, computers, chairs, signs, t-shirts, calculators, and everything else under the sun that gives them the impression that they have a busy business.

After their shopping trip is done, they sit back and admire their new equipment and feel like they can now begin selling. Wrong! Wrong! Wrong!

This story ends with the entrepreneur going out of business. Why? He financed the nice, but not necessary, things to have with his own money. Who should pay for this kind of stuff? Your customers, that's who.

Those things aren't necessary in the beginning. What is necessary in the beginning is having a customer. In fact, you want to have a lot of customers. Your $5,000 in startup cash should be spent on customer acquisition, not on a cool desk. Your customers should be your biggest financiers. Let them pay for the business.

Essentially we're talking about marketing here. Get your dollars into the right kind of marketing that will create a return for you. Examples might be:

- Building a website for less than $500 as we will teach you in later workshops
- Start a Google Adwords campaign and drive people to your site
- Hold a seminar for potential customers
- Create a marketing kit with your business card, brochure, and a sample of your product
- Approach another business in a complimentary but not competing industry to create a marketing campaign

The ideas are endless. Just don't waste your startup cash on stuff that won't pay you back. You want a return on your dollars. When you start spending your startup cash, I want you to ask yourself the following question:

"Will spending this money get me customers or will it massage my ego?"

You need to turn that $5,000 into circulating cash flow and not into office furniture.

Action work: Calculate your break-even point and determine how you will invest your startup cash

Now it's your turn. Don't you just love this part? Isn't it refreshing to know that you're taking action and getting it done? Congratulations on being one of the few who take action.

1. Fill out The 8-Week Break-Even Calculator I provided in your download file if you purchased this workshop from the8weekstartup.com. There is a sample image of it below.
2. Pay attention to how many units the spreadsheet says you'll need to sell monthly to pay for your bills. Can you sell that much? If not, tweak your assumptions and the business model until it makes sense and is realistic.
3. Start brainstorming how you'll invest your startup money and write your thoughts below. Make sure that every idea will help you to generate a customer.

_____
_____
_____
_____
_____
_____
_____
_____
_____
_____
_____
_____

Remember Ruth Handler in the beginning of this workshop? She created an empire, just like you will, and along the way she learned the importance of knowing her financial tools inside and out. Don't ignore what you learned in this workshop, or you'll pay the price down the road. If you do take the time to invest in acquiring customers and fully understanding your break-even point, you'll be depositing checks for your profitable company in no time.

The 8-Week Break-Even Calculator

8WeekStartup

Only Fill Out the Blue Squares

Step #1: What will you sell your product for or what will you charge to service one customer?

$ 99.00

Step #2: Enter your gross margin that you calculated from workshop #8

58%

Step #3: List all of the overhead items that you will have as ongoing monthly costs when you start

Your minimum monthly salary	$ 2,500.00
Rent	$ 350.00
Cell phone	$ 100.00
Insurance	$ 60.00
Internet	$ 75.00
Marketing costs	$ 500.00
Server or web hosting costs	$ 25.00
Utility bills	$ 75.00
Other	
Other	
Other	
Other	
Other	
Other	
Other	
Other	

Total Overhead $ 3,685.00

Step #4: Review your break-even point

$ 6,397.57

Step #5: This is how many products you will need to sell monthly or customers you will have to service to break-even. Can you sell that much?

64.62

WORKSHOP 10: How to Make Your Business Scalable

"There are no great limits to growth because there are no limits to human intelligence, imagination, and wonder."

- Ronald Regan

What is a scalable business?

A scalable business is one that can get bigger and bigger without spending proportionate amounts of money to achieve the growth. In short, if you have to spend more money on operations, staff, and resources for your business to generate extra revenue, it's not a scalable business.

A lot of businesses aren't scalable. Does that make them poor businesses? Not at all. However, we're looking for scalable business models in The 8-Week Startup, if possible.

Let me take you on a little adventure. It's the story of how I turned one of my very un-scalable businesses into a scalable business. As you probably know by now, Ignite Spot is a service based business that I own. We provide an experienced financial team to do the books, payroll, CFO work, and taxes for clients around the country.

When I started the business, it was as un-scalable as you could imagine. It was a bookkeeping business after all. If I wanted the company to make more money, I had to hire more accountants to do more work. It was a really difficult model to survive in, and here's why:

- I struggled to get myself out of day-to-day operations since I was the founder
- I struggled to generate the income that I wanted because I had to spend more money to grow the business all the time
- Since I owned an un-scalable service company, I felt like I was working 36 hours in a day. Try and figure that one out!

I remember reaching our growth ceiling. We couldn't get any bigger without my picking up some ulcers and trying to cram 48 hours into a single day. It just wasn't going to happen.

Then we had the scalability conversation. I sat down with my team and said, "Look guys, this isn't working. This isn't the kind of business I had envisioned when we started. What do we need to change in order for this model to become scalable?"

We had to find a way to achieve the following three things, and to do it quickly before I had an aneurysm. They were:

1. Reconfigure our revenue model so that we could make money without incurring more accountant time.
2. Restructure our costs so that other supporting expenses didn't increase with the onslaught of more clients.
3. Create a system where I could remove myself from the day-to-day operations and become more involved in strategy.

We realized that for our particular industry, the only way to achieve those goals was to stop being an accounting firm and start being an accounting franchise. That's right, we saved up what felt like a billion dollars and hired a franchise attorney. After a few months of rigorous paperwork, trademark applications, and jumping through legal hoops, we became the Ignite Spot Outsourced Accounting Franchise.

Our target customer was no longer the small business owner. It was the CPA.

We packaged up our business and began selling the model to CPAs around the country. If you know anything about franchises, it's that the CPA who is our franchisee pays an upfront cost and then a monthly percentage of his revenue to us for support.

Now we could scale! Within three months of opening our franchise doors, we were able to open four locations from Spokane, Washington to Cedar Rapids, Iowa.

Do you see why this business is now scalable? As we sell our business model to CPAs, they take our platform and start their own Ignite Spot accounting firm. As they get clients and service them, they pay us franchise royalties each month for use of our software systems, methodologies, and coaching.

We can now get bigger and bigger without having to put a proportionate amount of accounting hours into the firm. In fact, I no longer have to work 36 hours in a day. I could easily work 2 or 3 and get everything done.

As we open more and more offices, we will continue to build an ongoing monthly residual income stream that will be much larger than it ever could have been when we were doing the accounting ourselves.

If you're thinking about starting a service-based company, you don't need to rush off and make it a franchise in order to scale it. That's just one way to do it. Know this though: a service-based business is much harder to scale because it requires so much of you and your time.

Finding bottlenecks and breaking them

Why don't some businesses scale? It's all about the bottlenecks. If you think about the neck of a glass bottle, it narrows, forcing the liquid into a tighter space. Image if that bottleneck were so narrow that only a drop or two could get through at a time. You would die of thirst!

Some businesses by nature have extremely narrow bottlenecks.

Bottlenecks break a business. They're the equivalent of taking growth stunting pills for your company.

Some of the most common bottlenecks in a business are:

- Your limited time
- Your cost model
- Access to key resources
- Payroll structures
- Your management team and their leadership style
- Administrative work
- Poor technology

Let's talk about each of these for just a moment so that you can get a better understanding of why they can truly cripple your growth.

Bottleneck #1: Your limited time

You only have so much time in a day. Did you ever watch *Saved by the Bell*? I always admired Zack Morris and his ability to freeze time. Wouldn't that be great? If all you had to do was say "time out" and the whole world stopped moving, you could get so much done!

If you're too young to know what I'm talking about, just shake your head at my odd memories and move on. If you do know what I'm talking about, would you join with me in a silent moment of respect?

Since you're not Zack Morris, you only have 16 hours at most to work each day. You do need sleep, after all… as well as spend some time with the family.

If you have to put in more and more of your time as the business gets bigger and bigger, you have a serious issue. This bottleneck, in my opinion, is the worst of them all. That's because you can only put up with this lifestyle for so long. Eventually you'll crack, causing you to hate your business, your customers, and everything else in between.

I can guarantee you now that this is the largest hurdle you'll face if you set up a service-based business.

How to break the bottleneck:

There are several ways to get past this bottleneck. First and foremost is to find someone that can replace you. Get an expert that can do the work, train them to oversee the day-to-day operations, and then have a back-up plan in place for the days they are sick.

Bottleneck #2: Your cost model

This one is a bottleneck that most businesses share. If you have to spend more money on products, materials, labor, etc. to generate more revenue, than you have a cost bottleneck. For example, a furniture store has to buy more couches if it wants to sell more couches. An accounting firm has to pay its accounting staff for more hours if it wants to create more billable time. Such is the way of life for most companies.

There are a few that get around this though; tech companies and information companies for example. A tech company has a lot of upfront cost to develop its technology, but then after that, the company can sell to people in greater and greater numbers without having to create more technology.

A content company, like The 8-Week Startup, also gets to avoid the cost bottleneck. A lot of time went into creating these workshops…about 450 hours to be approximate. However, once the content is created, I don't have to do anything. People hear about our site through our marketing efforts or word of mouth and they download the workshops.

How to break the bottleneck:

Can you design parts of your business to act like a tech or content company? Is there something that you can do that may take some investment in time or money upfront that will create effortless dividends down the road?

Bottleneck #3: Access to key resources

Businesses often come to a grinding halt when they can't get access to resources that they need. These resources might be in the form of products, people, time, money, or information. What are the key resources that your business will need in order to breath?

It's a crying shame to see a business brought to its knees because it gets all of its product from a single vendor. There's a local BBQ joint in town that I absolutely love. I was talking to the owner a few months back and he was telling me about how they make their food taste so good. He talked about a specific kind of wood that they use in the BBQ pits to create their unique smoky flavor.

I asked him how business was treating him, and his smile turned upside down. I wondered why, since his restaurant was jam-packed full of people. He told me that he bought all of his wood from a single vendor and that the company just increased the price of the wood by ten-fold! I'm not kidding. There was no reason for the increase, either. When I told him to pick up some more vendors, he said that this was the only company that sold that flavor of wood.

How to break the bottleneck:

Avoid the resources bottleneck by doing your real job as the business owner. Instead of getting lost in the day-to-day operations, make sure that you focus on more valuable tasks like management of resources.

Bottleneck #4: Payroll structures

This is a common plague in a service company. In order to create more revenue, you have to hire more people. It can be painful, too, because you face the "chicken or the egg" complication. Do you hire more people first and then go out and get the customers to support their salaries, or do you get the customers first and then hire?

I obviously would vote for the latter.

Before Ignite Spot became a franchise, we faced this issue. There were times where I nearly broke the bank due to hiring someone. Supporting an hourly person was even difficult at times because they wanted so many hours to stay with the company.

How to break the bottleneck:

Find a win/win payroll structure that allows you to only incur payroll costs when there is work. At Ignite Spot, we decided to stop paying our staff salary and hourly all together. They get project pay. Since we charge each of our clients a fixed monthly fee, the accountant gets a percentage of that fee once their work is done. If they lose the client, they don't get paid anymore. If they retain the client through high quality work, they get paid a great rate for doing a job well done each and every month.

However you structure it, make sure that everyone wins and you don't get stuck with payroll costs that weigh you down.

Bottleneck #5: Your management team and leadership style

Micro managers are bottleneck makers. If you're a micro manager, you'll need to give up your excessive need for control or else you'll squeeze all the juice out of your company. Some managers insist that everything be run through them. They feel like they must review every task, procedure, communication point, report, and blink of an eye.

Growth cannot happen in such an environment regardless of how efficient the manager is. It goes back to bottleneck #1. The manager only has so much time which means that if everything has to be approved by him, we can only get done what an 8-hour day can handle.

How to break the bottleneck:

Make a list of all the tasks you will be doing in your business and find a way to outsource all but the strategic ones. It may take you several months or even years to get all the tasks into the hands of others, but do it.

Bottleneck #5: Administrative work

Some businesses are heavy laden with paperwork. Accounting is no exception. We became paperless, built our own custom software to automate much of what we do, and built a virtual firm allowing us to exist online. If you walk into our office, you won't see paper piles and rows of filing cabinets. You'll see open work areas and clean desks.

We do a lot of consulting with businesses that generate income by servicing governmental programs. Such businesses have a lot of red-tape and forms to fill out. This bottleneck is a killer. The business often has to build its entire process around dealing with paper flow.

How to break the bottleneck:

Take a day off and hit the whiteboard. Diagram all of the paperwork that will come in and out of your business on a monthly basis. Define where it comes from and why, then ask yourself if it's necessary. If it is, find a way to automate it with a software solution or outsource the task. If it's not necessary, why the heck would you do it? Scratch it off, and get it out of your world.

For example, we had financial reports that had to be sent to clients every month. When that time came around, it was a giant paper dance trying to get everything out the door. So, we began looking for software systems that would manage this for us. Over time, we ended up bringing on a freelance coder to build The HUB, which is the internal software at Ignite Spot that makes everything hum.

Bottleneck #6: Poor technology

I would argue that every company could grease the wheels and blow up a few bottlenecks with the right technology under their belts. Electricians, pizza shops, and lawyers could all take massive steps forward in their industries with a good shot in the arm of technology.

Don't just invest in technology, though. There are two rules to moving forward with this stuff:

1. It has to dissolve a bottleneck
2. It has to be simple and intuitive

When I was in my early 20s, I was the assistant controller for a local home builder. At the time, home sales were booming and we couldn't keep up. We had work coming out of our ears. We had one major bottleneck, though, that made it impossible to grow… purchase orders.

We didn't have a purchase order system to help us control the purchase of materials that were going into the homes we built. As such, it was nearly impossible to nail down the cost of a home and know how profitable we were.

We ventured forward into the unknown land of technology and implemented a purchase order system that was going to fix everything. In the end, we lost gaggles of cash on the thing and never got it up and running. Why? The dang thing was too complicated. Even the guy that designed it had no idea how to work it.

Had we taken the time to step back and simplify the technology, we would have dominated our market.

How to break the bottleneck:

List the bottlenecks that you'll have with your business and then do a quick Google search to see if there are any off-the-shelf software packages that will fix the problem. Make sure that the software actually fixes a bottleneck and can be operated by monkeys.

Action work: Make your business scalable in just five steps

Your homework in the workshop is designed to help you identify what bottlenecks you will face, as well as identify ways to overcome them. Given that you have probably never run a business like the one you are about to start, the mentors that you picked up in prior workshops will be extremely valuable here.

1. Identify all of the bottlenecks that businesses in your industry face.

   _____

   _____

   _____

_____

_____

_____

_____

_____

2. Call your mentors and ask if you can meet with each of them individually for a few minutes. Let them know that you're trying to understand what types of bottlenecks your company might face, and you would like to get their input on how to overcome them.

3. Present your list of bottlenecks to your mentors, brainstorm with them to see if there are any that you missed, and look for ways to get around them. Rely on their expertise. Most likely, they have encountered similar bottlenecks in their organizations.

4. Write down an action plan that you can implement for each bottleneck. Go home and create a plan to either bypass the bottleneck, using a simple and affordable software that you and your mentor found, or find a way to outsource the issue.

5. Thank your mentors for their help. This is important.

Remember, a scalable business can grow exponentially. A non-scalable business grows in a linear fashion with costs that parallel growth. Even if your business is destined to be non-scalable, don't give up on it if you are passionate about it. Many people told me that we would never be scalable as an accounting firm, but I found a way. Be creative and occasionally break the rules. You never know what you might find.

WORKSHOP 11: The Golden Nuggets of Competition

"Keep your friends close, and your enemies closer."

- The Godfather Part II

Your competitors shouldn't scare you. In fact, they're one of your best resources. Part of starting a business involves doing a competitive analysis to get a good lay of the land, however many people scout out their competition defensively. We want to take the offensive. Instead of researching our competitors to determine how they might hurt us, let's look for ways to use their track records, experiences, and customers to get ahead.

In business school, I was taught that I must do everything in my power to understand the competitive landscape. We were taught to learn their every move and then write a 40-page business plan to document everything that we learned. In the process, I was supposed to uncover how the competition was strategically positioned to squish me like a bug if I stepped out of line, the thought being that I would be able to foresee their intentions and avoid a death trap.

I took on those assignments but always dreaded them a little. Instead of approaching competitors like they were the "bad guys", I wondered what would happen if I approached them with a different mindset. What could I glean from my competitors other than fear? What could their experiences and customer interactions teach me about how to get ahead?

The quote above from the Godfather summarizes beautifully how most people feel about their business competition. Many people keep a keen eye on the competitor's movements and try to respond accordingly, the thought being that they have to stay close to their enemies in order to be ready to shoot on sight.

What I'm suggesting is that you stay close to the competition for a whole different reason. What I am about to teach you now will help you generate wealth much faster that your previously thought possible if you implement it.

Here it is: Since you're just starting out, use your competitors as a crash course in what not to do. They have most likely been in business for many years and have seen the highs and lows. You could also spend several years doing the same thing, or you could take a single day to glean information from them that will put you miles ahead in the market.

So don't do a competitor analysis because your bank wants to see one in your business plan in order to give you a loan, do it because you want soak up their years of success and failure into a few hours of research and instantly build the smarter company.

How to glean golden nuggets from your competition

I couldn't care less about putting my competitors out of business. To me, business is not war like many make it out to be. To me, business is a place to add value and solve problems. I would rather focus all of my attention on how to make my customers' experience better, versus trying to make my competitors' lives miserable.

With this kind of mindset, you end up having a happy customer while your competitors are running behind you trying to keep up. Isn't that what you're looking for? I've read countless quotes from notables on how business owners should work to bury their competition or drive them out of business. Good grief. Maybe I'm not as bloodthirsty as everyone else, but I don't want to be remembered for how many competitors I shut down. I want to be remembered as the guy that created a great business that addressed customer needs like no other.

That's why competitors are so valuable. You can watch and see how they are trying to solve your customer's problems. The best part is that you can then read reviews and client testimonials to see the good and bad feedback that they are getting for their efforts. Are they winning? Are they losing? You can figure that out with just a few Google searches or phone calls and it's free.

In this workshop, I want you to be able to walk away with a great understanding of what the other guys are doing, if it's working or not, and most importantly... I want you to have a better viewpoint of why your approach to solving your customer's problems will work or not.

How to scope out the playing field

Let's get this party started. In the homework section at the end of this workshop, I will have you choose three competitors that dominate your market. If you have a ton of competitors, you need to pick a more specific market to operate in. For example, there are a million online cooking websites and if you tried to create that, you would probably drown due to the competition. However, if you built a cooking website for backpackers teaching them how to create great energy filled food for out on the trail, you'll have a more specific target audience and fewer competitors.

If you don't have competitors, look harder. You do. There are always people doing what you are about to do. Given how many people are walking the face of this earth, I highly doubt that you are the first person to come up with your idea. You need to find people that are already at it so that you can learn from them.

As you do your research, there are several things you will need to look out for, and here they are:

What is their business strategy?

Back in workshop #6, we talked about business strategy. As you look at your three largest competitors, what is their strategy? Are they trying to be the low-cost leader or a high-end differentiator? I would venture to guess that many of them are trying to be a little bit of both which is why you can move ahead of them in time. As a reminder, it's not usually a good idea to try to be both.

Make sure you walk away from this exercise knowing who the low-cost leader in your industry is and who is winning as a high-end differentiator.

What is their niche?

Are they approaching your customers with a "we're trying to be everything to everyone" attitude or are they smarter than that and trying to service a specific group of people? If so, what group are they servicing, and are they doing a good job of it?

How do they reach that group?

Are they targeting the niched group via online advertising, radio ads, paper ads, or are they hiring people to dance on the side of a road in silly costumes holding signs? What are they doing to get noticed? Maybe they are spending a lot of time in forums with their customers or maybe they're not trying to reach their base at all. Most importantly, can you see an avenue of reaching customers that they aren't exploiting?

What mistakes can you avoid by looking into their past?

Do some research on where they have come from and where they are headed. Can you see anything in their past that they tried which failed miserably? Were there any strategic decisions that they made that propelled them forward?

This is a big one to take seriously. There are common pitfalls within each industry and you need to find out where your competitors all bit the dust. That way, you can sidestep those potholes and hit the throttle to the front of the line. If you don't take time to do this, you'll most likely get to scrape your knees just like everyone else.

What do they charge and why?

I want you to take the time to find out what your competitors are actually charging for their product or service. Don't guess or come up with an approximate value. Find out the real deal price tag amount and keep track of it.

I was working with a client once who said that he was going to price his product as the high-end differentiator in his industry. He was going to charge $150 a unit. I had no idea what the standard pricing was, so I asked him. His response was, "My competitors usually charge around $130." I then asked him how he came up with that figure and guess what he said? He said "Im guessing".

After I picked my jaw up off of the ground, I gave him some homework. I told him that we didn't have room to guess, since he was leaving his day job to do this. I sent him out to ten different competitors in his area and had him come back with iPhone photos of the price tags on the products he wanted to sell.

Needless to say, he wasn't very happy with me. This was going to take time. A week later, I had a phone call with him and I asked him how it went. He started talking and I could barely understand him because he was spinning so fast.

Apparently, most of the businesses were charging around $210 for the unit and one competitor in specific was charging $330. The low-cost leader was charged $99. I was floored. Had he stayed with his original price tag, he wouldn't have made a dime. Why? Because he was priced to be the average solution; the guy in the middle with nothing useful to offer.

When I asked him who was doing the best, he said the company that was charging $330! He was shocked. As we researched why, it was blatantly evident that this particular company had found a way to reach their market in a unique and useful way that nobody else was doing. Everyone else was trying to service the entire market. They were servicing a group within a market that had a specific need.

Interesting, don't you think? It goes without saying that he changed his price point. He decided to become a high-end differentiator and find a way to add a specific value set at a price of $330.

He is doing a great job within his market and the best part is that he is getting noticed.

When it comes to pricing your product, take the time to find out what others are charging. You might have your reality shaken up a bit.

What are their strengths and their weaknesses?

Most industries have the 800-pound gorilla. You know, the business that dominates and makes you think that you'll never have a chance of getting any customer share whatsoever. An example of this is Apple in the MP3 player space.

Sure, there are a lot of MP3 players out there, but does anyone care?

No. I don't. I have at least 4 versions of that dang Apple contraption and I can't get enough of it. Why are other businesses unable to knock Apple off the mountain? It's because they're trying to beat them at their strengths. Apple built a machine that's a sexy status symbol, and holds millions of songs in your pocket.

Why is everyone else trying to do that? If I was going to enter this space, I would build an MP3 player for kids in rock bands. They're a specific set of people that have specific needs far and above just holding music in a gadget.

My MP3 player would allow them to record their music, sync with a computer to mix and master it, and then share it with friends and family. I would add apps that allowed them to connect with iTunes to sell their music and advertise it on Facebook. The camera on it would branded as a way to take pictures of your band and post them to your blog on your website. There are so many things you could do for the rockers of the world.

I bet you if Sony built that, young rockers would line up. What do you think?

Whoever your gorilla is, wave them off without fear, pick a unique group of people with needs, and give them what they want.

Taking the time to list your competitor's strengths and weaknesses will give you a much better point of view as you create your position in the market. The last thing you want to do is build a USP, or unique selling proposition, that is already being replicated by the gorilla. If you do that, you'll lose. It would be like trying to arm-wrestle Sylvester Stallone. Don't do it.

What do their customers and online reviews say about them?

Here is where life gets interesting. You can usually find customer testimonials about your competitors on their websites. Read them and see what it is that they are raving about. These are the things that they are doing right. Write them down as "wow" factors that your market cares about.

Most businesses also have some people that are upset with them. Go find some online reviews of their product or service. This will allow you to dig up some great tips on what not to do. Think about it. Your customer market is saying "Hey, this happened and I really don't like it," or they might say "I would love this company if they just did this!" Ah ha!!! You just got a golden nugget. A customer is asking for something that your competitor isn't providing. Add it to your list of solutions you could provide.

Remembering the value of your niche

Once again, I just want to say that trying to be everything to everyone is a death sentence. As you do research on your competitors today, remember the value of your niche. The fact that you have zeroed in on a specific group of people with needs that aren't being met efficiently makes you valuable. People will pay you if you come up with a solution that actually meets their needs.

Warning: Don't start thinking to yourself that you're missing out on huge amounts of business by niching. All that you are missing out on is the dreadful feeling of not being noticed in a market where there are millions of other businesses screaming for a consumer's attention.

Think about all the white noise out there. How many advertisements do you see a day? Thousands. Everyone is trying to be everything to everyone. It's a hopeless shouting match. Trust me when I say this: You're not missing out on business by niching. You're actually becoming a useful business to a core group of people that will sing your praises and pay for your retirement.

Action work: Choose your top three competitors and do some reconnaissance

If I had my way, today's homework would get you out in front of your competitors today. I would have you on their websites, in their stores, and talking to their account reps. It's not going to be enough to do some research on the internet. Talk with them. Engage with them. Find out about them as though you were considering buying their companies. Most importantly, learn from them. Here we go.

- Determine who the low-cost leader is, as well as some of the high-end differentiators.
- From your research, find three competitors in your market that most directly compete with your new business.
- Get out of your chair and get the following questions answered about each one of them:
    - What is their business strategy?
    - What is their niche?
    - How do they reach that group of people?
    - What mistakes can you avoid by looking into their past?
    - What do they charge and why?
    - What are their strengths and weaknesses?
    - What do their customers and online reviews say about them?
- After you have done your reconnaissance, ask yourself the following questions:
    - Do I need to adjust my niche, price point, or business strategy?
    - What do I know about my market now that I didn't before I started this workshop?
    - What new opportunities did I discover that I can use to my advantage?

Pat yourself on your back. For some reason, this is the step that many people skip when it comes to planning their businesses. I guess taking the time to look into competitors is underestimated. Don't be like the masses, satisfied that you know the names of your competitors. You need to know much more, and with that knowledge, reign supreme.

WORKSHOP 12: Build Your Exit before You Begin

"Would you tell me, please, which way I ought to go from here?" "That depends a good deal on where you want to get to," said the Cat. "I don't much care where--" said Alice. "Then it doesn't matter which way you go," said the Cat.

- The Cheshire Cat – Alice in Wonderland

Beginning with an end in mind

Why on earth are you starting a business? Don't get me wrong. I think it's great that you're doing it, but what I want to figure out is why you're doing it. One of the most important things you can do for yourself is to determine the "why" before you get started down the path of business ownership.

I'm not just talking about what motivates you. I want to know what the end result will be. I was on a phone call yesterday with a very promising company. They're building a mobile application system that is growing like gang-busters.

Ryan Steck was on the phone call with me. As my business partner at Ignite Spot, he is someone for whom I have an immense amount of respect. He is our lead CPA and one of the best business consulting gurus I know. I love working with him, and being on this phone call was no different.

Ryan asked the entrepreneur his favorite question which is, "So where would you like to take your business? Do you want to sell it or do you want to live on it?"

The entrepreneur we were talking to was fully committed to selling for a large sum of money. His goal is to grow his company to a valuation of several million dollars over the next three years and then get out and start another company.

Wonderful.

That one decision alone changes everything. It changes how we get the company off of the ground. It changes who gets involved, how much funding is needed, how it will be marketed, what relations he will manage, and on and on.

Knowing your end goal is vital to starting and growing your company. Don't be like most entrepreneurs and simply start a business hoping to build more wealth. You can't simply start and then hope for a positive outcome. Engineer your outcome right now and make that the blueprint for your decisions as you move forward.

Building a business to retire with

If your ultimate goal is to build a business that will provide a continual stream of income to you and your family, then you're in it for the long haul. The goal here is to develop your systems and processes in such a way that the business will become self-sufficient and drive income to you in periodic installments.

With this end in sight, there usually isn't a big payday. Instead, you're working for a company that provides you with a steady paycheck. Many people choose this route with the thought that having a consistent income stream from an automated business will allow them the freedom to spend more time with their family and hobbies.

The downside to this plan is that you're still in the business no matter how you flip the coin. That means that when fires need to be put out, you're the one that gets the phone call at 2 a.m. You will always have a responsibility to your employees, customers, and culture. It will never leave you alone. Sure, delegation and systems will take care of most of the business's needs, but the buck will always stop with you.

As you grow older, you may find that your kids can take the business over. This is attractive to a lot of people since you are giving them an income stream to put bread on the table. It's not a bad deal.

Another thing to consider is that this lifestyle is not typically the lifestyle of the serial entrepreneur. If you're the kind of person that gets your kicks from creating, building, and growing new businesses, then you may struggle here. Some guys have a million ideas and want to do them all.

Building an early-exit business

Early-exit businesses involve building up your business to a point that a third party will come in and acquire you. If done right, it's a handsome payday.

This route is the more technical of the two since you're building your business in such a way that it will be attractive to buyers down the road. This means that you'll be dealing with valuations, investors, possible audits on your financial statements, and so forth.

It can be really attractive though if you consider getting millions for a business that you have been working on for 3 – 5 years.

Almost all of the mega-successful entrepreneurs that you hear about these days grow their businesses for an exit. Why? It gives them a large amount of money now instead of spreading that payment out over 30 to 50 years.

In the world of finance, there is a principal called The Time Value of Money. It says that having money now is more valuable than having money later due to inflation and other factors. The thought here is that if you had millions of dollars now, what could you invest it in to get billions of dollars?

So the end effect with early exit companies is that you tend to reach your mansion much faster assuming you're smart with your money and don't blow it all on video games and rice krispy treats.

What do you want to get from your company?

Here's the catch though: Not all businesses are capable of being early-exit businesses. Just because you want to go that route doesn't mean that someone will buy your business. For example, a technology company is much more likely to have potential buyers down the line than a dog grooming business.

You have to ask yourself if there are entities out there that would pay a premium for your business idea once you got large enough. If not, then you're probably on the road to a retirement business. Both businesses are great in my opinion. Many entrepreneurs only want to talk about the early-exit models though because those have a bigger bang for their buck.

If you really want to do an early exit business but you can't think of buyers that would pay top dollar for your business in 3 to 5 years, it may be time to go back to workshop #2 and generate a few more ideas. If you're happy with a retirement business, forge ahead and continue through the workshops!

Preparing for the tax consequences

Both models have different tax consequences. I would suggest that you get an accountant on your side at this point in the game. Forgive me for the shameless plug, but if you reach out to Ignite Spot for your tax accounting and bookkeeping, let us know that you bought The 8-Week Startup and we'll gladly give you a free consultation.

It's impossible to give tax advice in this setting since there are so many variables to consider. Just know that you'll need to consider many things including:

- What type of entity you'll be setting up
- What partners and investors will be involved
- What your personal tax goals are
- What you expect sales and expenses to look like as you ramp up
- What your other income streams look like
- When you plan to exit or gift the business to your kids
- Etc.

Planning for business valuation

Everyone wants to know what their business is worth as they grow it. The problem is that there's a million ways to value a company, and most of them are pretty complicated.

To start off, your balance sheet which your accountant creates each month has a paper valuation comparing your assets to your liabilities. In addition to that, there's the market valuation that gauges what the market is willing to pay for your business at a particular moment in time.

Creating a market value for your business is tricky and usually involves hiring an independent professional to make an assessment.

If you're going to build an early-exit business, you'll want to do some research to see how businesses in your industry are commonly valued. A good place to start is with an industry multiplier. Many industries have a multiplier that you compare to a base figure like gross revenues. For example, your industry may have a multiplier of 2.15 which would mean that you would multiply your gross revenues by 2.15 to determine a rough market value. So if your company did 5 million in sales last year, you would have a market value of approximately $10,750,000.

I'm oversimplifying valuation here, but it gives us a place to start. There are more ways to go about valuing a company, but the multiplier method is used quite a bit as a starting point for negotiations. When the time comes for you to hire a valuation expert, he will most likely use a multiplier in conjunction with several other factors.

Every industry has a different multiplier which will fluctuate based off of current economic conditions. That's the hard part about it. As you can imagine, a multiplier for a construction company may be really high in certain economic conditions, but in a housing market recession, the multiplier stinks.

Action work: Understand what you want before you start

It's time to determine what you want from your business. Setting the end result now will help you to stay focused as you make decisions and grow your empire. Once again, let me stress that both kinds of businesses, retirement and early-exit, are great options. It really comes down to the type of business you have and your own personal goals.

With all of that out of the way, here's your homework for the day:

1. What are your personal goals for a business? Are you interested in a steady stream of income over time, or are you interested in working your tail off for a few years and then

exiting big? List your thoughts and reasons for your thinking below.

_____
_____
_____
_____
_____
_____
_____

2. If you chose to be a retirement business, who will inherit it when you pass away? Write out your plans for making that happen and your reasons for doing so. Make sure that this person will actually want the business and will improve it when you are gone.

_____
_____
_____
_____
_____
_____
_____
_____

3. If you chose to be an early-exit business, identify at least three companies that would show interest in buying your business at a certain revenue point. Why would they want to acquire you? What would they need to see from you to make the acquisition? It might help to work with your mentors on this or even to call the companies and ask them.

_____
_____
_____

_____

_____

_____

_____

_____

_____

4. If you chose to be an early-exit business, what is your reason
   for doing so? What would you have to receive as a payoff in
   order to make it worth it to you?

_____

_____

_____

_____

_____

_____

_____

I know we're dealing with crystal ball stuff here. We have no idea
what the future will bring, but that's not our goal, entirely. Our goal is
to set a strategic target so that we have something to work towards
over the coming years.

As you complete today's homework, I want to you to close your eyes
and visualize what you have just decided for yourself. Visualize your
life as you achieve your desired result. How does it make you feel to
know that you are working towards a defined purpose that ultimately
will bring you the happiness and freedom that you're looking for?

Good job today. I hope that you feel the power behind mapping out
your exit. It's a valuable exercise that will keep you pointed north
during the many crucial moments of your company's birth and
maturity.

WORKSHOP 13: Forecasting the First 12 Months of Cash

"About the time we can make ends meet, somebody moves the ends"

- Herbert Hoover

Ever get that feeling in life that you just don't have enough money? It's like cash has decided to make you public enemy number one. I love the quote above. I think it summarizes pretty well how most feel when it comes to money. It's applicable in business too because once a company does get to the point where it's cash flowing, meaning that it has more coming in that going out, the business finds ways to spend more money. It's a booby trap designed to rob you of a good night's sleep.

What you need is a way to manage the cash as it moves through your business now and in the future. A simple cash flow forecast will help you take control and manage the dips in the road.

Change is the name of the game

Someone once described success as a squiggly line, rather than a straight shot from point A to point B. I would agree with that. I have yet to be in, or work with, a small business that isn't in a constant state of change. Change is caused by a million and one different things, from customers not paying on time to economic slumps and governmental regulations. We have a running joke at Ignite Spot that our business changes from day to day. It's not due to lack of vision, but rather necessity. Without change, you become stagnant, boring, and subject to the mercy of your competitors.

Small businesses are always on the move. Tomorrow's events, as they sit on the calendar today, will most likely be changed, monopolized, or conquered by other more pressing matters. I think this is one of the reasons that starting a business is scary for many people. The thought of waking up each day to an entirely new set of possibilities versus a set schedule takes a certain kind of stamina. I thrive on having a new day every day, and I hope you do too. The thought of living a concrete routine is not in my bag of tricks.

On a day-to-day basis, you may find yourself adjusting how you do business, why you do it, and what you hope the end result will be. With all that being said, one might wonder why we strive to plan at all. Why would we try and forecast cash if the business is going to be in a constant state of flux? We do it because having a plan is a heck of a lot better than not having a plan.

With a cash flow forecast, you can lay out your options in a financial model and then change things to see what the outcome will be. For example, you may be thinking of hiring an employee in six months which sounds great, but once you add the costs into your forecast, you realize that you better hold off until month ten, because otherwise your cash will go south for the winter.

Do you remember when you were little and your mom would ask you to take a bath? Once in the tub, she would shout through the door, saying, "Make sure to use soap!" You, being ever mindful of your personal hygiene as an eight year old, would go to grab the soap and it would pop out of your tiny hands. You would then spend the next 35 minutes trying to grab the bar. In the end, you never even got soapy! I hate to say it, but forecasting cash can sometimes feel like trying to pick up a bar of wet soap as an eight year old. Nevertheless, you've got to do it. If you actually use the tool I provide, you'll probably find yourself working on it daily once the business gets started. That's because your cash and assumptions will change daily, making it necessary to stay updated. After all, you'll want to know if a decision you make today will sink the boat three months down the road.

Why they call it a forecast

As you know, a forecast is your best estimate of the future. Just like a weather forecast that tries to predict when the storms will roll in, a cash flow forecast is your best estimate of the ups and downs in your cash balance. After all, cash is the most important part of your company. Without cash, you can't survive long so you want to make sure to put up your best defenses and protect it.

For many new entrepreneurs, forecasting cash will likely be a daily task. Until you become a large organization with in-house accountants, I would suggest that this be one of the tasks that you DO NOT delegate; keeping this ball in your court ensures that you're connected to cash and making the right decisions.

Many entrepreneurs tell themselves that they aren't detail oriented and determine to offload this kind of work ASAP. I'm fine with you delegating most of the administrative work, but forecasting cash should be your sole responsibility.

How to use a forecast

There are a lot of elaborate software packages out there that will help you forecast cash. In today's world though, Excel still reigns supreme. You probably already have the software on your computer and I'm guessing you already have a working knowledge of it.

We will be using Excel to forecast cash for your company. One of the most important rules for forecasting cash is to keep it simple. This is where Excel can be a detriment to society. Many people love making Excel complicated. They love using "if" formulas, macros, and a host of other doodads. As much as I love those things, we're going to keep most, if not all, of them out of the forecast.

Complicating Excel leads to errors, and we cannot afford to deal with errors when we are forecasting cash. So keep it simple.

The purpose of this tool is to help you manage "cash in" versus "cash out" and foresee when cash is in trouble. It's also a tool to help you envision when cash will be high, giving you opportunities to reinvest in your business and make it more efficient.

Forecasts are also only as good as the data that you put into them. If your data is garbage, no amount of Excel wizardry will make the future look bright. I can't tell you how many times I've seen people put together a fancy forecast while basic information like the beginning cash balance is wrong.

Don't let this happen to you.

Once you get your forecast built, you're not done. A forecast is a working tool. It's designed to help you make decisions on a daily basis. That means that you need to be able to enter "what-if" scenarios into it to see what will happen.

For example, what if you spend $50,000 to buy a piece of equipment? You'll need to put that purchase into your forecast to see how it effects your cash position over a 12 month period. You get in trouble when you don't use a cash flow forecast to make decisions like this one. It's easy to think that you have enough cash today to absorb the expense. Many people say to themselves, "Let's buy it since we have enough cash this month and we'll make it work." You don't want to go down that road. The term "We'll make it work" is really a code phrase for let's play Russian Roulette.

In short, make sure of the following:

1. Your forecast is simple
2. The data is understandable
3. You have the ability to add assumptions so that you can see what the outcomes will be

Using a tool like this shouldn't take more than 5 minutes a day, and in doing so, you'll do a better job of keeping the red out of your ledgers.

The Good, the Bad and the Ugly

Who doesn't like Clint Eastwood? That guy knows how to make a great movie. Every time I hear the title *The Good, the Bad, and the Ugly,* I think of him and cash flow forecasting.

Forecasting cash can turn you into a greedy you-know-what. As you start thinking about how many sales you're going to make, it's a natural human tendency to hope that your company will make buckets of cash. As such, your greed can sometimes skew the forecast to the positive.

I actually don't mind when that happens. We'll call that "The Good." At the same time, you need to have a second cash flow forecast that's "the Bad" and "the Ugly". This forecast needs to be your worst case scenario.

We need to have both scenarios because, in truth, you don't know what your future sales are going to be. A positive outlook will bring one set of circumstances and a slow outlook, another.

In The 12-Month Cash Flow Forecast tool that I added to your download file, you'll notice that there are two tables. The one on the left is the best case scenario and the one on the right is the worst case scenario. By default, the worst case scenario is set to reflect 30% of the estimated sales that you set in your best case. You'll be able to change this percentage in the tool to match your best estimates.

Understanding assumptions

When you forecast, you have to make some guesses. It's part of the game. To make this easier, there is a place on The 12-Month Cash Flow Forecast that allows you to enter some standard assumptions. Feel free to add more as they pertain to your business model.

As you build your cash flow forecast, you will need to make several assumptions including:

1. The growth rate of your sales
2. The seasonality of your sales
3. Your gross margin (which isn't a complete assumption since we calculated it in Workshop 8)
4. How long it will take your customers to pay you
5. When you will start incurring overhead
6. When to hire employees
7. What percent of your budget will go to marketing
8. Percent of labor, materials, and other cost of sales as a percentage of revenue
9. Etc.

There's a lot to think about, which is exactly why the tool needs to lay the data out in an easy-to-understand format.

Remember that assumptions change, and they can change daily. This is why using your cash flow forecast on a daily basis is so vital.

Action work: Fill out The 12-Month Cash Forecast

To really get the most out of this workshop, you'll need to get The 12-Month Cash Flow Forecast tool that I added into your download kit. If you bought this workshop form the8weekstartup.com, you'll have access to it. If not, I have attached a picture of the forecast below for your reference and you can use it as a model to build your own.

Also, be sure to watch the videos in your download kit. In the videos, I take time to fill out the forecast and show you what you should enter, and where.

To get started, you'll need a couple of things:

1. A working understanding of Excel
2. Your beginning cash balance
3. An understanding of your cost of goods sold from Workshop 8

Let's get started. Do the homework below. When you're finished, you should have your cash flow forecast filled out, giving you a good picture of what you can expect over the next 12 months.

1. Get the tool and fill in the blue cells: Start off by downloading the tool and watching the videos at the8weekstartup.com. As you move through the tool, you'll notice that some of the cells are colored **blue**. These are the cells that you are supposed to fill in. The remaining cells are formula driven and will fill in automatically. You'll notice that there aren't any blue cells in the worst case scenario. That's because the worst case scenario mirrors your best case with the exception of having lower sales. The goal is to show you what would happen if you kept your current cost structure, but didn't sell as much as you though you would.

2. **Get your positives and negatives right:** Note that when you enter a "cash in" item, make sure the number is positive. For "cash out" items, you must enter a negative number.

3. **Review your cash balances:** At the bottom of the tool, you'll notice the row that says "End of month cash balance." Do you see how those cells are colored from red to green? That's because they're formatted to give you a visual representation of your cash balance. If the cells are red, that means that cash is going more and more negative. As the cells move to green, that means that your cash position is improving. Obviously, we like the color green.

4. **Enter your "what-if" scenarios:** You'll also notice a section at the bottom of the tool called "'What-if' Scenarios". This is where you can add one-time income and expense items. For example, you may want to buy a piece of equipment in the future. Add those kinds of items here, so that they are separate from your standard ongoing costs and revenues. That way you can see them individually, and you can also see how they affect your cash balance.

5. **Adjust as necessary:** Once you get all of your preliminary figures in, look at your end of month cash balances and adjust as needed until your cash balance is positive across all months and you have enough of a buffer to sleep well at night. Keep in mind, though, that your adjustments need to be realistic. For example, if cash goes negative in month seven, you can't just triple sales in month six to cover the problem.

This topic is one that usually requires a lot of questions. Make sure you watch the videos to get a good grasp on how to use the tool and then feel free to jump on the forum at the8weekstartup.com to ask additional questions.

Good luck and happy forecasting!

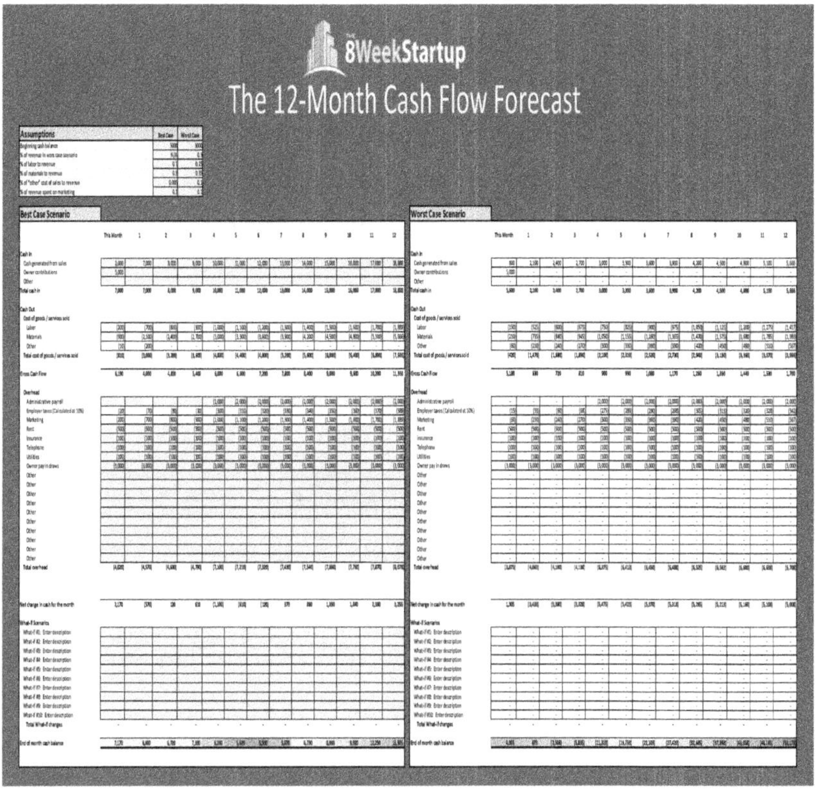
8WeekStartup
The 12-Month Cash Flow Forecast
Assumptions
Best Case Scenario
Worst Case Scenario

WORKSHOP 14: To Partner or Not to Partner

"I am certainly not one of those who need to be prodded. If fact, if anything, I am the prod."

- Winston Churchill

Why having business partners seems attractive

Having a business partner just makes everything feel safer, right? Well… that's not always the case. A lot of business owners start off by finding a partner and they end up regretting that they did.

Partners can be a great thing, but in many cases, they can destroy your company. It's a big decision to bring on a partner so you need to make sure that you are doing it for the right reasons.

Here are some of the wrong reasons for brining on a partner:

1. You're scared of running the business by yourself and you want someone to carry some of the anxiety.
2. You're best friends and you believe that that your friendship will make your partnership successful.
3. You need money in the company and the potential partner has cash.

In this workshop, we'll explore all of the good, as well as the bad baggage that comes with partnerships. Bringing on a partner will completely change the fate of your company. Given that it is such an important decision, you need to leave your personal feelings out of it. I know that having a partner would make owning your own business feel less lonely and less stressful because you have someone there with you to try and make things work, but you can't let that kind of emotional pull make decisions for you.

I'm not saying that partnerships are bad. In fact, when they're set up right, partnerships can exponentially add strength and value to your organization. It's hard to do though because you're dealing with people. Partnerships aren't a mathematical formula that we can calculate and forecast. People are moody, sensitive, happy, angry, and basically volatile depending on the circumstances. When you don't have partners, you avoid all of that.

What a good business partner can do for you

I am one of the lucky few. At Ignite Spot, I have a business partner that I get to work with every day. He is one of the best parts of the company and I am always impressed by his ability to help grow our business.

I didn't just jump on the partnership bandwagon though. Ryan and I knew each other for years before we finally partnered on Ignite Spot. During that time, we worked with each other, went out to lunch a million times, and built a relationship that began to transcend emotional squabbles.

We decided to become partners for several reasons. First and foremost, Ryan is a technical guru when it comes to accounting. He has a resume a mile long that impresses everyone who reads it. I needed someone like that in the firm that could oversee operations. Ryan goes far beyond operations, though... he has vision, and lots of it. As a matter of fact, the stuff pours out of his ears. Without the vision, Ryan would just be another employee. It's his ability to create his dreams that made him "partner worthy."

At the time, Ryan was working for a CPA firm and was planning on getting out to start his own practice, which is where I come in. I have a strong background in sales, web design, branding, and business development.

We were a natural fit for each other. I decided to ask Ryan to partner up with me and it was the best decision I ever made.

A good business partner will do many things for you and your organization. Just like Ryan does for us, your business partner should be able to:

- Encapsulate the same grand vision that you have
- Shake with excitement over the prospects of the company
- Be willing to do whatever it takes to achieve the dream
- Complete the skillsets of the management team
- Avoid emotional break-downs when times get tough

Let's talk about the third one on that list. A partner is the kind of person that will stay up until 3 a.m. to get it done. He will raise capital in crucial moments, make tough calls, and stand by you when nobody else will. An employee by nature will do none of those things. An employee typically shows up for work and leaves when its 5 p.m., with little more than a paycheck on the brain.

If you do decide to bring on a partner, you need to make sure you're not offering the position to someone who really is just an employee. That's why it took me and Ryan over three years to get to the point that we could trust each other. We had to know that the other person wouldn't let the dream die just because it was time to go home for the day.

What a bad business partner will do to you

Now is as good of a time as any to talk about best friends. I have seen a lot of people go into business with their buddies, which at first glance seems like it would be fun. My warning to you is this… money changes people. When money comes between you and your best friend, tensions will rise up and the emotions are ten times higher because you barbecue with this guy on the weekends.

Ryan and I have made a point not to be buddies. We don't hang out. We have never gotten together outside of work because we know that our relationship has to stay professional. We have to keep the emotion out of it. Period.

If you find yourself bringing on a partner for the wrong reasons and things go sour, you'll find yourself wading through a nightmare. Once a partnership has gone bad, it is really hard to save it. When that happens, your business will suffer in multiple ways including:

- Your business culture will crash and burn overnight
- You'll spend insane amounts of time fighting over ownership issues
- You'll end up having to constantly prod him to do his job
- The company will have to keep paying him regardless of his performance
- It becomes impossible to make decisions to grow the company because he'll fight you on everything
- You'll have to fork over gobs of cash to buy him out

It's for these reasons and many others that I would suggest that you start your business without a partner. It's probably safe to bet that you want a partner, and maybe have already picked one up. If that's the case, you may want to consider ending the relationship right now as it will be much easier than down the road when there is a lot of money on the line.

Later on, we'll talk about bringing partners into the mix once the company is up and running. If you are going to get a partner, I like this approach because you can more easily define what the partner will have to do to earn his or her way into the business. The partner will also be more motivated and see the grand picture if the model is making money.

You also don't want to have to pay wages or owner draws to a partner in the beginning. It is a huge drain on cash that can ultimately sink you.

How to know when you need a partner

You may never need a partner. If possible, try to avoid getting one unless there's good reason to do so. As the business grows, you'll soon find out where your strengths and weaknesses are. You'll also find areas of the business that need more help than others.

At Ignite Spot, we needed a tax division for our clients. Since I'm not a tax accountant, it was a really large hole to fill and Ryan was the perfect fit.

If you do need a partner, there are signs that will let you know. Remember that none of these signs are based on emotional fears or attachments; instead they are signs that will strategically move the business forward.

If you see these signs, you may need a partner:

- There is a specific part of your business that's out of your skill set and is too complicated for your mentors to help you with.
- The company needs to move in a strategic direction that you're unable to accommodate to.
- There are resources, contacts, market share, and knowledge that a partner could bring to the table that you can't.

Finding a great business partner can be challenging though. Think about job interviews for a second. I think it's fair to say that many people misrepresent themselves in a job interview because they want the position so badly. I can think of a few people that I've hired over the years that turned out to be no-gos, but were great in the interview phase. Partners can be the same way. Many people want to jump on a successful bandwagon, especially if they can get a piece of the pie. Many people will often become misleading with regards to their abilities, resources, and dedication when such a bright future is at stake.

That's why a partner has to earn the title. Never hand someone equity as a way of enticing them to join your company. I've seen so many entrepreneurs give up a piece of ownership to someone they felt would be a great asset on their team, but didn't feel like they had the cash to pay them in salary. I have yet to see that work out well.

The only time I have seen ownership splits work well is when the new guy has to earn his slice of the pie. In other words, don't offer the pie as an incentive to getting highly talented people on board; use your vision, excitement, and zeal as an entrepreneur to do that. Instead, get them on board with your passion and then, if they prove up to the task, approach them at a much later date and give them the ability to earn ownership and become a partner.

Dealing with the equity thing

Everyone wants to know how much equity they should give up to partners. Giving up equity will almost always lead to a blood bath down the road so make sure that you handle things properly at the onset and you should be fine.

If you do decide to give up equity to a partner, do it in phases, and never give up more than 49% in total. As they prove that they deserve ownership, they can increase their equity over time. Also, don't just give it to them. If having ownership in the company is important to them and they are dedicated to the cause, they should buy instead of being given the equity.

When people have to put their own money on the table, something happens inside of them. They have skin in the game now.

I can think of a client I advised a few years back who received several million dollars in venture capital funding. Despite my efforts, they blew through that money like it was nothing. I guarantee that if that had been their own money, they would have been sensitive as to how they spent every dollar, but because it was just handed to them, they burned through it in just a few months with little to show for it.

I could barely believe how quickly they spent the funds. They had no skin in the game, which meant that they felt no fiscal responsibility. If you bring on a partner, you want them to feel that responsibility. Make them buy in if they want ownership that bad. It'll be good for them. Trust me.

By the way, I'm not trying to scare you off of the whole partnership thing. I just want you to walk away from this workshop with a healthy dose of partnership reality, which is to say that they rarely work. In the end, someone almost always feel cheated which causes fights and eventually business failure.

To avoid the heartache that comes with partnerships, I would suggest the following:

1. Partner with someone for what they bring to the partnership, and not because he or she is your best friend.
2. Create a partnership agreement upfront which states who will do what in exchange for their ownership.
3. Review your financial statements together monthly and be open with each other about the financial position of the company. Usually partners split tasks up which means that one of the partners usually gets stuck with the bookkeeping.

Make sure that he is communicating with you and giving you an opportunity to review the books anytime.

Action work: To partner or not to partner

It's time to examine how you feel about having a partner. Have you thought about brining someone on at this point? Be honest with yourself as you go through this exercise. It's important that you realize why you want a partner, if indeed you do. If you don't want a partner, I would say you can skip the homework in today's workshop and have the day off.

Assuming you do want a partner, take time to honestly answer the questions below:

1. Why do you feel like you need a partner?

_____

_____

_____

_____

_____

_____

_____

_____

2. What is causing you to feel that way?

_____

_____

_____

_____

_____

_____

_____

3. Are you thinking about brining on your best friend as a partner? If so, do you really want money coming between you and this person?

_____

_____

_____

_____

_____

_____

_____

_____

4. Assuming you are still interested in having a partner, list out what this person would need to do to earn their ownership over time.

_____

_____

_____

_____

_____

_____

_____

_____

One final tip when it comes to partners. Be direct. Don't beat around the bush. After all, you're dealing with your business here. It's your future and you can't leave things to chance or bad partnerships. Tell them how you feel, what you expect out of the relationship, and why you are bringing them on. Tell them that you want to keep the relationship professional so that the business doesn't suffer from emotional break-downs.

I can't say it enough, but having a partner is risky business. Once you give them ownership, you can't just fire them and learn from your mistake. If you bring them on as a partner, you're married, which means that you better pick the right fish in the sea.

WORKSHOP 15: The Art of Recurring Revenues

"Profit in business comes from repeat customers, customers that boast about your product or service, and that bring friends with them."

- W. Edwards Deming

What are recurring revenues and why do we like them?

When you sell your first widget, you'll feel like you're on cloud nine. It's a great feeling to know that you built something that someone valued so much that they were willing to give up cash for it. I once sat in a small workshop with Rick Alden, founder of Skull Candy. One of the members asked him what he loved most about being an entrepreneur. He stated that he was recently at a store where his headphones were being sold and he watched a gentleman pick out a pair, walk to the cash register, and buy them. He said that watching that was his favorite part, not because he just made money, but because he helped create something that someone loves.

But is that all there is to business? The one-time sell? Absolutely not. Our goal today is to try and figure out how to create solutions for your customers that will keep them buying from you on a monthly basis. A one-time transaction is great, but if that customer never comes back, you're missing out on a lot of opportunities.

Today we build your recurring revenue model. Sounds like fun, doesn't it?! Well it is. Almost every business model has the ability to create a solution that would generate recurring revenues on a monthly basis. With a little creativity, you should never have to say goodbye to your customers.

We love recurring revenues for so many reasons. Let me spout off a few for you:

1. They allow you to continue providing value for your customers after the first purchase
2. You make a lot more money
3. They provide stability to your company's cash flows
4. They allow you to stay connected with your customers and make a difference in their lives

Whether you are a plumber, lawyer, accountant, Chinese bracelet salesman, or an artist, you need to find a way to get them coming back.

Later in this workshop we'll talk about how I've approached generating recurring revenue here at The 8-Week Startup. For now though, let's keep exploring what it means to you and your new company.

The lifetime value of a customer

What is the lifetime value of a customer to you? If you sell a product for $150 and then never see that person again, the lifetime value of your customers is just $150. That's not very good. We want to increase this as much as possible.

Let's assume that you come up with a way to get them to purchase with you on a monthly basis. Maybe you create a monthly educational class that costs $50 a month and lasts for six months. The lifetime value of that customer is now up to $450! You have grown the value by 300%! Not bad.

A local camera shop uses this model. I bought a Nikon from them a while back that cost around $700. They then offered me a discount on their photography classes, which lasted for three months, for a total of $300.

That approach does several things for them.

1. It increases the lifetime value of their customers
2. It gets their customers in their store at least once a month for three months which increases the chances that they will by more camera equipment
3. It allows them to upsell other services

If the camera shop had just sold me a camera and wished me well, they would have missed out on all of those benefits!

This is what we want to do with your company today. You need to brainstorm on what you can do to take your relationship past the first sale.

Looking beyond the single purchase

What is it that you are going to sell? Does your product or service lend itself to natural ways of generating ongoing revenues with your client? Obviously finding ways to build recurring revenue will be easier for some types of businesses than others. If you're having a difficult time trying to find ways to take care of your customer past the first sale, don't dismay. We'll go over a few different ways that companies do this in just a second.

Before we get to that though, I want you to open up your mind. Look past the first sale. Once your customer does pay for that first product or service, what do they naturally do next? Are there new problems or reasons for support that are caused by having your product? For example, if you sell a complicated piece of software, you may have given them tools to fix their initial problem, but you have now given them a whole host of new problems... Now they have to learn how to use the software!

You need to take some time to put yourself in your customer's shoes and ask, "If I had just bought this product or service, what would I think, feel, or do next?"

It's that moment in time that ideas for recurring revenues are born. As you begin to think this way, you'll find yourself realizing that the customer still needs you. That's a great thing! Now that you've built a solution to solve their initial problem, you need to build a solution to keep solving their problems.

Tips for generating recurring revenues

There are a lot of ways to go about doing this. Again, the type of business that you're starting will have a big influence on what you can do for your customer going forward. Let's look at some of the options that you have, but please keep in mind that there are other ways to generate recurring revenue. This list is by no means exhaustive.

Ongoing training

The software story that we used above is a good example of this. Is there a way that you can provide training to your customer after he or she has bought your product or service? Get creative with this, for heaven's sake.

I'm making this up on the spot, but what if you sold stoves? What could you do to generate recurring revenue in a business where people usually only buy stoves once every 20 years? What if you partnered with a local chef in the area and offered cooking classes at your shop? You could charge a monthly fee of $50 to your stove buyers and $150 to everyone else. The classes could be 2 hours long and when you finish up, you get to eat dinner with your classmates! Not only would it be fun to do, but it could be a great date night with the spouse as well – and all because you bought a stove!

Every business has the ability to pull this off. You just need to think outside of the box. Besides, do you know any appliance companies out there that are offering cooking classes from a top executive chef? I can tell you this: If I was in the market for a new stove, I know where I would go. That just sounds like fun to me.

Information Seminars

Great content is powerful. Is there a way that you can generate a monthly seminar or informational series for your customers? What can you do that will generate recurring revenues and provide amazing information for your customers?

The 8-Week Startup uses this model with something I created called the Entrepreneur's Club. I know that as people take these workshops, they're going to have a lot of questions. To address those questions, I have created two different options. The first is our online forums, which are free. You can go there to ask general questions, meet other entrepreneurs, and help others out.

The second option is The Entrepreneur's Club. For $49 a month, you'll have access to tools that are private to the world including:

1. A monthly entrepreneur's newsletter, written by me, covering new topics, tips, and tricks on getting your business up and running.
2. You'll be invited to a private weekly seminar online where I will teach a class in person. During that class, you'll have an opportunity to ask me questions where we can do hands-on

work together as we grow your business. Each class will last an hour and will have a unique topic that we will address for the month. It's our master class, where you can work directly with me and others in the class to get answers real-time.

If you are thinking about joining The Entrepreneur's Club, go to http://the8weekstartup.com/products-page/entrepreneurs-club/ and get signed up. I would love to see you there and get the chance to work directly with you on your business.

Is there something you can do in your business that's like The Entrepreneur's Club? I created The Entrepreneur's Club because of the need for further education. I know that when I read a business book, there have been many times where I wish I could reach through the pages and speak with the author to get my questions answered.

Servicing

Do you sell a product that requires maintenance? This model makes me think of the printer at our office. Each month, we need toner, maintenance, and the whole ball of wax to make the thing work smoothly. The company that sold us the printer also has a maintenance division that they use to capture that recurring revenue.

If you sell computers, could you sell a monthly performance checkup? If you sell cars, could you sell the oil changes? What do you sell and what consequences will your customer face by having the product? Find a way to ease those consequences and make life better for them ongoing.

Make sure that you don't shoot yourself in the foot with this one though. If you remember from past workshops, I spoke about my saltwater aquarium business and how my recurring revenues were going to come from maintaining the aquariums once I had built them. The problem was that the costs to do the maintenance just didn't make sense. It wasn't worth it.

Find a way to generate recurring revenues that creates a win/win relationship between you and your customer.

Members only

Exclusivity is cool. Being a member of something makes people unique. When your customers buy something from you, is there a members-only program that you can enroll them in? A lot of companies do this today. Just think about all of the cards attached to your key chain that make you a member of your local grocery store, hardware store, and book store.

Given that a lot of companies are doing the members-only approach, you need to be careful with this one. If you do create a member's-only system in your company, it actually needs to mean something. People have to be able to associate with your brand, your service, and see great value in it for this to matter. You can't just be another company in their life. You need to be vital to them. At that point, being a member creates pride and continual purchasing.

Once you do get a good member's only program in place, you can create products or services that are available only to members. This kind of approach tells your members that they are special and that you appreciate their business.

New features

Adding new features is a great way to generate more revenue. If you build your product or service and never improve it, you'll become stagnate to the market and your customers. If, on the other hand, you find ways to make your company more valuable, you need to be able to communicate that new value to your customers. A lot of people do this through newsletters or something similar.

Automate your recurring revenues

Once you do have a system in place that will keep your customers coming back for more, make it as easy as possible for them to buy from you. If they have to send you a check or come into your store every time they need to pay, then you'll hardly make any money. People get busy, which means that you can't fault them for forgetting about you. It's going to happen.

When and where possible, try and get your customers to sign up for the recurring revenue model via a credit card or bank card that can be auto drafted each month. Then it's up to you to do a fantastic job of wowing them every month so that they don't cancel on you.

You can get that set up when they're in your store making their first purchase, or when they hit your website. It's important to make your website payment ready so that you can generate revenues online. When we get into building a website in later workshops, we'll talk about how to integrate with a merchant like PayPal, so that you can take payments without a storefront.

Action work: Find a way to generate recurring revenues

It's that time of day again! Now it's your turn to focus the mirror on yourself. Take a look at your business and find a few different ways to generate recurring value for your customers, and therefore earn the right to generate recurring revenues.

Answer the questions below.

1. When your customer buys your product or service for the first time, what new set of consequences do they face?

_____

_____

_____

_____

_____

_____

_____

2. What recurring value can you offer to your customers that will make their lives even better after their initial purchase with you? Remember to get creative!

_____

_____

_____

_____

_____

_____

_____

3. Define ways in which you could provide ongoing training for your customers.

_____

_____

_____

_____

_____

_____

4. Define ways in which you could provide additional information or seminars for your customers.

_____

_____

_____

_____

_____

_____

_____

_____

5. Define ways in which you could provide servicing after the initial sale.

_____

_____

_____

_____

_____

_____

_____

_____

6. Is there a way to create a member's only program for your business? If so, what value would they get for being members?

_____

_____

_____

_____

_____

_____

_____

7. How can you introduce and communicate new features to your customers that will keep them coming back for more?

_____

_____

_____

_____

_____

_____

Recurring revenue is vital for a company's long-term health. Don't engineer your business to be a single transaction shop. Find a way to be more valuable, interesting, and fun. I can almost guarantee you that if a stove company started doing cooking classes, there would be a write-up about it in the paper.

Doing something unique that makes your customers' lives better makes you stick out, and sticking out is a great thing.

WORKSHOP 16: How to Get Killer Distribution

"I want to put a ding in the universe."

- Steve Jobs

You know that saying, "It's not what you know but who you know that counts"? Well, get ready to take it literally. When it comes to getting your product or service sold, getting it in front of the right people is vital.

We're looking for the people with megaphones. You actually have a few of these people in your personal network. You'll want to make use of those relationships to the best of your ability. Going beyond that though, we need to look at organizations and existing business arrangements that can propel your business forward at a thousand miles an hours.

Before we determine how to do this, let's talk about what the megaphone is. To me, a megaphone gives someone the ability to be heard above the crowd. It gives them magical powers to draw attention, look like a leader, and communicate a message that says, "What I am about to tell you is important."

If you can get your business into the hands of someone with such uncanny powers, you'll get a good boost, to say the least.

Let me give you an example of how I plan to do this with The 8-Week Startup. If I went the standard route, I would write this book and try to get it published as a one-off read. I could approach the topic like most authors and work my tail off to get a publisher to notice me. It may work, but even if I did get published, it would be tough to get noticed as my book is placed on a bookshelf with hundreds, if not thousands, of other business books. That doesn't sound too interesting to me.

What are my options? How can I be different, get killer distribution, and get noticed by the megaphone masters of my space?

Now we're asking the right questions. I think that questions are powerful. It's amazing to me how, with a few rearranged questions, you get a whole new perspective on life.

Let's attack these questions one at a time.

Killer distribution starts with being different

To get killer distribution, you have to be different. If The 8-Week Startup were distributed like every other book, few would notice it. That's a problem for me. So, I have to take the standard notion of a book, and turn it on its head. I'll do that by accomplishing the following:

- Write 40 distinguishable workshops that people can digest easily. I'm not shooting for long dissertations crammed into a huge book that overwhelm my readers. I want bit-sized workshops that create businesses.
- Take each of those workshops and turn them into audiobooks so that people can carry me with them wherever they go.
- Build custom tools for many of the workshops that take the reading to an action-packed level.
- Create video of me actually doing the program myself and starting a business.

The last one is the real secret sauce. If nothing else, many people will want to get the book and buy the workshop series simply to watch me conceive, start, and build a business right in front of them. That will get people talking far more than the standard "how-to" business book. Plus, once I get it into the hands of the megaphone holders, they'll have something to shout about.

In addition, I've made everything digital which makes The 8-Week Workshop far more versatile than most programs.

Notice that these differences are designed to add value to my readers. I didn't just create differences to be different.

Think of your business for a moment. How do people in your industry typically distribute their product or service? How can you turn model on its head in a way that adds value to your customers and makes the people with megaphones pay attention?

Get credibility to get noticed

Now that your business is ready to distribute its products or services in a unique way, you need some big names to smile upon you. For every industry, the big names are different. Your job is to try and get them to review what you are doing and give you a thumbs-up. Then you can take that recommendation, and share it with the world.

Why do you think that Pepsi hired Michael Jackson to dance around with their flagship soda in his hand? It gave Pepsi credibility and made people want to buy it. Did it work? Absolutely.

At The 8-Week Startup, my goal is to get some of the best business writers I can find to promote my series. I need to get there in steps though. Here is how I'm going to do it:

1. Upon completion of the workshops, I'm going to approach five professors from where I went to business school, and ask

them if I can do a live presentation of The 8-Week Workshop to the business students and staff.

2. I'm going to hold two to three seminars for these colleges and video tape them. My goal will be to get as much energy as possible packed into the events.

3. I will then approach local media outlets and contact journalists to see if I can add value to their business columns, thereby getting myself quoted in recognized media.

4. I will then send free copies of my entire workshop to my top 50 favorite business writers and entrepreneurs asking them to review it for me.

5. I will then use any reviews I get back as recommendations on my website, publications, etc.

It will be a lot of work, but it will be well worth it. If I can get notable business writers and entrepreneurs to approve of The 8-Week Startup, then their megaphones will ring loud and clear.

Have you ever noticed how all of the bestsellers have tons of recommendations from big name players? When you open the jacket, you're drenched with amazing people telling you how wonderful the book is. If a book has a ton of recommendations, I'm far more likely to add it to my library. This obviously works for more than just books.

Who are the notables in your industry? Don't just think of people either. Notice that I'll be doing seminars at business colleges. Try and think of people, organizations, etc. that have credibility. How can you utilize their credibility to get your name out there?

Get a distribution partner

Just having credibility isn't enough. Once you have some strong testimonials and recommendations from your industry big boys, you need to find ways to get out there. This is where the distribution part really takes effect.

If you've found a way to truly be different, and you've built up some recommendations, you can now approach market place leaders to help sell your product. Given that you have made so many in-roads, they'll be more interested in taking your business on.

Let's keep moving forward with The 8-Week Startup as an example. As I mentioned before, I could try to get published as my one and only goal. Getting a book on the bookshelf is a good way to distribute, but there has to be more…right? Of course there is.

Who sells information that would be willing to take on The 8-Week Startup and sell it to their customers? My first thought is with companies like App Sumo and Udemy.com, both of which have a large base of online users, and sell digital information that is right down my alley.

I obviously need to create content that is worthy for their customer base. If I can accomplish that, I'll be able to reach millions of people instantly. That's a lot more interesting that trying to sell a book out of my car trunk to uninterested pedestrians. Yuck!

Getting killer distribution is all about asking yourself, "Who already has massive reach to tons of my customers, and how can I get them to sell my product or service?"

Get away from thinking like the herd here. Don't look at other people in your industry and say, "I'll just do what they did". Actually, if they became overnight sensations, then do exactly what they did. Most companies however, do what everyone else does, which accomplishes little or nothing for them.

Running the numbers

Once you manage to get your product or service in the hands of the megaphone people, like App Sumo or Udemy.com in my case, you need to run the numbers. Whoever it is that will be selling your stuff will want a piece of the pie; that's a given. How much can you afford to give them while still making it worth your time and effort?

Remember back in Workshop 8, when you calculated your gross margin? That beautiful little percentage is back for some more action.

If the company wants more than your gross margin percentage, you can't afford it. Think about it.

Let's say that you sell a product for $500 and it costs you $300 to make in cost of goods sold. That would mean that you have $200 as gross profit and a gross margin of 40%. Do you remember how we calculated that? It's the $200 in gross profit divided by your $500 price tag.

If a company wants a commission of more than 40% on each item sold, you'll lose money.

Let's take a slight detour into accounting here. If it were my books, I would now include the commission that I pay to the seller as cost of goods sold. That means that if they want to charge 10% as a commission, or $50, my new cost of goods sold would be $350. This would make my new gross profit $150 and my new gross margin 30%.

Remember from Workshop 9 that the lower your gross margin goes, the higher your break-even point rises. That makes sense here since we're giving some of our profits to our distribution partner.

In this example, we lost 10% of our profit in order to get in front of our distribution partner's customers. Is it worth it? I would say so. I could probably only sell a handful of the product out of my trunk, but I could potentially sell much more with their bandwidth.

Who are the sellers in your industry that facilitate a large audience, but are not direct competitors with you? A lot of service businesses try to accomplish this by teaming up with other service professionals in other industries. For example, a lawyer may team up with a financial planner, accountant, or insurance agent.

If I were in that position, I wouldn't just team up with other service professionals though. I would find the biggest, most well-known guy in the industry, and focus on him. Then I would go through the previous steps described above, finding a way to be different and getting some recommendations from big name players. That way, when I approached him, I would make a great first impression and he would see value in partnering with me.

Trying to do it on your own

If it makes so much sense to find a distribution partner, why do very few people do it? It's because it takes work, creativity, and gumption. The very fact that you're here with me reading this means that you're that kind of person. You should be proud of yourself for going the extra mile.

Trying to reach a large market all by yourself is like trying to win a wrestling match with a grizzly bear. All alone, you're just that: the new guy or gal that nobody has ever heard of. Sure, you can spend oodles of cash trying to build a name for yourself, but you know better than that! We don't frivolously spend oodles of cash at The 8-Week Startup. It's a deadly sin that will destroy your soul.

Knowing all of this, many people still attempt it. I was in a marketing meeting with one of my clients a few years ago and they were dead set on making a name for themselves without using a distribution partner. They wanted to rent a billboard for $3,000 a month! I nearly fell out of my chair. The goal was to put the logo on the billboard with a tagline and their address. At $36,000 a year for one lousy billboard, I nearly cried. When I asked them what their motivation was, they said "There are a lot of people that will see it on the freeway. Besides, when I'm driving on the freeway, I love looking at the ads. There's one in particular that I absolutely adore." As she continued, she described a billboard from an insurance company that's known for their humor in advertising.

I sat back and thought for a moment. I then said, "How long have you been driving past that billboard?" She told me that she had been driving past if for nearly two years. I then asked her if she had ever taken the time to switch insurance and go with that company. She hadn't.

Instantly a light went on. I asked her if she really wanted to spend $36,000 a year to make people smile with a catchy ad, or if she wanted to find a way to link up with someone that already had a name so that she could start making some money. She chose the latter option.

Billboards work for some industries, but not for hers. Besides, nobody had ever head of her company so she was trying to create awareness. Every time I hear, "We're going to create awareness," what I really hear is "We're going to spend a bunch of hard-earned money on something we can't quantify and hope that it pans out sometime down the road."

Action work: Get a distribution partner

Getting your product or service out to the masses is like playing chess. With a few pre-planned moves, you can command the board without being written off as a pawn. The actions that you take today could make a huge difference in the launch of your company. Make the most of the homework and take charge of your future.

1. How can you deliver your product or service in a way that makes people talk about you and want to sell for you? Remember, be different in a way that adds value to your customers.

_____

_____

_____

_____

_____

_____

_____

_____

2. Since credibility is so important, what steps will you take to build your authority and get recommendations from the big boys in your industry?

_____

_____

_____

_____

_____

_____

_____

_____

3. Identify the megaphone holders who attract the customers you want to target.

_____

_____

_____

_____

_____

_____

_____

_____

4. How will you approach these megaphone influencers to get them to sell your product?

_____

_____

_____

_____

_____

_____

_____

5. What is your gross margin from Workshop 8? Reiterate why it is that you're not capable of giving more than this percentage away as a commission.

_____

_____

_____

_____

_____

_____

_____

6. Determine how much you can give up in commissions and still make it worth the work. Remember that the more you give up as a commission, the higher your break-even point will be. Once you do get a distribution partnership set up, you'll likely want to revisit Workshop 9 to calculate your new break-even point.

_____

_____

_____

_____

_____

_____

_____

There's no shame with riding on someone's coattails when it comes to business. Think of it as a catapult mechanism that will fling you towards growth.

Pat yourself on the back. You now have a distribution plan that will add jet fuel to your launch. Kaboom!

WORKSHOP 17: The 1-Page Business Plan

"Whatever you're thinking, think bigger."

Tony Hsieh – Co-Founder of Zappos

If you can say something in 1,000 words just as well as you can say it in 10 words, why not say it in 10 words?

Business plans are magnets for saying too much. If you've ever read one, you'll know what I'm talking about. Sure, I've read some business plans that were 40 plus pages which kept me interested the whole time, but they could have said the same thing in a much smaller space.

If you can tell, I'm not a huge fan of overly large business plans. Here's why:

- They can take months and months to write, which is time that you could be out learning from your customers instead of sitting at your desk.
- Entrepreneurs often feel like their business plans have to be a certain length to be impressive. They write more than they should and often load the pages with filler fluff.
- They're usually boring to read.
- Once you finally do get the thing written, you sit back and realize that most of your assumptions need to be changed. This means you have to rewrite and spend more time at your desk instead of in the field.

- Entrepreneurs often use them as a crutch for escaping the real work of starting a business.

The last point interests me quite a bit. As humans, we often take the easy road. As long as we feel busy, we feel productive. It's in our blood. Just like water follows the path of least resistance, we often tell ourselves that we are hard at work building an elaborate business plan, when in reality it's giving us an excuse to avoid getting out there and speaking with customers or selling.

Case in point. A gentleman called me about a year ago ready to start a business. I was so excited for him. He wants to start a retail location in his neighborhood that would actually do quite well. Before he called me, he acquired a location for his business and signed the lease for $2,000 a month.

I cringed a little since he didn't have any revenues coming in, but there was nothing we could do about it. The only answer was to start selling.

I gave him some homework to go out and begin speaking with his target market, but he insisted that he take time to work on his business plan. I didn't agree with the approach, but I wished him well and scheduled a follow up call for a week later. He felt that that would be enough time to get the plan finalized before he started selling.

A week went by at the blink of an eye. I remember calling him up and asking if the plan was finished. Unfortunately, it wasn't. He was 36 pages into in and needed more time to rewrite, check numbers, and on and on.

I just talked with him last week and it's been a year since our first call. He is still working on the business plan, managing his day job, and paying $2,000 a month in rent on an empty space.

I understand his desire to have a plan in place, but he's using it as an excuse to actually avoid starting a business.

It's easy to get into this mindset. He feels like he's busy, and in fact, he is. Unfortunately he's the wrong kind of busy. In his mind, he's working on his company. The sad truth though is that the market is passing him by. Plus, he's running out of cash.

If you think about it, it's often the most uncomfortable things in life that propel you forward the fastest. For example, spending the afternoon selling will make a lot more money than spending all day checking your email and surfing Facebook. If that's the case, why do so many people spend the day checking email? They do it because it makes them feel busy.

You do need a business plan, and by the end of this workshop, you'll have one. It will live on one page, get to the point, shout your value loud and clear, and get you back to doing more important things with your time.

If a banker or investor wants to see a gigantic business plan, feel free to write one for them. If it were me though, I would let them know that I have condensed all of the important information onto one page for their review and if they need more info on a given topic, I could provide it.

When they ask why I would go against the sage old wisdom of writing long and tedious plan, I would say that my goal is to get to the point, build a great business, and not waste their time with fluff. I'm not interested in become a business plan writer, I'm interested in being a business owner.

The five topics to cover

Putting your entire business on to a single sheet of paper can be a challenge. That's because you're forced to only say what's important, relevant, and useful. The rest of the stuff that would fill up 40 pages of dribble must be left out. If your word processor is like mine, that means that you'll be able to fit between 430 to 450 words on the page. This means that each word must have impact and meaning if it's going to earn its place in your business plan.

Given that we have such a small amount of real estate to work with here, we need to get an outline of the most important information we will address. Out of all the information you could write about, there are five areas that I care about the most when it comes to building companies. Let's dig into each one.

The Problem

Start by defining the group of people that you are targeting and the problem that they face. Try to get the description boiled down to 20 words or less. We don't need paragraphs here. Whoever reads the plan needs a clear description of the issue at hand and nothing else.

For example, if you are starting a company that sells a software solution to communicate with the parents of school children, you don't need to go into the history of school districts, the red-tape shenanigans that resides in government based organizations, etc. Keep it short and sweet. Such a company might say the following:

School systems are unable to efficiently notify the parents of children when there are snow days, activities, and emergencies.

It's hard not to start taking about the solution in this sentence. You want to jump right in and start talking about how your company will deliver a better way of living. Don't do that in this section of the business plan. Your goal is to define the problem and nothing more.

The solution

Now it's your time to shine. In this paragraph, you can talk about how you will solve the problem above. Again, try not to go into lengthy details that will bore people. All they want to know is what you're going to do about the issue. Try to keep it under 40 words. An example would be:

Our software will send a custom recorded phone message and e-mail to every parent in the district. If the parent doesn't answer, the software will redial them at a later time to ensure that the message is delivered.

It's funny, but in writing these examples, I found myself having to cut out unnecessary words and babble to make them fit within the word count.

The competition

We want to take a little more space with this one. If possible, try to get a clear description of your competitive landscape in 150 words. If the bankers or investors want more, feel free to provide them with all of your homework and supporting documentation that you did in workshop 11.

As you address your competitors, I would share who your top three competitors are, what they are doing well in the market, and how you plan to differentiate from them. This is where you add the business strategy you picked up in workshop 6. You'll want to define if you will be taking the low-cost leader approach or the high-end differentiator stance.

Here is an example.

Our top three competitors are ABC Company, Widget Works,

and Software Co. As the leaders in the market, they are focused on providing software solutions to grade schools throughout the country.

We will niche ourselves by focusing on preschools that need an additional level of support. On top of notifying all parents of major events, we have the solo parent feature. If a child wets his pants, the school can use this feature to reach out to an individual family instantly.

Our competitors charge a monthly fee based on the number of families that it tracks and e-mails. The average fee is $2 a month per family. Due to our ability to add extra features like "Solo Parent" we are approaching the market as a high-end differentiator and will charge $5 a family.

We have worked with over 30 preschools who have validated this price for the extra features.

As an investor in a company, a description like the one above is to the point and shows me what you have to offer. If I have to rummage around in 30 pages of poor writing to find the same thing, I'll lose my patience and move on to the next company.

The people

One of the most important aspects of a business is the team running the thing. You'll want to take a few moments to define your management team here. Take 100 words to describe why you are suited to lead the charge.

This isn't a time to go on about your philosophies in life or your childhood. Again, you don't have enough space for that stuff. Instead, talk about why your skillset makes you capable of succeeding.

Also in the section, you can take a moment to address the other people you have recruited along the way from workshop 7. If you'll remember, in that workshop we talked about the three most important resources of a company. One of those resources is people. We challenged you to go out and get three mentors, some groupies, and a management team. Within your 100 words, discuss who these people are and why they are on board with you.

Here's an example:

Bob Smith is the Founder of our company, Great Software Inc. He is suited to design, build, and maintain the software due to his 15 year career in software architecture with a national firm. In addition, we are mentored by Dan Jones, Joe Riley, and Mark Thomas who are successful entrepreneurs in similar industries.

We have built up a core group of raving fans that are spreading our message by passing out flyers to local preschools and blogging online. All of them are parents of preschoolers and are talking to their preschools about implementation.

The finances

The financial section of a business plan is often the most important. Since we are fitting everything onto one page, I would suggest that you use this space as a summary, and then attached your gross margin calculation and your break-even analysis from workshops 8 and 9 respectively. You will also want to attach your 12 month cash flow forecast from workshop 13.

In this section, you'll probably have about 150 words left before you spill over into the next page. In order to summarize everything, you'll need to address the key figures and assumptions without going into unnecessary details.

Here's an example:

The break-even point for our business is $2,350 a month in sales, which equates to 470 families at $5 a month per family that the preschool would pay. Given that the average preschool enrolls just under 100 children, we will need to get our software installed in at least five schools before we break even.

We have a high gross margin at 75%, and our first 12 months of cash flow remain positive as long as we can achieve our five-school goal within six months. We have already signed up two schools, thanks to our pre-opening sales efforts.

If you were trying to get a loan for your growing business and you handed that to the banker, he would be impressed. Why? Because you know your numbers and you have already got customers lining up. Most people go to their banker with a convoluted 1-inch thick business plan and pray for the best.

Is it any wonder that most small business loans are hard to come by? If nothing else, remember this… Make it easy for the banker.

How to use your 1-page business plan

Your 1-page business plan is a hang-it-on-the-wall reminder of what you are all about. It keeps the pure and sweet strategic points in plain view for you and your team to see every day. I like it because it states the problem and the solution clearly, who is going to fix it, and what financial metrics the company must hit to be successful.

Did you know that most business plans go into the garbage or rot on someone's C:\ drive? By keeping your business plan short, you can update it in less than a minute, take it with you wherever you go, and use it to inspire the folks in your organization.

Keep it simple and it will get used. Make it complex, and it'll be a heavy paper weight.

Why this isn't laziness

For all the naysayers out there who are proponents of intensive planning before doing, this section is for you. I'm sure you're ready to string me up by my neck and give me a beating for all I'm worth since I've discounted the glorious business plan. Many people will say that not investing the time in building a gargantuan business plan is just laziness, and that you need to do your homework before you risk your money on starting a business.

I can guarantee you this: By the time you have actually done all the homework in the 40 workshops that make up The 8-Week Startup, you'll be anything but lazy. You may not have a business plan worthy of breaking your back when you pick it up, but you will have this – a business that's open, makes sense to a core group of people, and is poised to make money.

Action work: Write your 1-page business plan

If you only had one page to describe your business, what would you put on it? Well, you're about to find out. After you complete your homework, come back the next day and read through your brand spanking new business plan to see if it reads well. Make sure that you got the important stuff down and kept all the fluff out.

1.   Describe what problem you are solving in 20 words or less.

_____

_____

_____

_____

_____

_____

_____

_____

2. Describe your solution in 40 words or less.

_____

_____

_____

_____

_____

_____

_____

_____

_____

_____

_____

_____

_____

_____

3. Describe your competition in 150 words or less.

_____

_____

_____

_____

_____

_____

_____

_____

_____

_____

_____

_____

_____

_____

_____

_____

_____

_____

_____

_____

_____

_____

_____

_____

_____

_____

4. Describe the people in your organization in 100 words or less.

_____

_____

_____

_____

_____

_____
_____
_____
_____
_____
_____
_____
_____
_____
_____
_____
_____
_____
_____
_____
_____
_____
_____

5. Describe the relevant financial metrics in 150 words or less.

_____
_____
_____
_____
_____
_____
_____
_____
_____
_____
_____
_____
_____
_____

_____

_____

_____

_____

_____

_____

_____

_____

_____

_____

_____

_____

_____

_____

_____

_____

6. Format your answers into a single-page document, pretty it up with proper formatting and headers, and shout for joy.

I have taken all of the above examples and condensed them into a sample business plan for Great Software Inc. and included that in your downloads folder.

If you feel like you have to write a 30 to 40 page dissertation on your new business, be my guest. I can promise you this though: Your business will likely pass you by. Many people never actually start their companies and I believe it's because they become authors instead of entrepreneurs.

WORKSHOP 18: Get a Great Name for the Business

"It usually takes me more than three weeks to prepare a good impromptu speech."

- Mark Twain

I love this topic. I'm a sales and marketing guy at heart so naming a business for me feel like naming one of my kids. There's actually quite a bit that you need to think about before you get to slapping a name on this puppy. As we move through the workshop, we'll discuss some of the best and worst practices when it comes to naming a business.

You want to get this right. Your name says a lot about you, the problem you propose to solve, and why you're special in the market.

The road trip game

My wife and I have a game that we play when we're on road trips. We play this game unconsciously, but none the less, we both seem to enjoy it. As we drive along, we gaze at all the billboards and business signs that litter the view. Every now and then, we'll come across a business name that throws us for a loop. We always end up laughing and wondering what the entrepreneur was thinking when he came up with that humdinger.

It keeps us busy and gives us a good laugh every now and then.

Have you ever done that? Have you ever walked past a business, read the name, and the shook your head in disbelief? A lot of people don't put any thought into their name, and it's a crying shame. After all, it's part of your first impression, and you really need to make a good one.

Keep your name out of it

One of the worst mistakes you can make is putting your own personal name into the name of your company. Please don't call your restaurant Bob's Diner. You name doesn't belong in your brand at all.

It amazes me how many people do this. I'm not sure if they do it to see their name in lights, or if they're truly uncreative. Either way, they stick their name in there, and we as the consumers are left wondering why they did.

If you name your store Jenny's Jeans, what is your customer supposed to get from that? Sure, they know that you sell jeans, but that's it. The name doesn't inspire the customer to investigate further, and every good business name should do just that.

If I saw a store named Jenny's Jeans at the mall, I would walk right past and probably never see the store. If, on the other hand, it was named "Stiches", or "Thread Bare", or "Frayed", I would pay more attention.

It's ironic that I'm taking about this given that I own an accounting firm. Most accounting firms are named after the founding partners. Something like Smith, Johnson, Dilbert, and Gooney, PLLC. Good grief guys! Could you come up with a worse name for a business?

Our accounting firm is called Ignite Spot. Why? Because we believe in taking the finances far beyond delivering monthly reports to our clients. We use that information to ignite their businesses to the next level with coaching and performance tracking.

Besides, Ignite Spot is a lot easier to remember than Smith, Johnson, Dilbert, and Gooney, PLLC. It gives you a competitive edge when everyone else has a terrible name. You're the one guy the customer can remember when it's time to buy.

Long e-mails suck

Assume that you work for Smith, Johnson, Dilbert, and Gooney, PLLC. Can you image the dang email? You would say, "Yeah, go ahead and send that over to:

dell@smithjohnsondilbertgooneypllc.com

and I'll take a look at it." Holy crap! Companies often try to make an improvement by turning the whole thing into an acronym just to have a manageable email. Now it's dell@sjdg.com which is stupid as well. What the heck is SJDG? That doesn't tell me anything about your business.

Have you ever been the person on the other end of the conversation trying to write down someone's ambiguous email? It's murder. You find yourself wanting to reach through the phone and smack them.

In essence, be kind to your email recipients and give them a business name that they can type without getting carpal tunnel and a serious hangover.

Paint a picture

It's not always possible to do, but if you can get your name to paint a picture in the minds of your customers, you've got a real winner. Let's look at some examples of great business names:

Twitter: It's short and sweet. It paints the picture of a little bird tweeting away which is essentially what the software allows people to do.

PayPal: Again, it's short and paints a picture. You now have a pal you can trust that helps you pay for stuff online. Who wouldn't want that?

Under Armour: Seriously… Can you think of a better name for this product? I can't.

JiffyLube: This is so much better than every other oil change company name out there. I mean, come on people, they're jiffy at it. Fantastic!

Wasn't that fun? When you think about a great business name, it's like tasting fine cheeses. You can sit back and savor how brilliant it is. I've never had alcohol so I can't relate to tasting fine wine, but I assume it's a similar experience.

All of the above names have the following in common:

- They help you understand what they do
- They are short and memorable
- They are fun to say
- They make for great emails

In all seriousness, keep your first and last name out of it.

Get it in a URL, get it in social media, and get it before it's gone

Here is where I'm going to make getting a name a little harder for you. Actually, I'm going to make it a lot harder for you.

It's one thing to say, get a name that paints a picture, and it's a whole different problem trying to find a matching URL.

A URL is a website address. What I'm trying to say here is that if you're going to name your new jeans company "Frayed", wouldn't it be ideal to have "frayed.com" as the URL as well? That's the problem. Almost all short URLs for the .com addresses have been taken. You can always make it a .co or a .biz but I really favor .coms for obvious reasons.

If you want to see if the URL is available, you can't just type it into a browser and see what pops up. The best way to do this is to head on over to GoDaddy.com and do a URL search on their website. These guys sell URLS to people like you and me. Once you find one that isn't taken, you can buy it, giving you the rights to put up a website at that URL in the future.

You also want the name to be easily accessible in social media. Down the road, you probably should have a company Facebook page, Twitter page, and anything else that will help you to get the word out. As such, you'll want to create accounts at each of the social media pit stops, and you're going to want the URL to be easy to remember. When you sign up with them, you can customize the URL. In the example we're using, we would want the following to be available:

- Facebook.com/Frayed
- Twitter.com/Frayed
- Youtube.com/Frayed
- Etc.

The best thing to do is to go to each of the major social media spots and check to see if people have taken that name. It's not always possible to get the social media URLs to work so it's not a huge deal breaker. The main thing is that you get a great name and a matching website address.

Last, but not least, you'll want to make sure that your name is available on the state and national levels. Take some time to Google "Business Name Search" for your state. Each state will have a database that you can search for free to see if the name is already taken.

It's important that the name be available in your state. Outside of your state, it's not as important but I still like to know that my business names are unique nationwide if I can manage it. To make sure of it, I Google "trademark search" and click on the link that leads to the USTPO.Gov site. It should be the first link on the page.

Once inside, I do a trademark search for my name to see if others have it.

Don't lose sleep over it

Trying to find a business name can be exhausting. I think that's why a lot of people take the easy route and come up with something long and off the wall.

I have stayed up until the wee hours of the morning banging my head on a computer trying to find the right name. Don't do that. Go to bed. The name will come to you. Ignite Spot took us a few weeks of searching. In the end, we found our name, got the URL, the social media channels, and a fun brand. We get comments on our brand every day and it was well worth the effort.

To make life somewhat more bearable, may I suggest getting a small notepad to keep in your pocket or a digital note you can keep on your phone? Every time you come across an idea in conversation, at work, or while lying in bed, write it down. You never know where you'll get your name.

When you're looking for a business name, the best thing you can do is to stop racking your brains and simply open your eyes and ears. Listen to words, read signs, and pay attention to messages all around you. Eventually you'll have a whole list of possibilities.

Action work: Start taking down names

What will you name your business? I can almost guarantee that the homework below will keep you busy for a while, so you may need to move on to future workshops until the name materializes. Have patience and know that a great name is worth the wait.

1. Get a notepad or a digital note that you can keep with you.
2. Begin writing down everything that sounds interesting and remotely useful.
3. Once you get a list of options, head over to GoDaddy.com and see if any of the URLs are available.
4. Make sure the name is available within your state and, if possible, nationwide.
5. If you do find a URL that's available for a name you really like, buy it at Godaddy.com. You'll end up spending roughly $15-$20 on the URL but now it's yours. If you come across a better name in the future you can always let this one expire.
6. Once you get your name, see if you can get it on the social media channels like Facebook, Twitter, and Youtube. If you can't, it's not the end of the world.

Coming up with the right name is stressful. Again, let me echo the sentiment of not losing sleep over it. The name will come. Now is a good time to start thinking of ideas, though. We waited until Workshop 18 to find a name because you didn't know enough about your business earlier on. Now that you know who you are serving and what problems you will fix, you can come up with the perfect name to paint that picture. Get to it, Van Gogh.

WORKSHOP 19: How to Get Paid the Right Way

"If you can count your money, you don't have a billion dollars."

- J. Paul Getty

The steps you take today will make things official. By the end of the day, you'll have an organized business, a bank account and a payment gateway so that you can legitimately accept payments from customers!

Taking care of the homework in this workshop will keep you square with the IRS. I have come across a few entrepreneurs who have skipped these steps and it's not pretty. Let me tell you a true story to show you what I mean.

A few years back, I met an entrepreneur at a business expo where we were presenting. She approached me and said that she had been running a company for nearly five years, and felt that it was time for her to get an accountant.

Naturally, I was excited to speak with her so we set up an appointment and I visited with her later in the week. I came to find out that she had never set up a business entity of any kind and she hadn't opened a bank account to track and manage her company's cash.

After she told me this, she walked over to a filing cabinet in the corner of her office and pulled out a letter that was from the IRS. Her personal taxes were being audited and in the process, the IRS discovered her secret business operation.

She was in a world of hurt. As I read through the findings, the IRS auditor had determined that she owed over $100,000 in taxes. I felt the instant sting of a headache pounding through my brain as I read the letter again.

To make things worse, the IRS doesn't like it when you owe them money, so they usually charge steep penalties and interest on outstanding liabilities. She was racking up huge amounts of fees for each month that she didn't pay it.

If she had set up her company properly in the beginning, she could have avoided almost all of the tax liabilities that she incurred.

Don't let this happen to you. Fortunately, it's easy to avoid. The IRS isn't so bad as long as you play by the rules. So what are the rules?

1. Register your business with the IRS and your state government
2. Get the right documentation for your company
3. Open a bank account and keep it separate from your personal funds and other businesses
4. File tax returns on time each year

You would be surprised at how many people don't file their tax returns. We get calls at Ignite Spot all the time from entrepreneurs that haven't filed in years. Every time I get one of those calls, I pause for a moment to pick my eyeballs up off the ground, dust them off, and put them back into my head.

I've never seen one of those cases turn out well. They're always a blood bath and I have yet to see the IRS lose.

How does this all start? For many, they start selling and don't have the proper bank accounts set up yet; they take their payment in cash or a check written out to them personally. This is a bad idea.

What happens is that they never get around to setting thing up properly and soon realize that they make more by getting paid under the table. Then one day the IRS sends them a fun letter and their whole world breaks down.

So, now that I have scared the daylights out of you, let's talk about what you need to do to get off on the right foot.

Choose an entity with your accountant

The first step to take in getting a legitimate business set up is to pick which type of entity you would like to be. Given that there are pros and cons to each, I would refer you to your accountant to pick the one that is best for your personal circumstance. Many choose an LLC as their entity type, but there is a lot to think about on this one.

If I were you, I would ask your accountant which one is best and why. He'll likely cover what your future tax strategy will be, what the business will accomplish, and what expected profits will be.

To help out, here is a list of the most common entity types and what they accomplish:

Sole Proprietor: This type of business has the least amount of legal hoops to jump through. You really don't have to do much other than open your doors to be a sole proprietor. There are some serious drawbacks to this structure though. In essence, you are the business. That means that you are personally tied to its operations. If the company gets sued, is really you that is getting sued since you are the business.

Even though this is the cheapest and easiest way to start a company, I wouldn't suggest it due to the liability that hangs over you.

Partnership: In this type of arrangement, you enter into a formalized partnership with one or more people. In this arrangement, you and your partners are still considered to be the business so if the business gets in trouble, you are personally liable. Something to be aware of too is that if a partner does something wrong, all the other partners could be held liable.

As with sole proprietors, I'm not a huge fan of general partnerships since the liability risk is so high.

Limited Liability Company or LLCs: This type of entity is pretty popular because you actually create a new entity. As such, the business becomes its own being and gets its own identification number with the IRS called an EIN or Employment Identification Number. The benefit here is that you're separated from your company now. That's why they call it "limited liability". There is now a layer of protection between you and the operations of the company.

For most people starting an 8-Week Startup, I would assume that an LLC would make the most sense. At a future date, you could convert your LLC into an S-Corporation to manage your tax bill. Again, work with your accountant to take the right steps for your personal needs.

C – Corporation: A corporation has the same wonderful protections that an LLC offers, but it is taxed twice and as such, I wouldn't recommend it for most entrepreneurs.

Get the EIN

Once you have met with your accountant and figured out which direction you want to go, the next step is to get an EIN if you are going to be an LLC or a Corporation. If you're going to be a sole-proprietor or operate as a general partnership, you won't have an EIN. Instead, you will use your social security number.

Getting an EIN takes all of five minutes and you can do it online at the IRS website. You can use your accountant to do this, but in all reality, you can do it yourself. It's not hard to do.

To get it done, head over to the8weekstartup.com/EIN. You'll find the link for the IRS application online.

As a side note, an FEIN is the same thing as an EIN just in case you come across the term. The term stands for Federal Employment Identification Number.

Register Your Business and Get the Articles

The next step is to get your business registered with your state. A lot of people register their business in the state of Delaware due to favorable tax circumstances. If you're particular state has a difficult tax environment, you may want to consider this.

At any rate, all you need to do is Google "Register a Business in _____" and fill in the blank with the name of your state.

The first link should be a government website. You'll know because it will end in .gov instead of .com. Click on the link and then follow your states instructions for getting registered.

This is where you officially declare what type of entity you are. If doing this kind of work makes you nervous, you can skip it entirely and have an attorney take care of it. That can get expensive though. I have heard of attorneys charging over $1,000 to set up an LLC. I set up my own LLCs and it takes me all of 20 minutes to do it.

At the same time, I can appreciate the anxiety of wanting to get everything right and if you've never done it before, it can cause some stress.

A decent option is LegalZoom. They do a great job and can get an LLC or entity set up for a fraction of the cost. Last time I looked, setting up an LLC would have cost around $100 plus the filing fees, depending on your individual state. Not bad.

Know that using a service like LegalZoom.com could take a week or two to get things wrapped up so that could put off your opening date a bit.

However you go about it, once you have your business registered you'll also set up your articles in the process. If you are starting an LLC, these are called Articles of Organization. If you are doing a corporation, they are called Articles of Incorporation.

Now that you have all of the boring stuff out of the way, you can finally set up a bank account and get paid by your customers!

Open a free checking account

You'll want to start off with a free checking account if possible. Some banks are notorious for charging a lot of fees to businesses so find a bank or credit union in your area that offers truly free checking for new businesses.

Also, think about your future. Down the road, you may want to get a business loan or line of credit with your bank. That means that you should pick a bank that is small business friendly and has a good history of lending. You don't want to get stuck with a bank that has impossible lending standards.

If I were you, this is a question I would ask my mentors. I would approach them to see who they bank with and why.

Most banks won't lend to new businesses until they have had a relationship for a certain period of time. You'll want to ask your bank how long they like to have an account open before they're comfortable lending.

Once you do find a bank or credit union that you like, it's time to get an account set up.

Every bank out there is going to want a few pieces of information from you if you're going to set up a business account with them. Make sure to take the following documents with you:

1. A copy of the IRS document you got which shows your EIN
2. A copy of the articles of organization or incorporation you received when you registered with the state
3. Personal identification
4. A check to make a small initial deposit

Don't let them talk you into any additional products right now. Your mission is to simply get a free checking account set up and that's it. We just need a place to stick customer money. We don't need CDs, upper-tier checking accounts, credit cards, or the like.

Get set up on PayPal or Square

Now that you're business has a bank account, you need a way to get money into that account. How are you going to accept payments from your customers?

The goal here is to make it as easy as possible for your customer to pay you.

Fireworks are a big deal in my hometown. I know when the 4th of July is coming because there are tons of firework stands that pop up all over the city.

I was actually driving to the office this morning and I passed two different stands right next to each other. One stand was a massive white tent that advertised all of the amazing explosives they have for sale. The other had a sign on the side of the tent that said, "we accept all credit cards". Can you guess which one had the huge line in front of it?

The guys accepting credit cards made it easy for customers to buy from them. You need to do the same.

In order to accept credit cards, you need to have a merchant account. This is essentially a clearing house. When someone swipes a card to pay you, those funds are wired to the merchant who then works with the credit card companies like American Express, Visa, and MasterCard to coordinate the payment. Depending on who you use, the funds could hit your bank account within a few minutes or a few days.

You do pay a fee for the convenience though. With many merchants, you will pay a monthly fee, usually around $20 - $30, and then you'll pay a per transaction fee every time you accept a credit card. The fee is a percentage of the sale amount and can range anywhere form 1.5% to 4%. Every merchant has different rates, so you'll want to shop around a bit.

My two favorite merchant accounts are PayPal and Square as of this writing. I like them because they have made convenience a top priority. Let's look at each of them:

PayPal: Almost everyone has used PayPal at some point in their lives which makes this merchant valuable. When people see that you accept credit cards and debit cards via PayPal, it makes them feel safe and that's important. They have a ton of features and different pricing plans. Their PayPal Standard account doesn't have a monthly fee so you only pay per transaction. It's a great solution for a new business. Down the road you can upgrade if it makes sense. This is the merchant that I use at The 8-Week Startup. I love them. If you want to see what they can do, head on over to paypal.com and review their pricing plans.

Square: I like square for how simple they make things. First of all, they popularized the iPhone credit card swipe. They have a little attachment that plugs into your iPhone and allows you to swipe a customer's credit card right from your phone. PayPal recently came out with their version of this as well. Beyond that, I like their fee structure. There is not monthly fee, and you pay 2.75% per transaction. That's it. Easy to remember, use, and track. You can get set up in minutes at squareup.com

Action work: Get official, get a bank, and get a merchant

It's time to make your business ready for payment. To do that, you're going to need the proper documentation to open and account and get a merchant. So, let's get started.

1. Work with your accountant to determine what the best type of entity structure will be for your business. Make sure he or she explains why to you.
2. Go to the8weekstartup.com/ein and follow the instruction to get your EIN.
3. Register your business with your state or with the state of Delaware if you live in a restrictive tax state. If you are uncomfortable doing this on your own, consider using LegalZoom.com or an attorney in your area if you can get a good deal.
4. Work with your mentors to find a bank that supports small businesses in your area.
5. Go to that bank and set up a free checking account.
6. Get set up with PayPal, Square, or a merchant of your choice so that you can start accepting cards.

Just think about how great it will feel when you can log into your bank account and see that customers are paying you electronically! It'll make all of this worth it. Best of luck!

WORKSHOP 20: Creating a Brand That Rocks

"A brand for a company is like a reputation for a person. You earn reputation by trying to do hard things well."

- Jeff Bezos, Founder of Amazon.com

I have a buddy that was born and bred a cowboy. He's the guy that wears wranglers everywhere he goes and I love him for it. To him, that's who he is and he's sticking with it. So much so, that he once went on a cruise to Mexico and wouldn't put on a swimsuit. Instead, he jumped in the pool with those dang Wranglers on.

I'm telling you all of this because his family has a brand; the kind that gets hot when you stick it in the fire and then leaves a scar on the cow when you press it into its rump. Cowboys brand cattle so that everyone knows to whom the cows belong.

I want you to think of your company's brand in the same fashion. Don't run off and turn your logo into a branding iron that you can squish into your customers' hind-quarters as they enter your store. That's not what I'm saying. If you do decide to do that, I'll see you on the news.

I want you to think of branding as a fairly permanent thing. A lot of people believe that a company's brand is nothing more than a logo and a tag line, which can be changed at any time. Not so. A brand includes those things, but is so much more. Your brand defines how your customer thinks about your company. It's what shapes how you're classified in the market and what makes you different. Because it's your customer's mental picture of what your company means to them, it's pretty permanent. Of course you can change your brand, it just takes a lot of time, marketing, and follow up.

Getting your brand wrong can often spell disaster. That's because you may be trying to be a high-end differentiator in your space, but if your branding screams "cheap", you're going to miss the mark. People won't understand your messaging and they won't buy.

That means that we want to get the brand right from the beginning. To do that, we need to go far beyond your logo and business card. Everything you have done in the prior workshops will help you today. You're going to need to draw upon a lot of what you have learned up to this point to get today's homework done.

I have broken up what I consider to be the most important parts of branding a business into three phases. Take your time to read through each one and apply what you learn to your business.

Phase 1: The positioning

What we need to determine here is how you want your business to be positioned in your customers' minds. If you did your homework in workshop 6, you should know by now if you're going to try and be the low-cost leader or the high-end differentiator. You should also have a 20-word or less description of how you plan to solve your customer problems.

Your branding needs to be saturated with those two things. Let's discuss.

Communicating the USP

In every piece of marketing that you create from your logo to your business card, website, and video – you need to communicate the

USP that you developed in workshop 17 when you built your 1-page business plan. That's not to say that you should plaster your USP word for word on all of your marketing collateral. What we want though is for all of your marketing to embody what your USP communicates.

For example, if your USP is:

"We help inventors manufacture small quantities of their idea and take it to market via our unique network of distributors."

How could you use that in your marketing? You wouldn't want that whole thing showing up in your logo or else you would have the world's worst logo. However, you could give this phrase to a logo designer and let them know that the image must represent an inventor finally being able to take his ideas to market. After all, without your company, an inventor may have to pay a standard manufacturing company a huge setup fee and thousands of dollars for a boatload of units.

Communicating the business strategy

You also need to address your business strategy. In the example above, the logo would look very different if you were trying to be a low-cost leader versus a high-end differentiator. For example, if you were shooting for a low-cost leader strategy, your logo would need to look affordable and economic. If on the other hand, you were trying to be a high-end differentiator; your logo would need to represent prestige, importance, and impact.

Every time you create a piece of marketing, a sales pitch, or anything else that is trying to deliver a message to your customers, you want that message to be the transportation device for communicating your USP and your business strategy.

If you forget to do this, you'll end up creating marketing materials that send crossed messages. When you do that, your customer gets confused and doesn't know what you're all about.

Looking at Ferrari again, you wouldn't know what to do if they printed flyers off of the CEO's home printer, made them in black and white, and advertised the message, "Get a Ferarri by the end of the month and we'll throw in a pair of movie tickets." Ferrari would never create such a catastrophe. As a high-end differentiator in their space, all of their marketing screams their ritzy positioning so that you'll never forget it.

Phase 2: The first impression

Now that we know what our marketing should convey, we need to work on the first impression. What are people going to think when they're first introduced to your business? What kind of wow factor will you provide that will make them want to know more?

You really do only get one shot with a customer so it better be good.

People buy shiny things

As we work on the first impression, I want you to remember a cardinal rule… People buy shiny things. It's true. If you put two cars next to each other in a parking lot, all things being equal, people will buy the car with the shiniest paint job, cleanest smell, and best detail.

You need to find a way to make every part of your business shiny; everything from your logo and website, to your product, company truck, and smile need to glisten.

Have you ever caught yourself doing this? You know, that feeling you get when you hold something in your hand and you fall in love with it because of how shiny it is.

Why do you think the folks over at Apple work so hard to make their products shiny? Because it sells. They put insane amounts of money into their displays and that's the main reason people buy iPads over other tablets.

If you're not the kind of person that has an eye for making things look great, find someone that is and get his or her help. You can't afford to miss the boat on this one.

Getting your logo designed

There are a lot of different ways to get a logo designed. Do yourself a favor and hire someone. Don't do the logo yourself unless you're a graphic designer.

In today's market, you can get a really good logo designed for between $100 and $300. There are a million shops online that can help you out, but my favorites are sites like 48hourslogo.com and 99designs.com. Instead of hiring a single designer to come up with a logo for you company, these sites have several designers. When you sign up, you'll fill out a creative brief describing what you want your logo to express and then you submit it. At that point, a contest is started and any of the designers can join your contest and start drawing logos for you. I like this approach because you get to see several different styles of artwork for you to choose from. This is how I designed the logo at The 8-Week Startup and it cost me $150.

Before you work with a company like this, you'll want to do a quick Google search to find examples of logos that you like which embody what you are trying to express. This will give your designers a heads up with regards to what you want. Otherwise, they may design something way out in left field.

Once you get your contest started, you should have your logo ready to go within a week or so.

Choosing your color palette

Color is extremely important to your brand. It's vital that you think about the emotional effects that your color palette will have on their experience. At The 8-Week Startup, I chose red and gold for many reasons including:

- Red is the power color. I wanted future entrepreneurs to be inspired by a color that speaks of taking control of their lives.
- Red is a high energy color.
- Gold is the color of...well...gold. If you're going into business, the thought of starting a business to make more money is somewhat motivating at times.

You might think that all of this is silly, but it's not. Color has a huge emotional pull on your customers and you want to get it right. At Ignite Spot, we rely on a lot of blues. That's because blue is a calming color that inspires professionalism and trust. Given that it's an accounting firm, that color scheme makes sense. You'll also notice a little orange at Ignite Spot. That is to let our customers know that we have a fun side to us, and that we like to stand out.

I would suggest that you get a primary color to represent your business and then find a secondary color to compliment it. Not all colors go together, so you'll want to do an internet search for "Complementary colors". When you do that, you'll most likely land on a website that will show you a color wheel. Find your color and then look at the colors and the exact opposite side of the wheel to see what matches the best.

You don't have to use complimentary colors, but it does create a stronger presentation that's easier on the eye.

Building your marketing collateral

Marketing collateral is anything you will create to convey your message. It includes business cards, banners, brochures, etc. I have found that online printing companies are a lot cheaper than brick and mortar locations in town. My favorite printer as of this writing is uprinting.com – their quality is really strong and their prices are usually very competitive.

In order to get your collateral designed, you have a few different options:

- You could pay a graphic designer to create a kit for you to include your card, brochure, stationary, etc. If you do decide to go this route, check out oDesk.com where you can hire contractors for one off projects. In the search bar, look for graphic designers. Once you find a few that you like, you can create a free account and then offer them a fixed price or an hourly gig to do your project.
- You could outsource to it companies like 99designs.com

Whichever option you choose, try not to spend more than $500 getting everything designed; that's assuming you're doing a business card, stationary, and a brochure. You may not need any of those items though. It all depends on your business.

Back at Ignite Spot, I needed all of those things in order to spread the word on our accounting services. At The 8-Week Startup, I don't need any of it because all of my sales are online.

Phase 3: The proof

The absolute necessity of living up to your USP

Once you do get your logo and collateral designed and printed, you have created a vehicle for telling people all about your USP. The most important part of building a brand that rocks is what follows. Now you have to live up to your USP.

If your marketing collateral says one thing and you behave differently, you're brand will be flimsy and transparent.

It's unfortunate, but a lot of companies are like this. Have you ever bought from someone that promised you the world, only to let you down once they got your money? It happens all of the time and it's not doing a lot for their brands.

A good brand is more than having pretty logos and cards. A good brand is about living up to the message on those cards.

Getting social proof

As you do get customers into your door, you're going to start getting feedback. Pay attention to it. Your goal as a business owner is to respond to any negative feedback as fast as possible and to frame the good feedback on the wall and in your website.

Social proof is the credibility you get from servicing customers correctly. It's when your current customers like you so much that they are willing to tell the world about you. For example, I jumped onto Google + yesterday and ran into a comment from one of our clients at Ignite Spot. She took time out of her busy schedule to post this without us asking her:

"Best thing I ever did for my small business was use Ignite Spot's accounting services. Worst decision I ever made was not using the services for a few months. I learned some tough lessons. A company can get in all kinds of trouble without the right financial guidance and accurate numbers!"

-Rebecca Sato, Daybreak Arts Academy

One of the best ways to get social proof is on video. If you can get your customers to talk about you on video, you have got something worth sharing. If you head over to youtube.com/ignitespot you can see some of the videos we have made with our clients.

Having social proof makes you credible to all of your future customers. Get as much of it as you can and your brand will flourish.

Creating a movement

The ultimate goal of having a strong brand is that people look to you as a leader in your industry. You see movements all the time, and you wonder how they get started.

Let me tell you about a little sandwich shop around the corner from my old office. The restaurant is called Moochies. They sell sandwiches and at any given time of the day, it's packed. More often than not, there is a line that goes out the door and wraps around the building.

Every restaurant would kill for that kind of crowd. The best part about it is that it's not fancy or outlandish. In other words, they don't attract their crowds by being weird for the sake of being weird.

So how do they get such huge crowds when so many other restaurants struggle to keep the doors open?

Instead of trying to be everything to everyone by having 30 to 50 different sandwiches for sale, Moochies has two main items that they sell: Philly cheese steak sandwiches and meatballs. This sandwich has gotten so famous that they even had Guy Fieri from The Food Network do a spot on them for his show, "Diners, Drive-Ins, and Dives".

Because Moochies has decided to do something better than everyone else, they are constantly packed, have gotten on television, and have created a Philly cheese steak movement. I've eaten there many a time and it's stellar.

Action work: Give Your Brand a Boost

Remember that we're going for a jaw-dropping first impression followed up by your product or service that supports your claims. Don't be like so many of the other business owners out there that put little to no thought towards this. Get it right.

1. Define your color pallet and why you chose those colors.

   _____
   _____
   _____
   _____
   _____
   _____
   _____
   _____
   _____

2. Find five different logos that you really like that embody what you want in your logo.
3. Get your logo designed using any of the methods or companies described above. Make sure to convey to the graphic artists what you are looking for, the color scheme you want, and the logo examples that you like.
4. Determine if you need marketing collateral. If you do, take your new logo to the graphic artist and have them design a

marketing kit for your business. Remember to try and keep it under $500 by using contractors at odesk.com or 99designs.com.

5. Ensure that all of your marketing materials contain the message of your USP.

6. Lay out all of your marketing materials and make sure that they look cohesive. If your business card looks completely different from your brochure, your message won't make sense.

7. Be thinking of how these designs will affect the look of your website that we will design in later workshops. Your site should feel like it fits in with each of these items.

8. Get testimonials from five customers that you can service now and use those testimonials in your marketing materials.

9. Make sure that you live up to your USP with every customer that you service.

10. Define one thing can you do better than anyone else that will create a movement.

_____

_____

_____

_____

_____

_____

_____

_____

Remember that people buy shiny things. If it looks good, it will inspire the customer to at least consider it. Take the time to get your first impression right and you'll create waves.

WORKSHOP 21: Setting Up Command Central

"I'm a great believer that any tool that enhances communication has profound effects in terms of how people can learn from each other, and how they can achieve the kind of freedoms that they're interested in."

- Bill Gates, The guy that started that software company that made a lot of money

Note to reader: I love technology, but I'm well aware of the fact that if you've never done what we are about to do, you'll likely have questions. If you feel overwhelmed, remember that I've recorded videos of myself walking through all of these steps so that you can follow along! To access the videos, look for them in your download folder if you purchased Workshop 21 at the8weekstartup.com.

The importance of command central

I just love the astronaut movies. When I was a little kid, I always wanted to don the white astronaut suite and float around weightless without restrictions. What kid didn't want to jump onto the space shuttle and fly to the moon?

It's the astronauts that get all the glory when it comes to space travel, but what about all the scientists sitting on earth working at Command Central? They're the ones that have access to the data, communications, and tools necessary to get the shuttle into the air and keep it there. We all know that the astronauts wouldn't have a hope and a prayer without Command Central.

If Command Central is so vital to the mission, what's going on inside its walls? Here's a short list of some of the more important things to note:

1. All communication flows through Command Central.
2. Command Central is the hub for technology. All of the gizmos and gadgets are operated from that room.
3. The entire mission's schedule is mapped out and managed from Command Central. It's important that they stick to set timeframes in order to keep everyone safe.
4. Course corrections are made from Command Central. If the mission is not going as planned, all of the above tools give the scientists the data that they need to make the proper adjustments to the flight plan.

I'm sure by now that you see where this analogy is taking us. Your business needs a Command Central - a single place that you can go to get all of your communications, technology and calendars so that you can make course corrections when your business is trending off mark.

Within the Command Central that we'll set up together, you'll be able to access your entire information network in one spot. I also want you to be able to get to that data from any internet connection at any time.

In this workshop, we'll create a place that will store and manage all of the following for you:

1. Your e-mail account
2. Your telephone system
3. Your calendars
4. Your important business documents
5. Your accounting records

6. Your customer interactions via a CRM (Customer Relationship Manager)
7. Pretty much anything else that's important for your business
8.

Enter Google Apps for Business

I am a huge fan of Google Apps for Business. Google Apps is designed to be the all-out, completely functional and mobile command center for small businesses at the flick of a switch. It's easy to set up, and gives you powerful tools right out of the gate that make you look professional.

Have you ever asked a business owner for his e-mail and he gives you something like widgetcompany@gmail.com? This is not a good thing. It tells people that your business is not a real business. Wouldn't you have expected bob@widgetcompany.com instead? This is just one of the many things that Google Apps for Business will do for you.

Before we set up Google Apps for Business though, we need to get some ground work done. Let me start off by creating an acronym, because I don't want to keep typing Google Apps for Business. From now on, I'll refer to it as GAB, if that works for you.

Secondly, we need to secure your website address if you haven't already done so. GAB is designed to function off of your company's web address, so let's get to that first.

Getting your URL

In prior workshops, we pointed you to GoDaddy.com as a great place to look for a URL which is geek-speak for a web address. Given that you picked out a name for your business in workshop 18, you should have already looked to see if the URL was available. We

also asked you to purchase it via GoDaddy.com in that same
workshop. If you haven't done that, go do it…we'll wait.

Do you have a URL now? Good! Also, don't lose your login
credentials at GoDaddy.com, because you're going to use them a lot.

Setting up web hosting

Obviously you are very familiar with websites, but you may not be
familiar with how they work. Essentially, a website is nothing more
than a bunch of files, pictures, and video sitting in a folder on a
server. A server is just a computer with some special software on it.
When you type in a URL, that command tells your browser to head
on over to that server, open up the folder, and display what's inside
to you.

If you are going to get a website, and I suggest that you do, you'll
need a server. Don't worry, it's cheap and easy to do. Given that you
got your URL at Godaddy.com, I would suggest that you also use
their server options to host your website.

In the next three workshops, we'll be building a website for under
$500 and we'll be using the WordPress.com platform to do it. For
now, don't worry about heading over to WordPress. Let's stay on
GoDaddy.com and purchase a place to host the website.

At the top of Godaddy.com, you'll see a button that references
hosting and servers. Hover over it, and a navigational menu will
appear. In that menu, you should see the option to purchase
"WordPress Blog Hosting".

You'll notice that there are a lot of different options. You can always
upgrade, so don't let it stress you out too much. Essentially, the more
money you spend, the more space you get on the server. For now, I
would just buy 12 months of the basic plan. I'm on their site right

now, and the pricing is $4.74 a month if I buy all 12 months which comes out to $56.88.

Once you have purchased your hosting account, you can move forward with setting up Command Central! To that we say, Woot Woot.

Setting up GAB

To get started, go to Google.com/a/ and click on the "Start a Free Trial" button. The free version of GAB is getting harder and harder to find, but even at that, the paid version is very cheap. You'll pay either $5 or $10 a month per user depending on which plan you go with. A user, to Google, is anyone that has an email address in your company. For now, you're the only one, so that makes it pretty cheap!

Set up the account by following the instructions on the site. It's pretty easy to get set up, but if you have any questions, you can always jump onto the forums at the8weekstartup.com, as well as reference the help materials from GAB.

Once the account has been created, GAB is going to walk you through a welcome session where you can get the basics set up. Take your time on this part, and make sure to watch the video that I created of myself setting this up for my new company. That way you can follow right along.

Also, if you are a paying customer, Google has telephone support that you can access if you get stuck.

How to get a proper e-mail account

Let's pretend that you bought widgetcompany.com as your URL and you now have the Godaddy.com WordPress hosting activated. Rock and roll!

You have to take a few extra steps to get your e-mail up and working. First, GAB wants you to verify that you, in fact, own your URL. To do that, Google is going to give you a piece of code which you will need to upload to your server. It sounds a lot harder than it really is. The only difficult part is explaining it in writing. That's why I have made the following videos for you to watch as part of the homework for today:

1. How to verify your URL
2. How to update your MX records

To get the code, go to the dashboard tab in your GAB account. You should see the iconic red and white envelop that Google uses for their e-mail. There should be a warning sign that says, "Activate E-mail". Click on that and you'll be taken to a page where GAB will walk you through the steps of setting up e-mail.

Once you've watched the videos, you should have your e-mail up and running! Good work. This is all worth it, I promise. In the end, you'll have a real e-mail account for your business versus a generic Gmail account which looks unprofessional.

Essentially all we are doing is hosting our e-mail with Google, thereby using the Gmail world of goodness as our e-mail platform.

Centralizing Your Important Documents

Now that GAB is set up and you have e-mail chugging along, do me a favor and look at the top of your screen. You should see Google's navigation buttons for all of the business tools. For example, you should see:

- Mail
- Calendar
- Documents
- Site
- Video
- Groups
- More

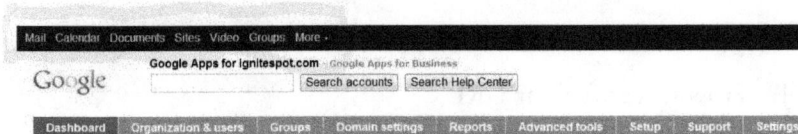

The mail tab will take you directly to the e-mail account that you just set up. Beyond the e-mail feature, I use "Documents" to host a lot of important reports and tools for my companies. You can create or upload Word, Excel, PDF, and other files to the Documents tab for easy access and sharing.

For example, instead of having your 12 Month Cash Flow Forecast stuck on your laptop, now you can upload the Excel file to your documents section and have access to it at any internet connection! Don't worry, it's secure. In order for someone to see it, you would have to share that document with them.

This is really convenient for when you get employees down the road. If you create a document that you need your team to be able to access, upload it to the Documents section and share it with your team members.

Understanding Google Calendar

In my opinion, Google has the best calendar tools on the market.

The layout is amazingly intuitive, plus you can create multiple calendars, overlap them to see where schedules conflict, and you can search your calendars for specific events.

Take some time to watch the video that I created on how to set up and manage your Google Calendar so that you can get the most out of it.

At the very least, make sure to connect your smart phone to your new e-mail and calendar accounts so that you can have access to everything on the go.

Understanding to Google Apps Marketplace

One of the best parts about GAB is the marketplace. There are hundreds, if not thousands, of apps that work with GAB! This means that you can essentially set up your GAB as your Command Central and customize it to your needs.

Know that many of the apps do cost money, but there are a lot of free ones out there, too. I wouldn't go crazy with the apps, at least at first. We want to manage cost and only get what we need to acquire and support customers.

To get started, go to the apps marketplace by clicking on the "More" tab at the top of the screen. When the menu pops up, click on the button that says "Find More Apps".

There are a lot of apps to choose from, but you'll notice that they are organized by type and category to make things a bit easier.

I would consider the following types of apps as a beginning point for any new business:

- **Customer Management:** Browse the Customer Relationship Manger (CRM) Apps to see what's out there. If you can find one that you like that's affordable, you'll be happy you picked it up. A CRM tracks all of your contact points with customers and new sales opportunities. The goal of a CRM is to help you close more deals with new customers and build on your relationships with existing customers. Examples of CRMs that integrate with GAB would be Nutshell, Capsule CRM, and Nimble.

- **Accounting:** QuickBooks isn't the only option these days. There are some new competitors on the scene and they pack a pretty big punch. The benefit to the new guys is that they are simple, intuitive, and accessible. Some of the apps that sync with GAB are FreshBooks and Xero which are two of my favorites.

-

Getting a telephone number

To stay with our goal of having everything in one place, I would support getting a Google Voice phone number for your business. That way, you're not giving everyone your personal cell phone number. Google Voice will give you a local phone number that has free U.S. long distance and low rates on international calls if you need them.

The number you receive is really just a forwarding tool. As you set up your Google Voice number, Google will ask you to which phone or phones you would like the caller to be forwarded. Since this is a new business, and we want to keep things simple, just have it forward to your cell phone for now. In the future, you can forward it to a service like Grasshopper.com, which is my favorite small business telephone platform.

To get set up, click on the "More" tab at the top of your GAB screen. If you don't see Voice in the menu, go to the bottom and click on a button that says "Even More". You'll be taken to a page with all of Google's business tools. Find Google Voice, click on it and follow the instructions that Google gives you.

Action Work: Set up your Command Central

It's very important that you take the time to get Command Central set up correctly. Once you have everything in place, you'll be able to run your ship with a single tool. It's no fun having to get your e-mail in one spot, your accounting records, team documents, and calendars in another, and then have to manage your phone, customer relationship interactions, and everything else in different locations as well. With Google Apps for Business, or GAB, as we have been calling it, you can put all of that into one spot that integrates as a whole.

1. Purchase your URL from GoDaddy.com if you haven't already done so.
2. Purchase 12 months of GoDaddy.com hosting for a WordPress Blog.
3. Go to Google.com/a/ and create a GAB account.
4. Go through the welcome and setup phases after you login to GAB.
5. Watch the following videos on how to set up your e-mail and follow along to learn:
   a. How to verify your URL
   b. How to update your MX records
6. Upload all of your 8-Week Startup documents to the documents section so that you'll have them with you wherever you go. Those documents include:
   a. The 8-Week Idea Map from workshop #2.
   b. The 8-Week Gross Margin Calculator from workshop #8
   c. The 8-Week Break-Even Calculator from workshop #9.

d. The 8-Week Cash Flow Forecast from workshop #12.
7. Watch the following video on how to set up your calendar and follow along to learn:
    a. How to set up your Google calendar
8. Browse through the apps marketplace to see if any of the apps make sense for your business. Consider apps for the following needs as a beginning point:
    a. Customer relationship management
    b. Accounting
9. Set up your Google Voice phone number and have it ring your mobile phone when someone calls.
10. Program a contact in your mobile phone so that anytime you get a phone call on your Google Voice number, the name of your business pops up and you know it's a business call.
11. Sync your email and calendar to your smart phone.

That's a lot of homework! You're going to be busy today. After you get everything set up, I want you to glory in your new-found power. You're now the equivalent of a NASA scientist sitting at Command Central in Houston, guiding the ship. All the necessary data can now flow to you, and with a single login, you can dominate the world. Bwaahahahah! For those of you that can't tell... That was my attempt at an evil laugh of domination!

WORKSHOP 22: Build a $10,000 Website for Under $500 – Part 1

"In marketing I've seen only one strategy that can't miss - and that is to market to your best customers first, your best prospects second and the rest of the world last."

- John Romero

Why you shouldn't hire someone to build your website

Ahhh… The ever-important and overwhelmingly mysterious website. It's finally here. You know you need one to compete in today's market, and you've been waiting for these workshops to get yours off the ground. A website is a must for almost any business, and a lot of companies are finally jumping on the bandwagon to get one. The problem is that most of the websites out there are pretty hard to swallow. They are poorly designed and barely functional.

You can't afford to have a website that looks like it was built by a second grader.

In order for someone to land on your website and feel confident in buying from you, it has to have the following features:

1. The first impression has to communicate that you are the best in your industry.
2. The content on the site needs to be useful, clear and to the point.
3. The site needs to load quickly.

4. There needs to be several "calls to action" for people in different phases of the buying cycle.
5. The site needs to inspire a sense of security – otherwise your customers won't enter their credit card information.

I was recently on Facebook and ran across an old friend that just started up a new business. I didn't know about it at the time, but he entered into a contract with a web design company to build him a website. When I called him up, I found out that it was going to cost him over $10,000 to build the thing.

What you'll learn in the next four workshops will give you a website that's just as good for an investment of less than $500!

I run into entrepreneurs all the time that are spending insane amounts of money on their websites. Every time I come across those stories, it kills me. I'm being hypocritical, though. When I first got started in business building, I did the same thing.

I didn't spend $10,000 but I did rack up a bill of around $3,000 with a local web design company. I remember the day that I signed the contract. I was so excited with the thought of having a professionally built website that I was beside myself. The thing took about four months to build because I wasn't the most important client on their schedule. After all, some companies were spending $50k to $100k on their sites. Once it was done, I loved it - for about a week. The problem with websites is that they're living and breathing animals that need to be updated, changed or improved. Every time I made a request to change something, I was charged an arm and a leg. It was legalized murder and I was the victim.

I eventually go so fed up with the whole thing that I decided to learn how to build a website myself. It took me about three months of late night studying, but I got it figured out. What I learned is what I will be sharing with you. The websites I build now, like the8weekstartup.com and ignitespot.com, are examples of what I've done for less than $500!

Every time I build a website, it takes me a few days to get it set up, architected, written out, and functional. The best part is that I can go into the backend of my websites at any time and change things without have to pay someone, and it only takes a few minutes.

At the end of the day, you'll be in control of your site and it will be something that you can be proud of.

Understanding the basics of WordPress

I use WordPress to build all of my websites. It's powerful, fast, cheap, beautiful, and pretty much has everything you need to build a Kick-A website. I love the platform because WordPress makes it so easy to generate new content. What you don't want is to build a website and then forget about it. The website is one of your main marketing tools, so you'll always be working on it. This means that you want a platform designed around generating new content on the fly.

WordPress started off as a blogging tool back in the day. Since then, it has grown to become one of the most popular website platforms on the market. Head on over to WordPress.com and take a look around for a minute.

Understand how WordPress works

WordPress can be used one of two ways:

1. You can create an account at WordPress.com and then pay for one year of hosting. This means that WordPress will be hosting your site.
2. You can host your site elsewhere giving you more control over what's going on.

I like option two which is why I had you buy the Godaddy WordPress hosting service in prior workshops. Since we will be hosting our WordPress site at GoDaddy.com, you'll need to make sure that your GoDaddy.com servers are ready to go.

To start, log into your GoDaddy.com account and go to your hosting control panel. You should see your URL listed on the screen. Click on the URL and find the section that says something to the effect of "Set up WordPress". Click the button and follow the instructions that GoDaddy.com provides.

What you are doing is installing the WordPress software on your GoDaddy.com server. As you do this, you'll be asked to create a login for your website. Make sure not to forget this since you'll need it to make changes to your site down the road.

To see if things are configured at GoDaddy.com already, simply open a web browser and type in your URL or web address. If everything is kosher, you'll see a basic website pop up. This is the standard template that WordPress comes with. As of this writing, the default template is called "Twenty Ten".

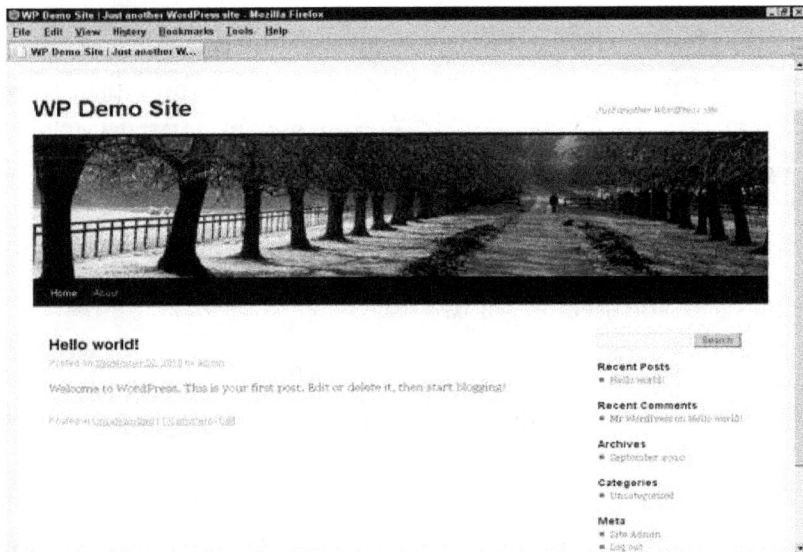

Don't bloody your knuckles or throw your computer against the wall if everything you do fails. Know that you can always call the GoDaddy.com support team and they can help you get your WordPress website ready to go.

A word to the wise… making changes to servers can often take 24 to 48 hours to take effect. GoDaddy is pretty good in this respect, however, which is one of the reasons I like them. I haven't had to wait for days for a change to occur on their server like I have had to with other hosting companies.

How to login to your website

Once you can see the default WordPress template by typing your URL into a browser, you're on your way! The next thing that you need to do is to learn how to log into the website so that you can make changes to it.

In order to begin building your website, you will need to login to the administration panel. To do that, you will need to type in your URL and follow it up with /wp-admin. For example, if your URL is widgetco.com, you will need to type in widgetco.com/wp-admin. You should be directed to a WordPress login screen.

From there, you will need to put in your username and password that you created when you installed WordPress into your Godaddy.com server. If everything worked correctly, you'll be taken to the dashboard for your website.

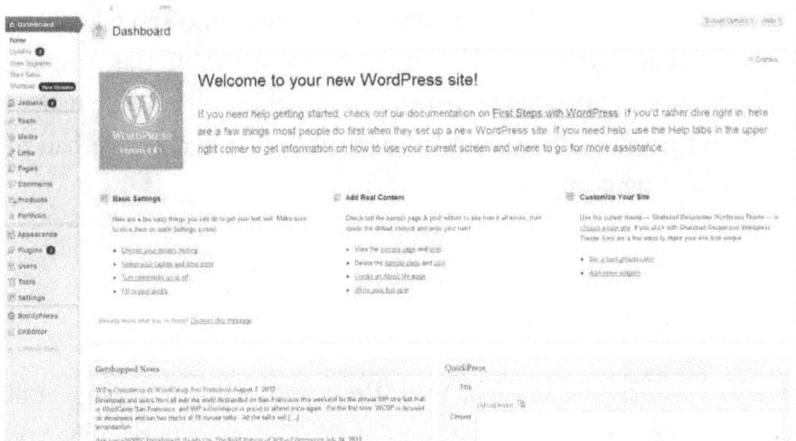

Also, remember that I have created videos of myself doing this for you to follow. After all, we're trying to make this as easy as possible.

The WordPress dashboard

The dashboard is where all of the behind-the-scenes stuff happens on your website. As you make changes here, they will be reflected on the website itself. Long gone are the days of having to know technical HTML and coding languages to build a fancy website. I will say this though… Having a basic knowledge of HTML is extremely useful. If you get the urge to take a basic course on it, good for you.

The dashboard is meant to be just what it sounds like – a dashboard where you can get access to all of the major functions of your site. From here, you'll be able to create new pages, menus, and products, as well as upload images, change the appearance of your site, and add functionality.

The WordPress navigation panel

On the left side of the screen, you should see several features for you to choose from. This is the WordPress navigation panel. From this blessed array of buttons, you can begin to tweak your site. Although you'll be using all of the options over time, there are a few that get used quite a bit and they are:

- **Posts:** This is where you create new blog posts
- **Media:** This is where you can upload new pictures and other media
- **Pages:** This is where you create pages for your website like an "About Us" page
- **Appearance:** This is where you change the look and feel of your website
- **Plugins:** This is where you can add additional software tools to your website that integrate with WordPress thereby making your website more functional
- **Users:** WordPress is, at its core, a blogging tool. Your visitors can subscribe to your site and this is where your "members" will be listed
- **Setting:** This is where you can change the general setting like the name of your website

Also know that as you add plugins to your website, you may end up with additional buttons in the navigational panel. For example, at the 8-Week Startup, I use a plugin called BuddyPress to create the community aspect of our site. This plugin gives us the ability to have a forum. When I installed BuddyPress onto my site, I ended up with a new BuddyPress button in the navigational panel. This allows me to configure BuddyPress to work the way I want.

Additional WordPress classes

Even though WordPress is set up to be intuitive, I would suggest that you look into some WordPress classes online. There are some really great ones out there for less than $100 that will teach you everything you need to know. If you go to Udemy.com, an online education site where gurus share their knowledge, you can find some great education. Simply search for "WordPress" and several classes will pop up.

Templates, and why we love them

So you want to know how to get rid of the default WordPress template and make a website of your own do you? That is where templates come into play.

A template is a website in a box. When you buy a template, you get the rights to use the website files as a starting point for your new website. Don't worry, by the time we get done with your site, nobody will recognize the template and you'll have a unique site that is all your own. This means that you can literally avoid thousands of dollars of design work for the cost of the template which is usually less than $50.

There are a lot of free WordPress templates out there to choose from, but I would say to pony up the cash and get a really good one. Most of the free ones are pretty basic. I have yet to find on that I'm in love with.

There are a ton of places to buy templates, but my two favorite sites are:

TemplateMonster.com: These guys usually have really good prices on templates and there are usually a lot to pick from. What I like about templatemonster.com is that they have partnered with a company to help you get the template installed on your site if you need it. The service usually costs less than $100 for them to do it. We'll show you how to install in though so you can save money here if you would like!

Note that not all templates will work with WordPress. Go to the top menu where it says "CMS&Blog Templates" and then click on "WordPress Templates".

Themeforest.net: This is another great place to pick up that "Pow" website template. Go to the top of the screen and click on "WordPress" to see all of the WordPress templates that they have.

How to choose the right template

Picking the right template is a lot more involved than just trying to find one that looks good. Your template needs to have several features that will make it a good candidate for a strong website. You're website needs to meet certain criteria to be both beautiful and functional. The most important aspect of a website is that it gives your visitors exactly what they're looking for. If the designer laid out the template in such a way that your visitors have to hunt and dig to make sense of anything, don't get it regardless of how cool it looks.

As you rifle through the templates, you can click on each of them to see them in action. There should be a button that says something to the effect of "See a Live Demo of this Template". When you click on that, you'll have the ability to experience the template as though it were a live website.

Here are the top ten tips for buying the best template possible:

1. Does the template pop? Does the look, layout, and feel make you want to stay on the site and poke around?

2. What's above the fold? The term "above the fold" refers to the parts of the website that you can see without having to scroll down. The content above the fold is the most important part of your site since many people don't take the time to scroll down and thoroughly explore a site. These days, people are in a hurry and what they see needs to grab their attention.

3. Does the section above the fold give you the ability to have a strong call to action? A call to action is a marketing term that refers to an offer that you make to your visitors. For example, if you go to the8weekstartup.com, you'll see that above the fold, I have rotating images that each have different calls to action. Each of then ask you as the visitor to get the workshops, register as a member, or take some kind of action to move our relationship forward. You want this space to convey your most important offers and to do it professionally.

4. Your template needs to be designed for WordPress. Again, make sure that when you are searching for templates, you are shopping in the WordPress section.

5. As you explore the template, make sure that it's user friendly and easy to navigate.

6. Make sure that your template matches the color palate that you chose in Workshop 20: Building a Brand that Rocks.

7. Avoid unnecessary flash. Flash is the stuff that makes things move and spin on a website. Too much flash is a distraction and doesn't impress search engines like Google.

8. Make sure that you like the blog layout of the template. You should be able to view the blog layout when you are previewing the template in the live demo.

9. Make sure that the template matches what you want to convey with your business strategy. Again, if you're going to be a high-end differentiator, you need a website that looks solid.

10. Get a good footer. At the bottom of your site, there's a footer that will show up on every page. Make sure that the footer in your template looks professional and gives people the information they need to contact your business.

What to do once you've found your favorite template

Once you have found your favorite template, purchase it. You will them be taken to a download page where you can download the template.

Our goal now is to take those files, and get them installed onto the Godaddy.com server. This will replace the default template that WordPress set up on your site. Every template is a little different, but what you'll get is a series of folders with .html files, pictures, and code. I have created a video of myself uploading a template to help out. Make sure to watch it and follow along!

If you can't watch the steps to the video, here are the basic steps for uploading your new template:

1. Login to the administration panel of your website where you can see the WordPress dashboard.
2. On the right hand side of the screen, hover over the button labeled "Appearance" and then click on "Themes".
3. At the top of the screen, click on "Install Themes".
4. When you get to the top of the install themes page, you should see a button that says "Upload". Click on it.
5. You will them be taken to a page that will allow you to choose a file to upload. Note that you have to upload a zipped file of your template. This can actually be a little

tricky. When you buy a template, it will be downloaded in a zipped format. When you unzip it, you should see a few different folders in there. One folder will likely have the same name as the name of your template. This is the folder that you need to upload to WordPress. However, you will need to zip up that individual folder. To do so, right click on it, select "send to", and then select "Compressed folder". The other folders in there are documentation folders for your benefit and do not need to be uploaded to WordPress.

6. Upload that new zipped file. It may take a few minutes to upload everything depending on your internet connection.

7. You will then be taken to a page that shows you have uploaded the template. You should see a button that says, "Active Theme". Click that in order to replace the current theme with your new one.

Also, save the files that you received in a location where you'll keep all of your business documents. Having the original template files down the road may come in handy if your website ever has issues.

Action Work: Set up WordPress and get a template installed

By the end of today, you'll be able to go to your URL and see your template up and operating! It should look just like the live demo that you played with before you purchased it.

1. Log in to your GoDaddy.com account and install WordPress on your server by following the GoDaddy.com instructions. If you are struggling, simply call their support and let them know that you want to get WordPress installed on your hosting account.

2. Check to see if everything worked by going to your URL. If the Twenty Ten default template is up and running, then you've got everything set up correctly.

3. Log in to your default template and take some time to explore the WordPress backend.

4. Go to templatemonster.com or themeforest.net and find a WordPress template that meets the ten tips above.

5. Buy the template and download the files.

6. Watch the video of me uploading a new template to WordPress and follow along. To get access to the videos, you'll need to have purchased this workshop via the8weekstartup.com so that you can get all of the download files that come along with it.

In the next workshops, we are going to discuss how to set up your template and make it your own. After the next few days, your new business will have an amazing website and you'll be $9,500 richer than all other entrepreneurs out there who spend an arm and a leg to have someone do this for them.

You gotta love it!

WORKSHOP 23: Build a $10,000 Website for Under $500 – Part 2

"Everyone lives by selling something."

- Robert Louis Stevenson

Your website is like a foot soldier that works for you 24 hours a day, 7 days a week. It's always out there, looking, selling, and making an impression. If you ask me, that's a pretty good tool to have around. It's the employee that never sleeps, is always looking for customers, and is usually your first impression on a customer.

In our last workshop, we worked pretty hard and got an actual WordPress template up and live at your URL. Obviously, this isn't what we want people to see, though, when they type in your web address. We are going to need to change quite a few things in order to make this template your actual site.

Over the next few workshops, we will be working on the following:

- How to create the layout of your site
- Creating the navigation and menus
- Changing the pictures, logo, etc.
- Changing the content to your own words
- Adding widgets and plugins to make your site unique and functional

By the end of today, I want all of the navigation and menu items in your template to be customized. I also want the pictures changed and customized to reflect your new business. After all, we don't want to use the templates photos of generic scenes, now do we?

Architecting your site for usability

When a customer does land on your site, it needs to be a good experience. They need to be able to get around without too many questions. The biggest sin that most new website builders commit is to just start creating pages for the site. They build the about us page, the product page, and so forth. Before you do that, you need to think about how your visitor will move through those pages. If you take a moment to draw out your website onto a sheet of paper, you'll be able to organize the pages in a way that makes sense.

Rule of thumb: Thin websites are much better than fat ones. What do I mean by that? You'll want to avoid building a website where you have to go through more than two clicks to get to a page. If you have to navigate through seven clicks to find a page, that page will never get found. Having a page that's deep is also bad for search engines like Google. The search engines won't "go deep" so it's best to keep all of your pages within one to two clicks.

So here is what you do. Think of this like an organizational chart. In a company, you would have the CEO at the top, and under that position you would have managers which would then oversee individual employees.

Draw your website the same way. At the top where the CEO would go, I want you to write home page. Under that, branch out to the main menus of your site. For example, you may have a services or products menu, a blog, an about us menu, and so forth.

Once you get your menus listed out, define the individual pages that will make up those pages. For example, under the about us menu you may have a page for your staff bios, a page for your contact information, and a page for your customer testimonials.

At this point in your graph, you should be three levels down, but notice that the first and second levels don't represent a click to your website visitors. The first level is the page that people see when they land on your website. The second level just represents the menus that you'll have in your navigation. As a user hovers over your menus, the template should then display the individual pages available to them within that menu. That means that the user only has to go through one click to get to any single page.

Creating the navigation

Once you have your layout in mind, I want you to log in to your website so that you end up on your WordPress dashboard. Click on the "Pages" tab on the WordPress navigation panel. This is where you'll create your menus.

Start by clicking "Add New" at the top of the screen.

This will take you to a form where you can create the pages that will eventually become your website!

As you fill out the form, you will need to complete the following steps:

1. Enter the title of your page in the field at the top of the screen. This title is literally the wording that your website visitors will see within the menu and navigation panes so keep it short. Make sure that the name clearly defines what the page will be about so that the website visitor doesn't have to guess.

2. In the large box below, this is where you add the text and pictures that will fill up that particular page. You'll notice that the image that I have added below has a lot of extra formatting options that yours probably doesn't have. That's because I use a plugin to give me extra functionality. We'll cover that plugin tomorrow so don't worry about it for now. As of today, simply create your pages and add some holding text like, "This page will have customer testimonials on it".

3. On the right hand side, you'll notice a drop down box that says "Parent". If you leave it with the default selection of "no parent", then this page will be one of the main buttons on your websites navigation. These types of pages are represented by the second level that you drew out in your diagram. Any individual pages that should be within a menu will need to have a parent page. As such, create all of the level two pages first. Then come back and create the level three pages and choose which level two page will be the parent. Once you do this, your visitors will be able to hover over a navigation button on your site and see the individual pages in that menu! See, I told you this would be easy.

4. As you work, feel free to click the "Preview" button to see what your work will look like. Once the page is built, click "Publish". After a page has been published, you can always come back and edit it to add content, pictures, and even change the name of the page. Clicking publish just means that the page can now be viewed on the live website. Given that you won't have any traffic on your website, don't be shy about publishing your pages for right now.

Do you have all of your pages draw out and entered into your website? Keep in mind that you can always change things around. WordPress is very flexible and that's why we love it.

As a side note, you may have a default page or two in there from when you downloaded WordPress and installed it. Make sure you delete all but the blog page, so that they don't show up in your website menu.

Understanding sidebars

When you created your pages, you probably noticed a section called "Sidebar Selector". This is a really important feature that we'll get into in the next workshop. For now, know that WordPress uses something called Widgets which add applications to your website. We will discuss in Workshop 24 how to create sidebars and assign widgets to them.

Once you have done that, you can come back to your pages and choose which sidebar you want to use on a particular page. This essentially gives you the ability to determine which widgets you want showing up on each page.

How to add pictures

One final note about creating pages, and that's on how to add pictures. There are a few ways to get pictures into your website.

1. You can add pictures into the content of a page by uploading and inserting the image in the page creator space.
2. You can add pictures and other media into a widget.

We'll cover the first option today since the next workshop covers widgets in detail. If you go back to where you created your pages, you'll notice a button at the top of the box were you add the pages content. It says "Upload / Insert" and has a little camera and music notes next to it. This is the tool that you'll use to add pictures within the text of a page.

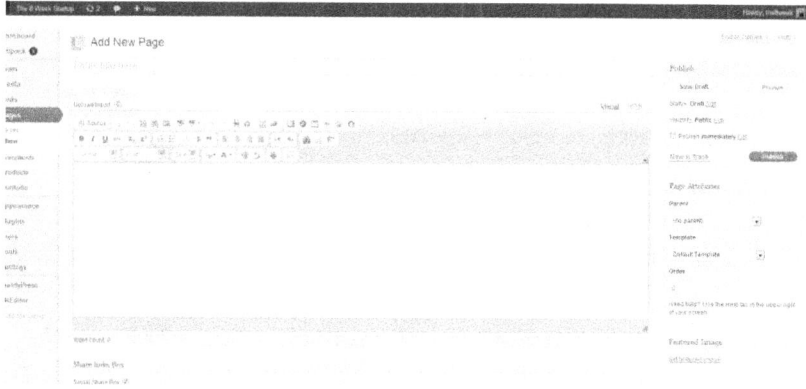

Once you get some text into your page, put the cursor at the point where you want your picture to show up. Then click the "upload / Insert Button" and follow the instructions.

Make sure that you fill out the title of the image along with the other fields. This help Google to know why you're displaying the picture on your website. That's a good thing because it tells Google how to treat your page when people search for a product or service like yours.

Once you're done, the picture will get dropped right into the text where you put your cursor. It's like magic... I know! And you thought you were going to have to sit through hours of HTML and coding lessons.

The whole point of WordPress is to make it possible for people like you and me to take matters into our own hands; to be able to use our creativity, imaginations and spunk to produce amazing websites on the fly.

WordPress is a type of CMS or Content Management System which means that all of the hard work is done. All you need to do is get a template, modify it, and add the content and pictures. You shouldn't have to spend hours digging through code like you would in one of those $10,000 custom built sites. Who needs em' right?

How to add a blog, and yes, you need a blog

Every business should have a blog. Why? Because a blog is what attracts visitors. A blog is the engine for creating new and interesting content for your audience. If your site is never anything more than the same ten pages you created in the beginning, people won't have a reason to return. Plus, having a blog is one of the best things you can do for your SEO which stands for Search Engine Optimization.

SEO is the practice of trying to make your website more visible to Google. The better your SEO practices, the higher your website will rank when people search for a business like yours. Eventually, you'll want to be on the first page for the keywords that define what you do. Having a blog that is updated at least twice a week is a great step towards making that happen.

Just make sure that you don't blog about your cat or your family vacation to Maine. If you own a business that sells custom printed playing cards, your blog posts should be about how you just did a custom set of playing cards for a customer who added her kids pictures onto the back of the cards. As such, she may type "Custom printed playing cards" into Google. If you have blog posts that talk about that, Google will be more inclined to direct her to your website. If on the other hand, you are blogging about your adventures in Maine, Google will think your website isn't relevant and not being relevant is bad. In fact, it's suicide.

This is another reason why we love WordPress so much. Their blogging platform is bar none the best in my opinion. Your template should have come with a blog since you bought a WordPress template.

To actually start blogging, you'll need to log into your website again and look at the dashboard with me. Do you see that button in the WordPress navigation panel that says "Posts"? Click on it for me. This is where you create a new blog post.

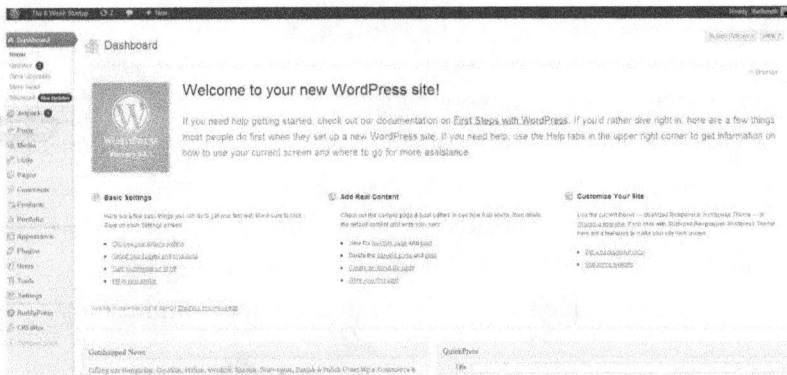

This process is almost identical to creating pages for your website. The main difference is that the content will end up in a blog post versus a static page located within a menu on your site.

Tweak Your General Settings

One final note for today – lets adjust the general settings on your site. In the WordPress navigation panel, you should see a button called "Settings". Hover over it and a sub menu will appear, from there click on "General".

This is an important step because it allows you to title your website and adjust a few other settings. The title of your website is what appears at the top of the browser screen when people type in your URL. It helps people to know what your website is all about, plus it give Google clues as to what you are up to.

If you go to the8weekstartup.com, you'll notice that the site title is "The 8 Week Startup" and the Tagline is "How to Start a Business in 8 Weeks." When you land on the page, look at the top of your browser and you should see those exact words looking right at you.

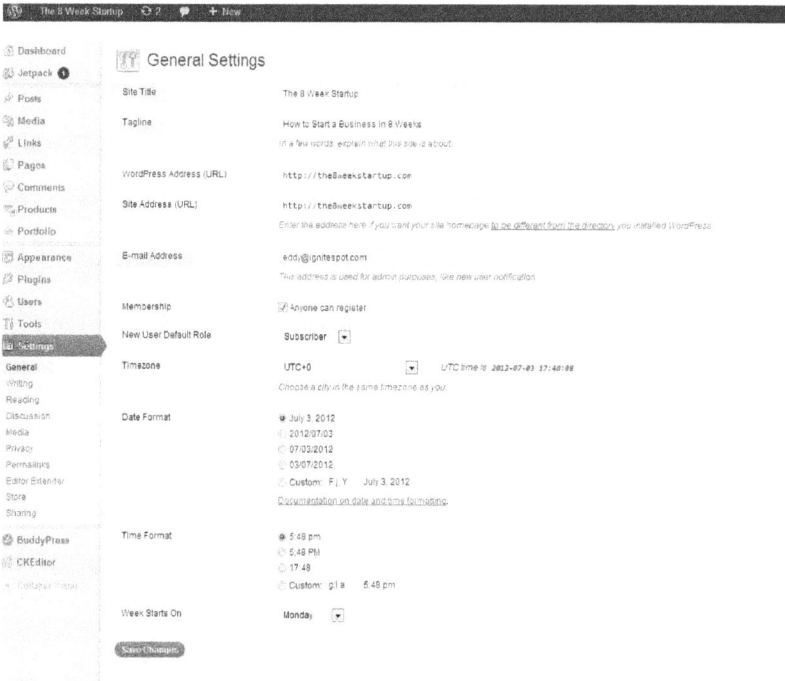

Action Work: Create your menus and pages

It's time to build the skeleton of your website. Today's work is important because you're creating the foundation of your online marketing presence. Don't let that scare you, though. As I said before, you can always change, delete, and move things around.

1. Draw out the hierarchy of your website. Try to make it so that your visitors don't have to click more than twice to get to any page.

2. Log into your website and create the parent pages that will make up the menus on your site.

3. Create the pages that will be located under each of the parent pages.

4. Practice adding text and pictures to your pages.

5. Make sure that you can access your blog from the main navigation on your site.

6. Create your first blog post and write about what your business does best. Try to avoid sales jargon in blog posts. Instead, focus on adding value and giving your visitors something worthwhile to read. A good blog post will be between 300 and 500 words, have at least one picture or video clip, and be relevant to your future readers.

7. Go online and do a website search for blogs in your industry. Subscribe to a few of them and begin reading them daily to see how others blog in your space.

There you have it. In your hands, you hold the beginnings of a great website! As I mentioned before, we will be looking at adding widgets and plugins in the next workshop.

Until then, have a happy WordPress day, you animal you.

WORKSHOP 24: Build a $10,000 Website for Under $500 – Part 3

"I was a functional addict."

- James Taylor

Having a website is nice and all, but if it doesn't do anything, it's not very useful. Your users need to be able to experience your website, not just look at it. In the past, this functionality is what you really had to shell out the big bucks for. You would have to hire a coder to integrate a shopping cart, forum, sign-in page, or anything else that required more than just putting some words and pictures on a page.

Thanks to the miracle of WordPress and other similar platforms, coders around the world have created widgets and plugins. What this means for you is that you can now install these things right into your website and with the click of a few buttons, you can have the same kind of functionality.

At the8weekstartup.com, I have quite a few widgets and plugins working behind the scenes. I installed them within a few hours, got them up and running, and now you as the visitor can chat with other entrepreneurs in our forums, login as a member of the website, purchase workshops, and more. How much did the entire website cost me to build? You guessed it! Less than $500.

The difference between widgets and plugins

Let's talk about what these things are before we start installing them on your website.

Plugins – Your site wide software

A plugin is a piece of software that works across your entire website. It essentially makes your entire site more functional. An example of a plugin would be the CKEditior for WordPress. When you install this plugin, it gives you many more options for formatting your blog and page posts. Instead of having the basic formatting tools, this plugin gives you all of the options you would be used to if you were using something like Word to write. For example, after you install this plugin, you can easily change the color, size, and font style of your text. You can add hyperlinks, align paragraphs, and much more.

For those of you reading this workbook versus listening to the audiobook, I've added a screenshot below of what the CKEditor added to my WordPress capabilities.

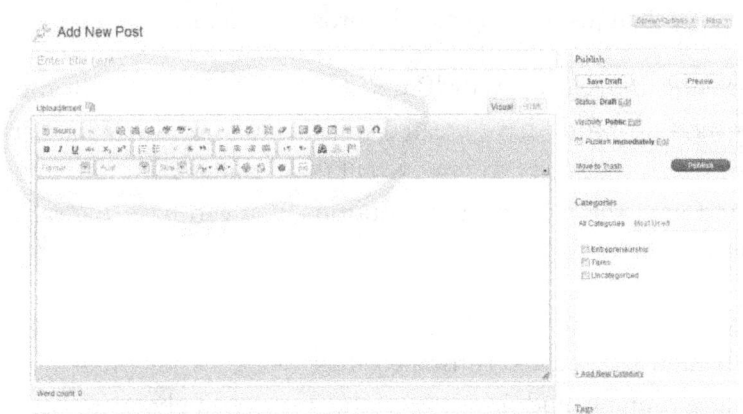

Here are a list of my favorite plugins and why I think they are so useful. I'll teach you how to install them a little later on.

- **CKEditior:** Again, this plugin allows you to have full flexibility on how to format your pages and posts. It's a must.
- **SABRE:** If you have website where visitors can log in, you'll want this plugin. Otherwise you'll get a lot of spammers registering on your site and causing havoc. Essentially, spammers have created software to look for unprotected

websites. When the software finds such a website, it creates a fake user so that the spammer can start posting on your site. Sabre keeps this from happening by making all registrants complete a simple test when they register to prove that they are human.

- **BuddyPress:** If you want to create a community on your website, BuddyPress is a good option. There are others out there. I just don't have any experience with them. BuddyPress is the plugin that I use at the8weekstartup.com to create our forums. This can be a difficult plugin to get configured properly, though, due to its possible incompatibility with your template. I found a WordPress guru at oDesk.com to help me get mine up and running properly and it cost me less than $100 for his time.

- **WP e-Commerce:** If you need to add a store to your website, the WP e-commerce family of plugins are great. The basic plugin can be downloaded for free at getshopped.org. From there, you can purchase premium plugins that work on top of that basic package to make it even better. There are premium add-ons and free ones. I use this platform for the online store at the8weekstartup.com. To get all of the add-ons that I needed to make the shopping experience the way I liked it, I ended up spending $219. Like BuddyPress, this one takes some time to figure out, but you can do it. I didn't have any experience with the software before I got started, and I had the store set up in no time.

One thing you can do is to run a Google search for "Best WordPress plugins" to see what other people are adding to their websites to make them more functional. There are so many good ones out there that we could spend months talking about them.

Widgets – Your sidebar gadgetry

A widget is very different from a plugin. Widgets do not affect your entire site. Instead, think of them as little tools that you can stick in different parts of your website. WordPress gives you the ability to create spaces for you to stick your widgets and these spaces are called sidebars. Note that some WordPress templates do not allow sidebars. If the template you purchased is this way, you will get an error when you try to add widgets.

A sidebar is literally a piece of real estate on your website that has been designated for widgets. A sidebar can be on the side of your website, in the footer, or elsewhere. The template that you chose will come with a set amount of sidebars that will work within its design. Some templates are better than others though and will allow you to create your own custom sidebars.

Examples of widgets are things like a user registration form, a Facebook like box, an advertisement, or a calendar on a specific page.

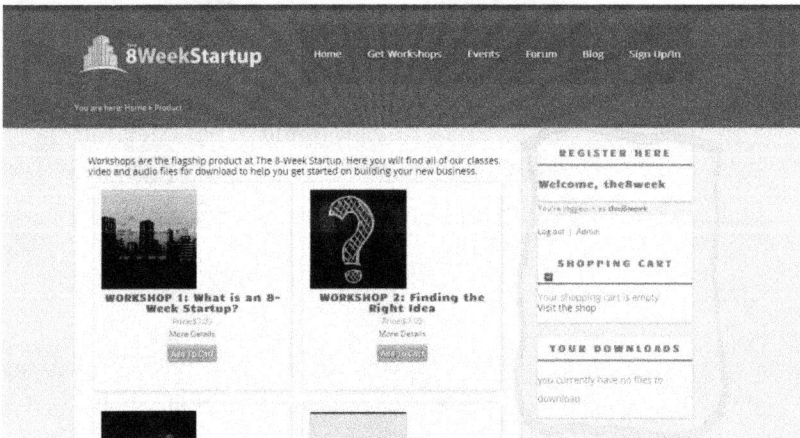

At the8weekstartup.com for example, our registration form, shopping cart, and downloads manager are all widgets in a sidebar. I have placed that sidebar on our products page so that people could see what was in their shopping cart and what they have downloaded with us.

When you install a plugin, it may come with a feature that allows your visitors to interact with the website. For example, the shopping cart plugin that I got from getshopped.org installed a few widgets for me to use, including the shopping cart widget and the downloads manager widget. It was then up to me to decide where I wanted those widgets to live on my site.

Let's talk about how to do that next.

How to install and use plugins

Since a lot of our widgets come with the plugins that we get, we first need to understand how to add plugins to our site. Remember that not all plugins are free. If you have to pay for a plugin, you'll most likely be taken to a 3rd party website that is not within WordPress, where you can enter payment information and download the plugin.

At any rate, here is how you do it.

Log in to your website so that you're looking at the WordPress dashboard. On the left is the WordPress navigation panel. You should be getting pretty used to it by now. You should see a button that says "Plugins." Click on it. You'll then be taken to a page that will list the plugins that are working on your site. Since you haven't installed any yet, you shouldn't see much other than some default plugins that WordPress puts there for you.

At the top of the screen, you should see a button that says "Add New". Click on that to be taken to the plugin directory.

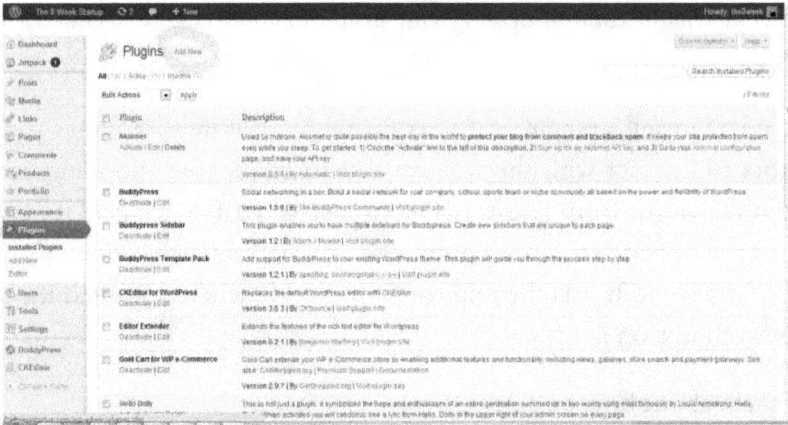

Once inside of the directory, you can search for new plugins, read about them, read user reviews, and install. It's a really easy process.

To get you started, lets install the CKEditor so that you can have all the tools you're going to need for writing pages and posts.

Step 1: Type CKEditor in the search bar. Then click the "search plugins" button to find it in the directory.

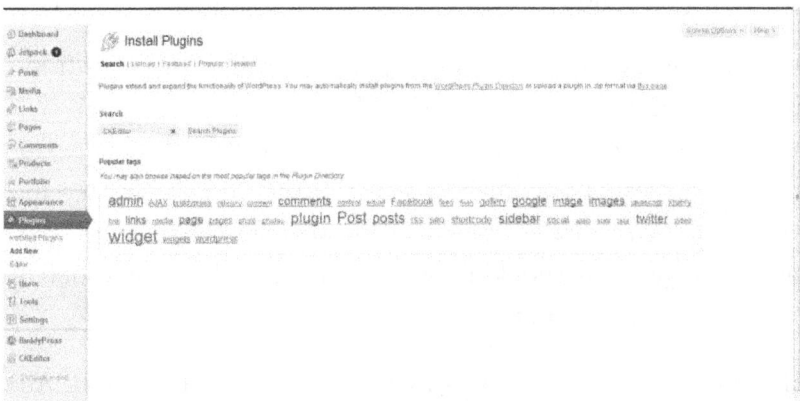

Step 2: Click on the "Install Now" link below the plugin.

Step 3: Once the plugin is installed, you'll need to activate it on your website. To do that, click on the "Plugin" button in the WordPress navigation panel again, just like you did in step 1. Then find your new plugin in the list on the screen and click the "activate" button just below it.

If you followed the directions above, you should have your first plugin installed. Well done! You didn't even break a sweat! I told you this would be easy.

To test out your plugin, try to create new page or post to make sure that all of the extra formatting tools are there for you.

The plugin may also add a new button to your WordPress navigational panel on the left side of the screen. When that happens, click on it to further customize the plugin. You'll notice that the CKEditor should have added a new button to your navigational panel.

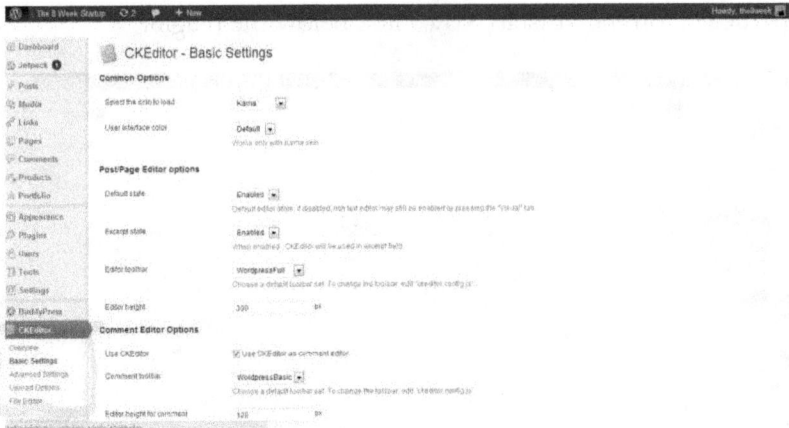

How to customize your widgets

After you get a few plugins installed, you'll want to get the widgets set up on your website. Again, some plugins come with widgets. You also need to be aware that WordPress has default widgets available to you. One of my favorite is the "text" widget which allows you to add a unique piece of text or html to a sidebar. There will come a time when you'll want to add a tool to your site and the developer will give you some code to paste in. An example might be a calculator or a weather widget. You could take that code and insert it into the text widget so that it displays on your website.

Enough jibber-jabber. Let's get the widgets.

Step 1: Log in to your website and hover over the "Appearance" button in the navigational panel. You should see a sub menu drop down which contains a link called "widgets" – click on it. This will take you to the portal where you add widgets to the sidebars that are included in your template.

In the center of the screen are the available widgets that you can use, and on the right are the sidebars where you can place your widgets.

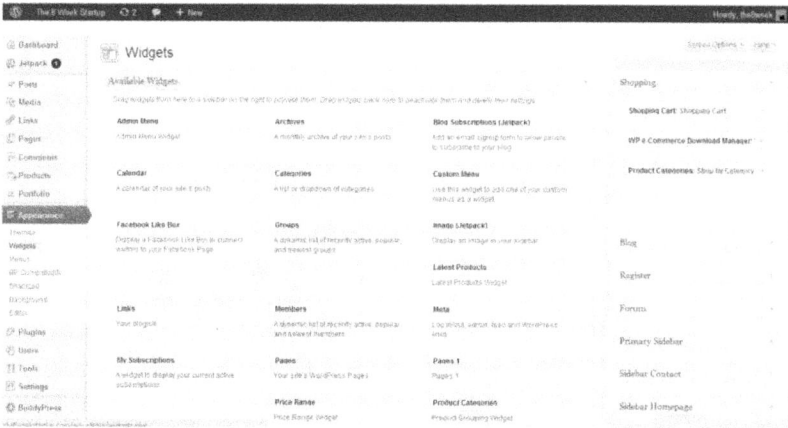

At the8weekstartup.com, my template allows me to create custom sidebars which I'll show you in a second. For now, I want you to understand how widgets get into the sidebars, how you customize them, and how you assign sidebars to pages within your website so that they appear to your users.

I created a sidebar called "Shopping". In that sidebar, I added three widgets for my visitors:

1. The shopping cart
2. The download manager
3. Shop by category

All of these widgets came with my WP e-Commerce plugin and the premium add-ons that I purchased.

When I installed the plugin, the widgets automatically showed up in the center section titled "available widgets." Once I created the sidebar called "Shopping," all I had to do was drag the widget from the center of the page into the "shopping" sidebar. Now, any page that displays the "Shopping" sidebar will show those widgets on it!

As you do this, you'll notice that each widget located in a sidebar has a little arrow to the right of its name. When you click on that arrow, the widget will expand, allowing you to configure it.

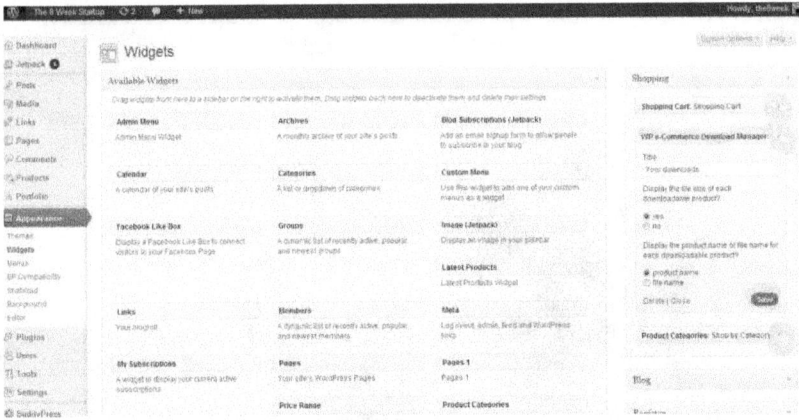

When you open up the widget like this, you can give it a title and change any available options.

Next, we need to understand how to assign a particular sidebar to a page on your site so that those widgets show up where you want them.

If you'll remember when you created pages for your site, there was an option to assign a sidebar to that page.

Go ahead and click on the "pages" button in your WordPress navigational panel, so that you can see all of the pages that you have created.

Open up any given page and scroll down towards the bottom to a section called "sidebar selector." You should see a drop down box that will all you to pick from any of your sidebars.

At the8weekstart.com, I have a page titled "Workshops" which is where our visitors can go to buy new workshops. Given that this is a page where I would like my shopping widgets to be displayed, I assigned the "shopping" sidebar to that page.

Creating sidebars with my template

Although not all templates work the same, let me walk you through how my template allows me to create sidebars.

In the appearance menu, I can see the name of my particular template. When I click on my templates name, I have the ability to customize my template a bit. One of the options is to add sidebars.

All I need to do is click the add button and title it. Then I head back over to the widgets area, which is ready for me to assign widgets to it.

What to do from here

We have covered a lot today, and I fully understand that there is no possible way that I could have answered all of your questions when it comes to installing plugins and widgets. Make sure to watch the videos in this workshop to get a better sense of how all of this works. In addition, you can always ask questions on our forum or you can sign up for The Entrepreneurs Club at the8weekstartup.com for more support.

Action Work: Get plugging and widgeting

What you learned today is probably the most difficult part of WordPress to wrap your brain around. If you can understand how widgets and plugins work, you're going to have a great website. If you are struggling with the concepts, don't worry – just take time to practice with them. I like to have two computer screens going at all times so that I can learn faster. I usually have my WordPress dashboard up on one screen, and my live website up on the other. As I make changes by installing plugins and adding widgets, I refresh the live website to see the changes. If the website didn't do what I expected, I take note and adjust as needed. Overtime you'll get a good grip on how to do things.

Here's your homework for today:

1. Install the CKEditor and activate it.
2. Install SABRE so that you can avoid spammers.
3. Do a Google search for "best WordPress plugins" and see what's out there. Add any plugins that you feel will add to your users' experience on your site. Avoid any plugins that detract from their experience or make your site feel unorganized.
4. Create sidebars if your template will allow you to do so.

5. Search for widgets that will make your site more functional and download them to your site.

6. Visit the widget area and begin assigning widgets to your sidebars.

7. Assign sidebars to the specific pages of your website.

8. Review your website and move the widgets around until you're happy with their location.

One final note... There are going to be times when you'll get frustrated with building you site if you have never done it before. That's due to the learning curve. Be patient with it and know that you're not shelling out $10,000 for this thing.

With time, you'll get it. I can usually get my websites up and running within a few days, but I am always looking for new plugins, widgets, and other ways to make it better, so the process is always ongoing.

In the end, you'll be in full control of your site. It will look great and you'll have spent less than $500!

WORKSHOP 25: Build a $10,000 Website for Under $500 – Part 4

"Human beings must have action; and they will make it if they cannot find it."

- Albert Einstein

By now, you should have a website up and live, with some plugins and widgets installed. Congratulations on getting this far! You have done what few entrepreneurs have dared to do and you have saved a bundle of money in the process.

Now you're at a point where you have to add something substantial to the website... Words. Writing the content for a website can be a bit time consuming, but it's important that you do it well. Don't outsource this function to someone else. They don't have the same knowledge and passion for your business as you do.

Why a lot of websites fail

A website is built for several reasons, but first and foremost is to generate new business. It is the portal by which people learn about your products or services. It's too bad then that many people build their websites with other purposes in mind.

Have you ever visited a website that does nothing more than drone on and on about technical mumbo jumbo or, even worse, about the accomplishments of the CEO? A lot of websites seem to use words like: "me", "us", and "we" instead of "you" and "your".

You're building a website for your customers, not for yourself. What we're going to cover today will help you to craft the kind of content that will make your visitors feel like you care more about them than you do yourself.

One of the secrets in sales is knowing that your customers don't care about you… They care about themselves. That's not derogatory. It's true. We're all too busy to care about much more than what's happening in our own worlds.

Customers are looking for a solution. If your website doesn't deliver that solution, they'll leave. That means that you don't have time to talk about yourself. Instead, you need to be talking about them, their problems and the solution that they can enjoy by working with you.

Your website needs to create conversions, not fuzzy feelings.

What is a conversion?

In website lingo, a conversion is a desired action that someone takes on your website. For example, you may want your visitors to fill out a form, call a phone number, initiate a chat request, or subscribe to your blog. All of those actions move your relationship to the next step, and that makes conversions valuable.

Your customer is willing to take such an action only when the website gives them exactly what they are looking for. Going with our theory that they didn't land on your site to read about your philosophies on life, but instead went there to get a problem solved, your website needs to give them several opportunities to do that.

So here we are, ready to throw content onto your site. As you start thinking of what you're going to say, I want you to keep a few things in mind:

- Write for your customer and not for yourself
- Determine what actions you want your customer to take on your website before you start writing content, then design your content so that your customers know what you want them to do
- Don't use a salesman tone of voice, instead make sure that your content is informative and useful
- Try to make each of the pages on your site distinct from each other
- Assign a keyword to each page and use that keyword in your writing so that Google users can easily find the page when they search for the keyword

Designing for conversion

Getting leads from your website has a lot to do with how you design things. If your website, the content, and its overall presence are sloppy you won't get any leads. If you picked a decent template, then the layout and presence of your site should be pretty sharp. Now it's up to you to get the right words in there.

To help out, let's head on over to your website. Type in the URL and let's take a look at it together. Without scrolling down, what do you see on the home page? This is the most important part of your site. It is the first, and most often, only section of your site that visitors will see. This section of your website is "above the fold" which means that they don't have to scroll down to see it.

An important tip is to not put your most important information below the fold. If you place your main offer at the bottom of the home page, you'll never get customers.

Let's call this prime piece of real estate, "center stage". If you had less than ten seconds to wow your customer, what would you put on center stage? At the8weekstartup.com I currently have a rotating image with different calls to action. We'll learn about calls to action a bit later.

On our center stage, the first thing that people see is an invitation to get the workshops.

You get the point. Our visitors come to the8weekstartup.com to learn to do one thing – start a business. So, that's what I'm offering on my center stage.

Levels of the sales cycle

Here's the catch, though: Not everyone is ready to buy. That's a problem for most websites, because websites tend to only cater to those ready to pull out the credit card. It's a fatal error indeed to not support the people that are just looking around.

As an entrepreneur, you have now taken on the sacred badge of salesman or saleswoman. It's your job to generate sales for your company, and every good sales person knows about the sales funnel.

Imagine, if you will, a funnel that has three layers to it. At the top, or widest part of the funnel, are all of the people that will land on your site for whatever random reason. Those are the people that are just looking. We'll call these people tire kickers.

The second level down represents all of the people that want to engage with your company, but may not yet be ready to buy. We'll call these people engagers.

The final level of the funnel represents the people that trust you enough to buy from you. We'll call them customers.

We use the shape of a funnel for a specific reason. That's because there are always more tire kickers than there are customers. Your job, and that of your website, is to try and move as many people down through that funnel as possible.

What this means is that if you only have offers for customers, you're missing out on some pretty big opportunities.

As we move through the next sections, we are going to want to focus not only on the customers, but also the tire kickers and the engagers.

Crafting calls to action

A call to action is just what it sounds like. It's a statement that asks your visitors to take an action on your website.

There are all sorts of calls to action out there. Some of them include:

- Click here
- Download this eBook
- Sign up today

Now that we know all about the sales funnel, we want to come up with an offer for each type of visitor along with a related call to action that makes sense to them.

As a side note, the term "call to action" is often shortened to CTA, which we'll also do going forward.

CTAs for tire kickers:

What kind of information are tire kickers looking for when they visit your website? These are the kind of people that don't want any interaction with a salesman just yet. They also aren't too keen on giving up their personal information like phone numbers and such. As a matter of fact, they really don't want much engagement at all other than to do some research.

Since that's what they're looking for... let's give it to them.

A great way to address their needs is to write an e-book with valuable information in it. The e-book would be something that they could download off of your website in exchange for their e-mail address. Giving up an e-mail address isn't a huge risk for tire kickers, so many of them are willing to do it as long as the e-book is informational.

To do this, you'll want to write a 3 to 7 page educational book that solves a problem that your common customer would face. For example, if you own an online store that sells power tools, you could write an e-book that teaches shoppers what to look for when trying to buy the perfect drill.

Once you get your e-book written, take some time to pretty it up with pictures, your logo, correct grammar, and beautiful formatting. Then you can create an offer on your site, like the following:

Click Here

Download the top 10 tips for buying the perfect drill!

The goal would be to lead the visitor to a page on your website that describes the e-book and has a form on it. The form would ask for their e-mail address only. Once they fill out the form, the e-book is sent to their email address.

You can automate this kind of process if you set up your forms correctly on your website. To clarify, a form is nothing more than a place for your visitors to enter their information and click "submit" in exchange for something from you. We'll talk about how to create forms in a moment.

The overall goal with tire kickers is to get their e-mail address, so that you can send them an e-mail occasionally. We do this so that they remember who you are and visit your site again down the road when they are more prepared to buy.

CTAs for engagers:

Engagers want something more. Getting a download isn't enough for them. Instead, they are looking for ways to engage with your company. They want to dip their big toe in the water to test the temperature, but they're not quite ready to commit and cannonball in.

Think about your business for a moment. What could you do for engagers that will give them this opportunity?

A lot of websites do free webinars. A webinar is nothing more than an online class that you offer. They can essentially attend the class, interact with your company, and get a sense of how good you are at solving their problems.

Going back to our power tool store, the website could advertise a monthly webinar that shows a member of your staff building a woodworking project. The visitors could watch from their home computers, chime in to ask questions about the tools, and get a sense of your expert status.

There are a lot of software platforms out there that make it possible for you to hold webinars. If you decide to go down this road, do a quick internet search for "online webinars".

Your call to action could be something like:

Register for our FREE Power Tool Class

Watch the tools in action, as we build a dog house this month

When they click on the button, they'll be taken to a landing page that describes the class and has a registration form for them to fill out. Engagers are willing to give more information since they are further down the funnel so it's fine to ask for their name, e-mail, and even their phone number.

Webinars aren't the only way to meet the needs of engagers. The goal, though, is to find a way for them to experience your product or service without having to pay for it. Give them a taste and they'll soon be moving down the funnel to customer land.

CTAs for customers:

Customers are ready to buy so we want to make sure that you have a call to action for people who have their wallets open. These are the calls to action that say:

- Buy now
- Get it here
- Start today

Those are just a few examples, but you get the idea. When people click on this CTA, they should be taken to a page that describes what they are getting in exchange for filling out the form. At Ignite Spot, for example, people click on the CTA "Get an Accountant," which takes them to a page that asks for the contact information. The page also describes what will happen once they fill out the form. In essence, it tells them that an accountant will call them to do a free consultation to see if we are a good fit for their business.

Adding buttons to your site

You may be wondering how to add a CTA to your website. That's a great question. A CTA is usually a button that people can click on your website. On a website, a button is usually an image like a .jpg file.

The image of the button has the CTA on it.

Get a FREE Consultation

You may need someone to help you create these buttons unless you are proficient at creating images. I eventually broke down and bought Adobe Illustrator so that I could create my own, but there are other software packages out there that can do the same.

Since we are in a bit of a hurry, though, I would suggest turning to oDesk.com and hiring a graphic artist to create 10 or so buttons for you that match the look and feel of your website. They could do in an hour or so and you'll only be out $30 to $50.

Make sure that you know what you want your CTAs to be before you hire them.

Once you do get your images, you can insert those images into various parts of your website and hyperlink them to the landing or offer page that they represent.

Make sure to watch the videos that I have created for you in your download folder. You'll be able to watch me create buttons, add them to the site of my new business, and hyperlink them. All you'll need to do is follow along!

Adding forms to your site

Forms are what make your site valuable to you. They are what allow you to generate leads. That makes them pretty important in my book.

Forms can be pretty complicated, which is why online companies like Wufoo.com and Contactme.com have come out in recent years. They give you the ability to create your own custom forms via an easy to learn wizard tool online.

Once the form is created, you can copy the html code and paste it right into your website!

I use Wufoo.com for my websites because it's easy and I love the flexibility. The best part is that I can tell Wufoo how to update me when I do get a new lead.

At Ignite Spot, it's vital that I respond quickly when people request a free accounting consultation. As such, I have configured Wufoo to send me a text message every time I get a new lead. I always try to call my leads within 10 minutes!

Again, make sure to watch the videos in your download packet for this workshop and follow along as I add forms to my website.

As a side note, the forms don't always look pretty when they are installed. At times I have had to pay a coder for an hour of his time to make them fit well within my templates. For the $50 - $100 it cost me to make the forms look pretty, it's always a great investment. I have a friend that does this form me. If you know of a coder, make sure to approach him or her if your forms need to be spruced up. If you don't know anyone, you can always get a coder at oDesk.com

Action work: Call your visitors to action

Let's get a good understanding of what your sales funnel is going to look like, and let's craft an offer and a CTA for each phase. Once we have that, we'll get those juicy CTAs up on the website for all to see.

1. Visit some of your favorite websites and see if you can find their CTAs. What did they do? How are they trying to engage with customers? Remember that not all sites are good at doing this.
2. Find other websites in your industry and determine how they are using CTAs.
3. Create an offer for your tire kickers that will allow provide them with a valuable solution. Consider writing an e-book.
4. Create an offer for your engagers that will give them the opportunity to engage with your business without having to fully commit.
5. Create an offer for your customers that will entice them to sign up.
6. Create your CTA buttons either yourself or by hiring a graphic designer at oDesk.com
7. Place your CTA buttons in strategic locations above the fold so that visitors will see them.
8. Create individual pages on your website for each of the three offers.
9. Hyperlink the CTA buttons to their respective pages.
10. Add a form to each of the pages so that you can collect your customer's information and provide them with what they are requesting.

As you work on your website, you'll almost definitely find new and better offers. For me, adjusting my offers is a never ending process. I'm always looking for more and better ways to connect with the visitors on my websites.

WORKSHOP 26: How to Get Customers by the Truckloads – Part 1

"A satisfied customer is the best business strategy of all."

- Michael LeBoeuf

Everything we have done up to this point has rested on our ability to do what we will accomplish today, and that is to get customers.

If you've been doing your homework, chances are pretty good that you've had that nagging feeling in the back of your mind that's spouting off common entrepreneurial doubts like:

- What if I can't get any customers?
- I don't know how to sell anything… maybe I should try and hire a salesman!
- What if the customers come too slow and we run out of money?

All of those concerns are pretty valid and are normal at this point in the game. It's not unusual to be worried about your abilities to bring in the dough. That's why the next three workshops are targeted toward how to sell.

I love selling, and it's for reasons that you may not suspect. For me, selling is all about finding solutions for people. It's not about reaching quotas, getting bigger commissions, or the like. I get a real sense of satisfaction when I can actually help someone with an issue that plagues them.

Let met give you a quick story to show you my point of view.

When I was 21, I took a job selling financial services to families in distress around the country. I worked in a call center and it was my duty to reach out to these people, assess their personal situation, and try to match them up with our in-house financial specialists.

When I took the job, there were 150 salesmen on the floor. We spent the first week in training, which felt a little silly, to be honest. They had us memorizing scripts that dawdled on about the financial experts background and why we were the best company to get them out of their financial woes.

After training, we were placed on the call floor and expected to get at least two families a day to sign up for a free consultation. After a week or so of sounding like a robot and not getting any sales, I was about to quit when a thought occurred to me. I realized that I was talking to families that really needed help, but didn't want to talk to a salesman. Dealing with financial stress is an emotional experience even for the most stout of heart and to have a salesman call them up to try and get them to buy something was nothing more than annoying to them.

I determined that I would change my approach. I was going to throw the script out. If I got fired for doing so, it didn't matter, because I was ready to quit anyway.

The next day I showed up for work with a new goal. Instead of trying to get two families to sign up for free consultations, I decided that I was going to ask a single question and then listen. That question was, "What is it about the finances in your family that is causing you the most stress?" I literally took three pages of script and whittled them down into one single sentence.

By the end of the day, I had 12 families signed up for financial consultations. The sales managers were floored. So was I, actually. I did it again the next day and signed up 9 families. After a few months of beating sales records, the owner of the company asked me to redesign the entire sales program, train the staff of 150 sales people, and oversee new client acquisition.

All of that came about because I threw my sales hat away and put on my "I care about you" hat instead.

With that kind of attitude, selling is actually quite fun. As we go through the next three workshops, please remember to wear the right hat, so that you can enjoy finding and working with new customers.

The art of prospecting

Selling starts with prospecting. When we think of prospecting, we think of gold diggers; the guys up in the mountains, wearing overalls and standing knee deep in a stream, sifting rocks in a tin while they swat flies out of their beards.

What are those guys doing? They're looking for gold. As an entrepreneur, you can leave your overalls at home, but you will need to get out into the stream and start sifting.

In the world of sales, prospecting is literally the process of finding potential customers. There are hundreds, if not thousands, of ways to do this, but not all of them are suited to your personality and the characteristics of your business. Do you place an ad, start cold calling, set up Google Adwords to drive people to your website, or do you hold seminars, just to name a few?

By the end of the workshop, my goal is to help you determine which form of prospecting is right for your business, implement that strategy, and refine it.

Also, notice that this section is called The "Art" of Prospecting.

That's because selling isn't a science. There are emotional, psychological, and financial considerations that make selling for every business unique. I wish that there was a perfect formula, but there's not. As an artist, you'll need to keep your mind open to all of the possibilities available to you as well as be willing to go outside of your creative space to do something that you may not be used to doing.

Where to look

The problem with new businesses is that they usually start prospecting the same way... with an ad. That ad is usually in a phone book, a newspaper, or something similar. Once that ad is live, they wait for the phone to ring and when it doesn't, they loudly declare that that type of advertising doesn't work.

Let me start of by saying that we want to invest our money into mediums that will sell our product or service. At this point, we're not terribly interested in advertising. What's the difference, you ask? Advertising is, in the sense that I am using the word, when you spend money to reach the masses. It's buying a billboard, television ad, or something similar.

It's an expensive route that doesn't make a lot of sense for us, at least out of the gate. Down the road, advertising will likely be helpful once you have enough resources to support the budget.

For now, we want to avoid advertising and focus on selling. Keep that in mind as we discuss different ways in which you can prospect for your customers.

The first question you need to ask yourself though, isn't "How should I spend my marketing money?" If you go all the way back to workshop 2, where you defined the needs of a specific group of people, we want to bring them back into focus for a bit. The real question you should be asking yourself at this point is, "Given that I am going to help group X with their problems, where does group X usually hang out?"

Since so many businesses don't service a specific group of people, they tend to spend their marketing money on a wide array of things hoping that one of them will stick. Since you're smarter than that, you've picked a specific group of people which allows you to communicate with them in their language.

You need to meet your customers where they are. In other words, find out where they hang out. That's where you need to be.

Let's look at an example. Assume that you are starting a business that digitizes blueprints for engineers. If you've ever been to an engineer's office, you'll know that it's usually overflowing with tubes upon tubes of blueprints. Your service might be to visit their location weekly, digitize their new prints, and make them available online so that they can review, modify, and manage them anywhere they want to, including on their job sites.

Who are the main prospects in this example? They're engineers, and more specifically, the firms for whom they work. If you can get an entire firm to be your customer, you'll have a much bigger and profitable account on your hands.

Knowing that you are trying to get engineering firms to sign up, how would you spend your marketing dollars? Remember, the best question to ask ourselves is, "Where do engineers hang out?" Where do we meet them?

I would venture to say that putting an ad in the phone book for a business like this would most likely be a waste of money. Most engineers probably don't hang out in the phone book looking for people to digitize their blueprints. They've got more pressing matters to deal with.

Let's make a quick list of where engineers hang out, just to see what our options are:

- They spend a lot of time in their offices
- On the job site, if they do engineering on development-type projects
- At educational seminars to improve their skillsets
- A lot of engineers use CAD software tools to design

If this were my business, I would look at these options and then ask myself, what is the most natural selling vehicle that fits into each of those hang out spots? Let's brainstorm for a minute to see what we mean. Given that engineers do hang out in their offices quite a lot as desk jockeys, you could visit in person, create a demo video of your solution and send it to them to watch, or you could offer to digitize a blueprint for free and give them a 30 day trial to thank them for their time.

You may consider contacting the companies that sell CAD software to see if you can partner with them. Perhaps they would let you sell your services on their websites for a portion of the profits.

You could also invest some money in an expo booth, make a list of every engineering conference and seminar around the country, and begin attending them as a sponsor and presenter.

Although there are many more ideas for selling to engineers, we have touched on a few that will allow you to communicate with your audience directly. The biggest rule of thumb in prospecting is to invest your dollars where your customers are, and not on a big ticket ad that speaks to the whole world.

Sticking with a strategy

Once you have determined where your customers mingle and you have come up with a few different ways to reach them, you need to build long-term strategy that will deliver.

This can be more difficult than it looks depending on how spontaneous you are. It's tempting to look at new and wonderful ways of selling to get customers. What I have found personally is that trying to do a little bit of everything gets you nowhere. Instead of trying to present at expos, visiting engineers at their offices, and partnering with CAD sellers, consider choosing one of these and getting really good at it.

Because selling is an art, you need to be able to stay focused on your strategy and refine it as you learn. This is done with testing. If you have your marketing and selling program distributed into several channels, you won't have the bandwidth or wherewithal to be good at any of them. As you get better, feel free to add other channels down the road.

Have a clear process in place

Once you have settled in on how you are going to target your prospects, you need to develop a clear step-by-step process for how you will move them through your sales pipeline.

Let's keep up with our digitizing blueprint company and assume that you feel that presenting at expos will be the best route for you. That's great! The next step is to decide what that could possibly mean.

Once you invest in the tools you'll need to start your selling campaign, you'll likely begin meeting a lot of prospects.

I want you to be able to answer the following questions clearly so that you can get the most out of your strategy:

1. What will you do when you meet a prospect?
2. Where will you keep their contact information?

3. How can you set up an automated follow up system if they like what you have but aren't ready to buy yet?

4. How much will you need to invest in your system in order to meet a new prospect? Obviously, we want this dollar figure to be as low as possible so that you can talk to more prospects for the same amount of marketing expenditure.

5. What will you offer them that's low or no-risk that will get them interested?

6. What kinds of questions will your prospects have for you? How will you respond to those questions?

7. Once someone does buy from you, what happens next?

You'll want to have mapped out a clear process for what the prospect will experience as he or she moves through to becoming a fully-fledged customer. At the same time, you'll want to include in that process what you'll do to manage all of the people that slip through the cracks.

A good example of this actually occurs at expo shows. Have you ever presented at one before? If you have, you'll know that you get a lot of business cards. It's sad to say, but most people throw those cards away after a show because they can't remember who was who. If your strategy is to do expos, you'll want to make sure that you have a way of capturing those relationships and turning them into opportunities.

Ten time-tested prospecting methods

Here' a list of ten different ways that you can prospect for customers. Again, there are many more than this, but it will get your brain thinking about ways that you could reach your customers:

1. **Door-to-door sales or cold calling:** The age-old way of selling still works and it works well when done right.

2. **Google AdWords:** I would recommend getting a book on how to master Google AdWords before you go dumping money into this one. You can spend a lot here before you see a return if you don't know what you're doing. At the same time, if you do know what you're doing, you'll make a killing.

3. **Facebook:** You can advertise on Facebook and the best part is that Facebook allows you to target and sell to niche groups of people. In essence, if you only want your ad to be shown to Engineers, you can make it so when you set up your campaign. It's genius.

4. **Seminars:** These are used a lot by businesses that sell intangible services. You'll see many professional firms, financial planners, coaches, and the like in this arena.

5. **Expos or tradeshows:** These can be fairly expensive to get into since you need to have a decent looking booth to compete for attention on the floor. However, if you can get into them, it may be a great way to meet a lot of targeted people very quickly.

6. **Piggybacking:** This is the process of finding someone who sells a product or services that compliments yours and then partnering with them. In our example above, the idea of building relationships with companies that sell CAD software would fit here.

7. **Demonstrators:** Tis the way of many multi-level marketing companies these days. If you have a product or service, you can get people to demonstrate it and share in the commissions.

8. **Referrals:** A happy customer is always your best way to market.

9. **Events:** Some companies have gotten really adept at holding events to generate their marketing conversations. For example, one company here in town recently rented the theater the day before a blockbuster movie was to open and they had hundreds of prospects come to the event.

10. **Location:** If you're a brick and mortar store, location is everything. Make sure that you're not just in a good spot in town, but that you're located in a place where your niche is likely to hang out.

Skip the sales jargon and listen

Whatever method you decide to master, remember that you must drop the sales lingo and become a better listener. Instead of using sleazy high-pressure sales techniques to try to close a deal, consider asking a valuable question and letting the customer sense the need for what you do.

Going along with our example, you might ask, "Mr. Engineer, have you ever noticed that dealing with stacks and stacks of blueprints is affecting your work in a negative way? If so, how would having all of them digitized so that you can get them on your laptop or iPad improve what you do?"

Action Work: Develop your prospecting strategy and implement it

It's time to start prospecting. Right now we need to be completely focused on how to meet as many potential prospects as possible for as little of an investment as possible. Let's get started:

1. Take some time to describe the group that you're going to be solving problems for. I know we've done this in past workshops, but I want you to write it out again so that they are clear in your mind. Describe who they are, what they do, why then need you, and so forth.

_____

_____

_____

_____
_____
_____
_____
_____

2. Define at least five different places where these people hang
out:

_____
_____
_____
_____
_____
_____
_____

3. What forms of prospecting will allow you to naturally
communicate with them in their hang out spots?

_____
_____
_____
_____
_____
_____
_____

4. Of the different prospecting ideas you just listed, on which
one will you focus and become great?

_____
_____
_____

_____

_____

_____

_____

_____

5. Describe the steps that you will take to implement this new prospecting strategy.

_____

_____

_____

_____

_____

_____

_____

6. What step can you take right now to get started?

_____

_____

_____

_____

_____

_____

_____

As you can guess, the last step of your homework today is the most important. Why? Because I don't want you putting off the action of getting started. Once you take the first step, you'll be well on your way to getting customers. Make sure that you don't just answer questions one through five and then tell yourself that you'll get to it when you have more time.

Right now is the only time you'll ever have.

WORKSHOP 27: How to Get Customers by the Truckloads – Part 2

"Salesmanship is limitless. Our very living is selling. We are all salespeople."

- James Cash Penney

Yesterday we focused on getting people into your business. We were prospecting. Hopefully you were able to complete your homework, which means that you now have a strategy in place for how you are going to begin generating prospects.

You'll want to turn on your prospecting machine as soon as possible. A lot of people feel like they have to have everything perfectly polished before they speak to their first prospect. If that were the case, you would never get out there and speak with anyone.

The fact of the matter is that your presentation, sales skills, and ability to get new customers will increase with each new person that you talk to.

You'll get feedback on your business cards, brochures, presentation style, and so forth if you get out there now and start talking. If you don't, your message will never improve.

So, whether you decided to go with cold calling, expos, Google AdWords, or some other form of prospecting, turn it on now. I want conversations about your company to begin yesterday.

Did you know that a lot of people fear this step for one main reason? Do you know what that reason might be? It's that they don't know what to say to a prospect when one finally shows up.

It's a fair concern and I think that we should address it, so that you feel more comfortable.

Once you get them in, what do you say?

It's not so much about what you say as who you are. People buy from other people that they like. If you spend your entire time pitching a script to your prospect, they'll turn off after the first sentence. If, on the other hand, you look him in the eye, smile, and connect with him as a person you'll have a much more interesting conversation. Just don't give him googly eyes or he might get the wrong idea.

A lot of people ask me what I say when I sell. I tell them that I don't say a set thing. Instead, I make friends and then I listen to my new friend's problem to see if I can help.

Here's the twist, you have to be a friend back. That means that you have to be completely honest with them and not be a salesman. That means telling them that your product or service isn't the best solution for them if that's truly the case.

It means caring about them more than you do the sale.

It means doing what is right for the customer at all times.

When I tell people this, they say, "That's great, but I stink at making friends with complete strangers." You know what? Most of us do. It takes a lot of practice to make a total stranger instantly feel comfortable around you. That is your task though. From now on, your job is to build this skill within yourself. Every time you meet a new person, get serious about your selling abilities and try to buddy up with them. It's called building rapport.

If you're new to building rapport, here are a few things that you can do that will make you more successful:

Mirroring

When you look in the mirror, what do you see? You should see yourself, unless you're a vampire in which case you might as well give up now, because nobody is going to feel comfortable around you.

If you're not a vampire, then bravo. You have a fighting chance at being liked… and seen in the mirror.

My point here is that a mirror gives you a direct reflection of yourself. Do you remember when I said that people like buying from others that they like? Have you ever bought something from a salesman that drove you crazy? You know that guy that just got under your skin? Maybe you couldn't figure out why he was so annoying, but you just knew that if you bought from him, you would have to go home and gargle with mouthwash.

We want to avoid being that kind of salesman or saleswoman. One of the best ways to do this is with a principle called mirroring. Here is how it works. The next time you're with someone, I want you to reflect them in a natural and caring way. In other words, I want you to mirror or match their tone of voice, energy level, and body posture. Those are the magic three when it comes to doing this right.

What this means is that if your prospect is moving a million miles an hour, amped up with excitement and can't stop talking, I want you to increase your energy level to his, get just as excited, and answer all of his questions.

If your prospect is sitting in a chair, arms folded and leaning back in a dignified manner, your job is to do the same without looking exactly like him. Such a person may speak more slowly and thoughtfully with little or no hand gestures. Guess how you're going to speak... thoughtfully, without a lot of hand gestures.

What is this going to accomplish? It will help your prospects see themselves in you. They'll feel far more comfortable around you and will be more interested in opening up to you.

If you're by nature a high-energy person and you keep that personality when you go to present to a dignified and thoughtful speaker, do you honestly think that he will like you? He may, but chances are that you'll probably annoy him to the point that he'll think that you're immature and not taking his concerns seriously.

If on the other hand you speak slowly and more dignified to a high-energy prospect that's spitting out idea after idea, that prospect will likely think that you simply don't care.

Do you see why this works so well? You need to become a gecko when you speak to strangers.

You may be thinking that this feels fake. You say that you just want to be yourself and that will get you the most sales. I would agree that it's important to be yourself, but you're probably a pretty annoying person to a certain part of the population. I know that I am. Everyone is.

In sales, we do things like mirroring not to trick people into liking us, but to help them feel comfortable with us so that we can help them with their problems.

This principle works on the phone, too. You just have fewer tools with which to work. In phone sales, you need to mirror the prospect's tone of voice and energy level.

Get rid of the sales stigma

You've probably heard that people don't like to be sold to but they sure do like to buy. I'm like that. I usually cringe when a salesman approaches me because I know what's coming. As business owners, we need to get rid of the sales stigma. That means getting rid of anything that feels greasy or underhanded in our presentations.

I'm not a huge fan of high-pressure, buy or die, sales techniques and sales environments. It's a no-brainer to assume that our customers don't like them much, either. So what does a customer want? They want a solution and someone that cares enough to help them find the best solution for their budget.

Getting your customer to see you as a friend and a consultant is far more powerful than having them see you as the tweed suit wearing, greasy moustache man with a catchy sales line.

Understanding the psychology of buying

When you customers buy from you, they are going to go through a process in their mind. It's a psychological journey that they don't realize they are taking, but they travel it nonetheless. If you have every bought something that costs more than $100, you've been on this journey too.

No matter what you are selling, you need to understand what is going through your customers' heads, so that you can walk a mile in their shoes and help them find the ideal solution, be it yours or another.

Most people start in panic mode. Something has gone wrong and now they're stranded. It has happened to them so many times that a light bulb finally turns on and they realize that they need to find a solution.

That's when the euphoric phase starts. The thought of finding a business to solve this issue of theirs becomes so exciting that they start researching their options. That usually leads them to either Google or asking their friends for recommendations.

Here is where some of the problems start. As research begins, they get presented with your product and every other one on the market. After a little bit of searching, the options, features, and advances make finding the right solution rather difficult to do. So, they nominalize the shopping experience down to the one factor they that they understand fully… price.

In the end, they get so anxious over all of the options out there, that they tend to find a solution based on price alone.

What causes this? The consumer knows that price isn't the most important factor most of the time. The main cause of stress is usually risk. For a prospect to buy from you, you have to get rid of the risk. This risk is caused by several factors including:

1. They may have never heard of you or your company
2. They don't fully understand your offer and the benefits they'll receive for paying a higher price
3. They may not have known what the product or service should actually cost, and as such had a much smaller figure in their minds
4. Timing – If they feel like they are being rushed then the feeling of risk is often much higher

To help your buyer overcome the feeling of risk, there is a secret weapon that you can employ. I call it leveling up.

What is leveling up and how can you use it?

Before we get into the throws of leveling up, I want to you remember the last time you went on a first date and ended up really liking the girl… I'll assume you're a guy for sake of ease in this example. Image in your mind what happened that night. Can you see where you were? It might have been at a restaurant, sports event, or your grandmother's bingo party – I'm not really sure.

However you met her, the important thing to remember is how you felt right when you saw her. Do you remember how beautiful and stunning she was? I'm willing to bet that you didn't walk over to her and say, "Hi, my name is Mark. Will you marry me?"

That's called going from zero to sixty in the blink of an eye. No woman would say yes to that unless you were famous, owned your own private island, and had seven homes across the world. She might say yes then, but even if she did, she would be really stupid. Why? Because marriage is a big deal. You're going to be living with this person for the rest of your life, so you better darn well like each other.

So what did you do? You leveled up. You probably started off introducing yourself and having small talk. Assuming that you made a good impression on her, she may have agreed to a date.

Once the first date rolled around, you probably did everything you could to spiffy up including taking the time to trim up the unibrow and buy some breath mints. While on the date, you wouldn't have held her hand yet, because you haven't earned that. What you have earned is the right to have a more in-depth conversation.

As long as you don't put your foot in your mouth, the conversation may lead to future dates. At some point in the future, hands will be held and there will be a first kiss. Ooh, la la.

One day, a few years later, of course, you find yourself on bent knee, asking this goddess to be your lawfully wedded roommate – or so the story goes.

Do you see how leveling up works? It's the principle of increasing commitments over time. If you apply this psychological process to your business, you'll get truckloads of customers. If you ask them to give you a huge chunk of change right at one set, you'll likely lose out.

Designing your increased commitments

This works for any company regardless of what you sell. Start off by looking at the end goal. What you need to do is determine how you can invite your prospects into more and more committed relationships with you over time.

The first commitment should be low risk of course. What could you do to get your prospect to go on a first date with you? Now remember, you don't get to hold hands or kiss yet!

Take some time to discover three to five different levels of commitment that you can walk your customers through from the time you meet them to the time that you become lifelong companions.

Do this and you'll prosper.

Action work: Begin selling your stuff

Let's start making some real money now. Generating a strong customer base takes time, patience, and the willingness to course correct as often as is necessary. Let's get you on that path and never look back.

1. Make the decision to mirror everyone that you speak with. Don't copy them exactly or else you'll be found out. Just mirror them naturally and try to connect with them on a

higher level. This will take a lot of practice so start now and never stop doing it until you kick the bucket.

2. Turn on your prospecting system. If you are doing door-to-door sales, go out this afternoon and start knocking doors. If you are doing Google AdWords, get it turned on. Whatever you are going to do, do it. Remember not to give up after a few days. You need to really focus on your prospecting method and refine it.

3. Brainstorm three to five layers of commitment through which you can walk each of your prospects. Figure out a way to implement those commitments in your sales strategy, starting with the lowest risk commitment.

Ultimately, let the buyer buy and enjoy the process, while you become a trusted friend that is helping them find the best possible solution. Every time you come across a sleazy sales technique, drop it and focus on the relationship instead. No amount of sales tactics will ever be as strong as you actually caring about them and trying your best to help them succeed.

WORKSHOP 28: How to Get Truckloads of Customers – Part 3

"Try, try, try and keep on trying is the rule that must be followed to become an expert in anything."

- W. Clement Stone

Today is all about you. You are the secret sauce to tons of sales. A lot of people look for that magic bullet to making millions and closing mass amounts of deals when the answer is right under their noses. There are tons of different selling programs out there, and a lot of them are pretty darn good. At the end of the day though, the most important element in the sales equation will always be you.

If you were the kid in high school that everyone liked, you'll probably find this workshop a bit easier. For all of the rest of us, it may take a little work to become likeable. That's the honest answer to getting a lot of sales, though. You have to be likeable.

I have already said it in the past, but today we are really going to dive into the fact that people buy you and your personality before they buy your product or service.

Once they have decided that they like you, then they start looking at what you have to sell. If the product or service meets their needs and solves a problem that is painful to them, you have a new customer.

So today is a lesson on how to be liked. By the end of this workshop, I want you full of confidence, energy and the right attitude.

Working on you, your confidence, and your likability

Have you ever noticed that a really good salesman glows with personality? Confidence is a great asset when you're selling, but too much of it comes across as cocky.

At my home this summer, we had some issues with our driveway. The concrete had sunk and cracked, so we decided to hire a company to come out and level it. The guy that showed up was obviously a body builder. He wore a skin tight t-shirt and skinny jeans. When I opened my door and saw him, I thought, "Wow, this guy's in shape". Everything was fine until he spoke. Here's his exact introduction word for word.

"Hey bro! I'm here to bid on your driveway. Do you got a second to come and look at it with me, my man?"

It was by far the worst experience I have ever had with a salesman. He was so in love with himself that I couldn't tell if we were talking about concrete or his biceps.

At one point, my wife came out to see what was going on and he actually started posing in front of us. When he left, my wife busted up laughing.

Again, let me say that confidence is essential to getting customers, but cockiness is just awkward and insulting.

What we are about to do may be difficult for some of you, but I want you to do your best with it. Some people naturally don't like themselves. There is usually some aspect of your personality, body, or other characteristic that you don't like. If that weren't the case, we could safely say that you're not human. If you are going to be successful, you're going to have to learn to look past those things and truly learn to appreciate who you are.

If you have serious self-confidence issues, I want you to try the following on a daily basis:

1. **Join a gym and actually go every day.** If you work out, you're going to gain confidence. Just don't turn into our concrete salesman. As you get stronger, you'll feel healthier, happier, and more successful.

2. **Go to bed.** Stop staying up so late. As an entrepreneur, you can't afford to stay up until 2 a.m. and get four hours of sleep. It's called beauty sleep for a reason, so hit the pillow starting tonight. I go to bed at 10 p.m. and get up at 6 a.m. every day. You can't appreciate yourself if you feel like a walking pile of you-know-what.

3. **Pretend you're on camera.** Whenever I film a video for a company of mine, I always laugh at the director. Picture me sitting in front of a camera doing my best to be entertaining and the director is back there saying, "Not bad. This time, increase your energy and excitement ten- fold - Action!" In life, movement instantly changes how you feel. I want you to actively focus on your hand gestures, body posture, stance, and excitement level. Now bump it up by tenfold. Use powerful hand gestures, stand or sit with successful posture, and inject excitement into your voice, facial features, and mannerisms. I guarantee you'll instantly feel better and more successful.

4. **Get some new clothes.** Start dressing in a way that builds up your confidence. This has changed over the years for me. When I started my career, I always wore a suit everywhere I went. Doing so made me feel more professional, confident, and in command. Now that I have my own businesses, I wouldn't be caught dead in anything other than shorts and flip-flops. For me, I get confidence from that knowing that I have earned a lifestyle that lets me dress like an entrepreneur. With that being said, it's ironic but I just went out and bought a bunch of really high quality shorts and shirts. It sounds

weird, but your clothes directly affect how you project yourself and how you feel about yourself.

5. Look for the good in everyone you talk to. Your assignment is to start complimenting people, and to do it sincerely. Every time you meet someone, you should be mirroring them, which you learned in the last workshop. Now I want you to also find ways to sincerely build them up. As you do so, you'll get really good at finding positive things about people, and guess what the natural product of that will be...? You'll get good at noticing positive things about yourself.

6. Look around you and feel grateful. I actually have what I call a success journal. In that, I have written down everything that brings me joy and happiness. When I'm feeling burned up, I always read it and realize that I'm the luckiest guy in the world. If you were to peek in it, you would see pictures of my family as well as pictures of things that represent goals I want to achieve. Being grateful is a huge step towards self-confidence so start saying thank you.

Having self-confidence is actually a skill, not a characteristic. So many people think, "I wish I was as confident as that guy!" They make it sound like he's become something they're not. All he's done is learn the skill of being self-confident. He's learned to wake up each day and tell himself it's going to be a great day. He's learned to dress sharp, go to the gym, and do all to other things which naturally lead to confidence. If you lack self-confidence, all you need to do is acquire the skill.

It's important because you're going to have bad days as an entrepreneur. Something will go wrong and you'll often be the one having to lift yourself up. When you have a day job, you can stay depressed and expect someone else on the team to execute while you wallow in your misery. As an entrepreneur, you can't do that.

Ask for a commitment

When you are selling, there is going to come a time when you need to ask for the sale. You will need to look your prospect square in the eyes and ask him or her to buy from you. This is obviously a lot easier to do if you have some self-confidence.

A lot of people don't ask for the sale. Do you know what happens in those types of conversations? You should because you have been in them yourself several times, only you were the prospect. To sum it up, the prospect tells the business owner that he or she will think about it and get back to them. The business owner then gets it in his head that the prospect will eventually come back and buy, but they hardly ever do.

I mentioned previously that I'm not a big proponent of greasy sales techniques. I want to make that clear. A lot of you may be thinking to yourself that asking for the customer to buy falls right in line with something that you would expect to come out of the stereotypical salesman's approach.

In all reality... It is. What we need to understand is that by asking for the close in the wrong way, we will come off as a greasy salesman or saleswoman. When done correctly, we create the impression that we are trusted consultants that are trying to craft the best possible solution for them.

Here is what you don't do:

"Sally, I think that we are the best solution for you. Go ahead and sign your name on the dotted line and we can get you set up right away!"

Yes, it's a confident approach but it's also too forceful for my tastes. When it's time for me to ask a prospect to buy, here's what I say:

"Sally, based on everything we have talked about today, It seems like this would be a great solution for you. Would you agree?"

If she says yes, then I sign her up. If she says no, I can ask her why she feels that way and try to resolve the concerns she may have.

However you ask for the close, you'll likely need to get good at it. Make a promise to yourself right now that you'll never leave a sales call without asking for the close. So many people are afraid to offend the prospect so they never ask and as such never get the account.

Welcome to your new career

Selling needs to be treated as a profession if you're going be good at it. If you merely have selling as a to-do list item in your daily schedule, it will ultimately get pushed around by other less important tasks. If you make it your profession, you'll get a lot of customers. If you make it a to-do list item, you'll never do it.

I spoke with one of the best salesman I know recently. He also happens to be the owner of his own company. When I asked him what a CEO should be doing with his time, he said "Selling." A CEO should be the best salesperson in the entire organization. It is his or her job to be on the leading edge of getting customers. I couldn't agree more.

With that being said, I want you to realize that by becoming a business owner, you're really starting out on a new career path in sales. In order to do well in your new career, you need continual training. This workshop alone will not be enough to make you a master salesperson.

The best sales professionals in the world realize that selling is not like riding a bike. Keeping up on your people skills is a lot of work. This means that they are often investing in themselves and their sales training.

Regardless of how good you are at sales, I would highly recommend taking the time to attend a selling seminar. There are tons out there. Do your homework to see which ones are right for you. Each seminar will approach sales in a different manner, so take some time to learn about the philosophy, technique, and success rate of the seminar. Also, you may need to do some traveling to attend the seminar. That's all right.

In addition to going to seminars, I would get as many books on selling as I possibly could. If you were to look at my personal business library, I would guess that 75% of the books are on selling. Authors like Brian Tracy, Jeff Thull, Jeffrey Gitomey, and many others have so much material out there that it's insane not to learn from them.

Get a selling mentor

Do you know someone who is great at selling? If so, bring them on board. Get that person as a mentor and pick his brain. The more time you spend with the person, the better. You want his approach, confidence, technique, and charisma to rub off on you.

Most of us have someone within our network that is great at sales. Take some time to figure out who that person is for you. When you do find someone to mentor you, ask him the following questions:

1. How do you prepare for your sales day?
2. How did you get self-confidence?
3. What sales books do you read?
4. Is there a particular sales strategy that you follow?
5. How can I get better at connecting with people and building rapport?

Soak up as much knowledge as you can from these people. You'll know that they are good at selling because they'll be financially well off. Oddly enough, a good sales professional is often the millionaire in the room.

Action work: Get polished

If you are already meeting with prospects, good for you! If not, get out there and get started. As you do this, I want to make sure that you realize just how amazing you really are. Let's boost your confidence level today and keep it there.

1. Apply any or all of the six self-confidence boosters that I taught you earlier which included going to the gym and dressing well. As you do these things, I want you to take note of you how feel.
2. Commit to always asking for the close when you speak with a prospect. Determine the right wording for you and practice it in front of a video camera. Keep recording it until you feel comfortable.
3. Get a great sales mentor.
4. Climb to the top of your roof, spread your arms out wide, and shout "I love myself" three times... all right I'm just kidding on this one. If I get emails from your neighbors stating that you did this and it's all my fault, I'll be a happy man.

I know that some of the things we've talked about today may feel a little hokey, and that's all right. Learning to change your confidence level often feels that way. I've seen a lot of really intelligent entrepreneurs struggle because they had no belief in themselves. At the same time, I'm never surprised when I see an entrepreneur with enough confidence to break down walls. She wins every time.

With confidence, everything else will fall into place because you'll have the oomph to make it happen.

WORKSHOP 29: How to Escape Accounts Receivable

"Communication – the human connection – is the key to personal and career success."

- Paul J. Meyer

Accounts receivable is a bad thing. It means that people owe you money for work that you have performed on their behalf. The idea is that you do the work for someone, and they get 30 days to pay you.

In a perfect world, that should work fine, but the trouble with receivables is that people don't always pay on time. Quite often, they take 60, 90, or even 120 days to pay. Shoot, some people don't pay at all! This is a huge problem for a lot of businesses because they run out of cash waiting for checks to show up in the mail.

This problem plagues some industries more than others. In construction for example, a company may perform work and not get paid for months. It's pretty common. On the other hand, if you own a retail store, the customer is paying at the cash register. They can't leave with the merchandise in hand until they pay. As such, retail stores don't have accounts receivable.

If you are starting a business that doesn't require the customer to pay now, this chapter is for you. Our goal here is to cancel out that issue or, at the very least, limit it as much as possible.

I'll be sharing three different techniques with you today that you can implement into your business that will obliterate your receivables and get you paid much faster.

Elimination technique #1 – Half down and half upon delivery

If you are doing project work for someone, it is vital that you set the expectations upfront with regards to how your company bills its customers. In order to get paid on time, let your customer know that your standard billing system requires a 50% down payment to cover the initial costs of doing the work. Once the work is complete, let them know that the remaining 50% will be before the project can be delivered.

If you are providing something tangible to your clients, this is a really easy process to implement but it takes a good business owner to enforce it. Here's a little story to illustrate what I mean.

I have a client that builds large custom projects for businesses. The price tag can range anywhere from $1,000 up to $150,000 depending on what his customers order. When we started consulting with this particular client, they had a lot of receivables for work that they had done in the past. In other words, they had become the bank to all of the customers and had financed a lot of the purchases. You can image what this did to the cash flow.

I was talking with the business owner one day and we decided to require a 50% down payment on the project when the customer placed an order. Once it was built, the customer could come to the warehouse to inspect it. Upon final approval, the customer would have to pay the remaining 50% before he was allowed to take it home.

It was a simple solution to eliminating the receivables for the company and it worked… For a few months. Over time, my client had customers that would give him excuses for not being able to pay when they picked up their product. Being a nice guy, he let them take it, with the promise to pay as soon as possible. It's unfortunate, but the client is back to square one with receivables and he is once again the bank for all of his customers.

My point here is that if you decide to operate this way, it has to become a part of your model, not just a fleeting thought that you'll try out. You need to implement this billing structure into your entire operation cycle so that everyone involved knows that it's how things are done. When you get a new customer, there needs to be clear communication that this is how you do things.

Customers are actually really nice and cooperative when you communicate with them. If you tell your customers up front that this is how you operate, they won't question you at all.

As I mentioned earlier, this strategy works well if you are delivering a tangible product because you can hold it hostage until the final payment is made. That sounds harsh I know, but it has to be done. You can't afford to let your customers control your cash flow. If you do, you'll go out of business.

Eliminator technique #2 – Get their banking information

More and more businesses are paying for their bills with an online bill pay service or an auto draft. If possible, set up your business so that you get paid that way. If you can eliminate the standard invoicing procedure, in which you send out an invoice and then wait for months to get your check in the mail, you'll sleep better at night.

This is a technique that we use at Ignite Spot. Since we provide an intangible service, we have one favor that we ask of all of our clients, and that's the ability to receive our fee via a monthly automatic bank draft. Since we come up with a set monthly fee that we are going to charge, the client has no issues with it.

We love it because we have no accounts receivable... Ever. If you look on the books of most accounting firms, they are laden with receivables. I don't know about you, but I like to get paid for the work that I perform.

To set this up, all you need to do is add a paragraph in your customer contract that states that you will draft for your fees. You then make this very clear when you are signing up a new customer and you supply them with a form that requests their banking information.

A lot of people feel awkward asking for such personal information as their clients account and routing number.

Here is the secret to getting past that... If you make a big deal out of it, then it's going to be a big deal. If you just make it one of the minor steps that need to get completed to onboard a new client, your client won't think twice about it.

At Ignite Spot, we have been accepting payments this way since we opened our doors and guess how many people have given us grief about it... only one. That's because I know that people are used to paying for things via their bank account with today's technology so I don't stress out about it when I ask them for the information.

You will need to work with your bank to make sure that they have the ability to draft your client's bank accounts. If they don't, you may need to switch banks. If they do, set up an appointment with your banker to get the service added to your account. You may pay a small monthly fee for it, but that fee is a lot better than having thousands upon thousands of dollars sitting out there in receivables land. I believe that we pay roughly $25 a month with our bank.

Eliminator Technique #3 – Try to get paid upfront

This one isn't always possible, but hey – it's worth a try. If you can set up your business so that you can get paid up front, then you will not only avoid the trap of accounts receivable, but you will also have given yourself some options with how you invest your cash.

Cash literally is the blood of your business. Your blood carries oxygen and other goodies to different parts of your body; without it you'll die. In business, cash does the same thing. It carries oxygen to the various departments of your company and allows everything to work properly. It makes sense then that having the cash now instead of later is pretty helpful.

If you want to get paid up front, you will have to give your customers a reason for doing so. With this technique, all of the risk is placed on your customer, which isn't good. If you can make it worth it for them, then you have a win/win situation.

A few ways to make it worth it to them are:

- You could create a guarantee that states that you'll refund their money for any unused portion less a small fee.
- You could show them how the money will be invested to create a solution for them.
- Offer a free consultation before you take payment to show them what you're capable of doing.

However you do it, the idea is to try and soften the risk on their part, so that they feel comfortable with paying upfront.

Doing more than one at a time

It goes without saying that if you can set up your business to do more than one of the eliminator techniques described above, it will only make your life easier.

For example, if you are going to do the 50/50 split, you could combine that with requiring payments to be made via a bank draft so that the customer doesn't have to fiddle with a check.

Try and get creative with how you structure your payment system so that it fits nicely within the type of product or service that you provide. Again, these tips lend themselves better to some industries more than others.

If you have a business wherein you'll be servicing a customer more than once, getting the bank information for drafting purposes makes a lot more sense than if your customers only buy once.

At the end of the day, it's important to realize that you're not going into business to be a bank for your customers. You're going into business to provide a great product or service to them, and because of that, you need to get paid for doing so.

Clear communication upfront, as well as having the fortitude to stand by your business strategy when your customers ask for an exception, is important if you want to avoid receivables. I know the customer service person inside of you is probably saying, "Isn't the customer always right? Shouldn't I give the customer what she wants so that she stays happy with my company?" My answer to that is no. You do want to give your customers a great experience when they buy from you, but you also need to make sure that your business will be in a better spot for having served them. A business transaction must be a win/win proposition; if it's not, why would you do it?

For businesses that absolutely have to invoice

If you must invoice due to the type of work that you do, then do yourself a favor and have a system in place. A lot of companies could get more cash in the door if they took the day off and organized their invoicing system.

Essentially you need to optimize your invoicing world. Here are a few tips and tricks to getting the most out of your invoicing system so that people pay you quicker and more efficiently:

1. Invoice as soon as the deal is made. A lot of companies wait to invoice at the end of the month. By the time your customer finally gets his invoice, he may not remember what it's for. That means that the invoice will sit on a desk for weeks as they research it.

2. Use a simple invoicing application on your smart phone to be able to invoice while you're in the field. A lot of the apps that are built for invoicing will sync with your QuickBooks file making life really easy.

3. Ensure that your invoices are emailed to your customers instantly and sport a neat little "Pay Now" button on them. When your customers get the invoice in their email box, they can click on the PayPal link and pay you immediately.

4. Make your invoices look professional and make sure that all of your contact information is on them. This gives the payables clerk everything he or she needs to pay you without asking any questions.

5. Make sure that your invoice is in the format that your customer needs to process the payment. Some companies are picky about paying invoices if they don't clearly define the work that you did. Ensure that you have detailed your work well so that there is no ambiguity.

This entire workshop is all about greasing the cash flow wheels. I want your business to have as much cash running through it as possible, so that you have options and the ability to grow. Don't be afraid to use today's technology tools to eliminate receivables in your life. In all honesty, its good for business and it makes things a lot easier on your customers.

Action work: Eliminate receivables

1. Do you have the ability to request 50% down and 50% upon delivery with your product or service? If so, what can you add to your customer onboarding process that will communicate those expectations clearly?

_____

_____

_____

_____

_____

_____

_____

_____

2. Do you service your clients on a regular basis? If so, contact your bank to see if you can add a bank drafting feature to your business checking account. Then tell all of your customers that you receive payments via a monthly bank draft.

3. Can you justify getting paid up front for what you do? What are some ideas that you can think of that would reduce the feeling of risk for your customers so that they will pay up front?

_____

_____

_____

_____

_____

_____

_____

_____

4. If you absolutely must invoice, take the day off and design an invoicing system that will easily create detailed invoices in the field that you can e-mail to customers. See if you can get the e-mail to link up with your merchant account like PayPal so that they can pay you right from the e-mail.

5. Design your invoice to have all of your contact information within a professional layout.

Getting rid of receivables isn't hard to do as long as you set your business up to avoid them from the beginning. Take some time today to think about how you can eliminate the receivables in your business so that you'll have enough cash to properly focus on your customers and take care of them.

WORKSHOP 30: Automating Operations – Part 1

"Efficiency is doing better what is already being done."

- Peter Drucker

Why automation is hard for most businesses

Automation is the process of investing time and energy into the betterment of your company. It's the kind of thing that requires the extra push above and beyond your normal call of duty.

Have you ever had a car that you actually improved? I'm not talking about doing the oil changes and vacuuming the thing out when your kids spill milk in the back seat. I'm talking about actually making mechanical changes to enhance the performance of your car.

For example, I am an avid Jeeper, which I have mentioned in prior workshops. When you buy a stock Jeep, it's capable of going off road, but if you really want to take it off road you need to lift it, put massive tires on it, swap out the axles, add lockers, and do all sorts of other improvements to make it a rock crawler. It's not a cheap hobby, I know. My wife makes sure to remind me of that every now and then.

Here's the great part, though... Once the improvements are made, your Jeep is bigger, tougher, and far more capable. It can go places that most vehicles can't. If you want to drive right through a huge boulder field, go for it. Your Jeep can handle it.

Taking the time and money necessary to add systems to a Jeep to improve its performance is a lot like automating your business. A lot of people don't do it because it takes time, research and elbow grease. Just like the Jeep, though, once the improvements are made, your business is bigger, stronger and more capable.

With the right systems in place, what could your business achieve? With that in mind, I would urge you to be the kind of entrepreneur that is committed to doing whatever it takes to get things automated. Put in the time, energy and commitment up front and you'll be able to stand back and watch your factory churn out widgets before you know it.

The number one poison of automation and its antidote

The biggest enemy you are going to run into when trying to automate your business is time. For some reason, there is always something to do, someone to talk to, or some fire to put out. There is never enough time in the day to be able to invest in improving performance. At least that's the excuse we tell ourselves constantly.

In all honesty, that's all it is – an excuse. We all know that we could be fitter, wealthier, and happier if we stopped making excuses and did the work to change our fates. When our parents told us that we could be anything we wanted, they weren't lying. They just forgot to train us on how to eliminate the excuses that sabotage those dreams.

It's important that we know this now and recognize it. We need to be able to plan for when your excuses will plague you.

So how do you beat the monster? You have summits.

At Ignite Spot, for example, we have a summit on a regular basis. This literally is a day in which everyone walks away from their to-do lists, e-mails, cell phones, and scattered schedules to sit in a room together. What do we do for the whole day? We build our business. The entire day is focused on solving a business process that is slowing us down.

With the combined brain power of the entire team, we find that we can come up with great solutions. Here's the catch… We actually have to build and implement that solution on the same day. It's never enough to come up with a great plan in a meeting and then assign someone to implement it at some point in the future. That's a recipe for a lack of execution.

No. Your summits must actually accomplish something so that by the end of the day, you will have automated and improved upon a piece of your business.

When you have your summits, here is what you need to do:

1. A few days before the summit is to take place, determine which business process is causing your company the most grief.
2. Let everyone attending the meeting know that you will be solving that particular problem and remind them to bring their A game to help fix it.
3. Remind everyone that summits are a day for fixing the company and not for dealing with to-do list items that can wait until tomorrow.
4. Hold the summit and spend the first part of the day brainstorming the solution as a team and the second part of the day working together to implement and document it.

In the beginning, you won't have a team to work with since it's just you. That's all right. You still need to hold summits all by yourself. Schedule a day on a periodic basis where you will do nothing other than focus on a business process, fix it, and automate it.

When I first got started, I would do this in my living room. It worked great. Oh, and just in case you are wondering, I would hold a summit monthly. If that's too much for you, don't go longer than quarterly or else your business won't improve.

Avoid the silo strategy

Another problem with businesses not being able to automate anything is that they think in silos. The term "silo" comes from farming and references a place to store bulk materials like grain. They look like large free standing tubes in the middle of a field.

As a small business grows, it gets new employees who do their best to add value to the company, and in doing so create their own systems that nobody else can operate or understand. Each of those solutions are individual silos that hold information, data, or knowledge on how to do something. If the employee leaves, it's like having the silo burned to the ground along with everything inside of it.

As a new business owner, you need to begin today by creating an atmosphere that encourages a centralized storehouse of knowledge, data, and tools. It's actually pretty easy to do, but you have to start today or else you'll never get around to it.

The goal is to have a place where your employees can turn to and better understand the company, their jobs, and how to get things done. With such a tool in place, people will stop coming to you for everything, which gives you more free time. That's why we're starting a business, right? You do want more free time, don't you?

This is how we do it here

What I'm getting at is that you need a guide. I'm not taking about the 300 page employee manual that huge corporations hand out to every new employee. Those things don't get read, anyway. Have you ever gotten one? I have. They end up sitting on a bookshelf collecting dust.

Why don't a lot of employees read those things? First of all, they're on paper. Nobody wants to read through a huge manual to try and find one little piece of information that they need. It's just easier to go and ask the boss, since he wrote the dang thing. The second reason why nobody reads them is because they get outdated. Businesses change constantly and most businesses don't take the time to update the manual, reprint a copy for every employee, and pass them out every time a change occurs. As such, you end up reading a manual that was created 10 years ago.

To be clear, that is not what we are after. You do need a guide, though. I like to call them playbooks. For me, a playbook is something that is more like a field guide. It's easy to use, update, and carry with you. Also, everyone on the team has the ability to make changes to it, update it with current processes, and share it with the entire team at the click of a button.

If you set up your Google Apps for Business account like we discussed in prior workshops, you will have access to Google Documents. I use this feature to create my playbooks and it works great.

Here is what you do:

1. Log into your email account and click on the "documents" at the top of the screen.
2. Create a new word document and title it something like "Company Playbook".
3. Share this document with anyone currently in your company and with all new employees.
4. Create a table of contents that lists the major processes within your company. Don't feel like you need to list out everything that your company does. For now, just type out the major operational tasks that you do.

5. Also in your table of contents, create a section called "Job Descriptions" and list all of the different job descriptions that you'll likely have within your company as you grow.
6. Add any additional information to your table of contents that you feel is important.

It's that easy. Now all you have to do is open up your playbooks every time you have a summit and document your new process so that everyone understands how to do it. As the company continues to grow and change, your employees can login to update it with the new how-to lingo.

There are a few great things about having a playbook on Google Documents which are:

- You can search its contents. If your employees want to know how to do a specific task, they can search for it in the search bar instead of having to thumb through pages and spend hours researching.
- It can go with you and your employees anywhere. All they need to do is log into their email accounts and they can get to it.
- Once you add your job descriptions, you can easily train people new people and give them a quick and easy reference for what is expected on the job.

The playbook will actually become a team document. Use it in your meetings, trainings, and everything else so that it becomes a central part of who you are and what you do. That way, everyone will reference it when they need answers to questions.

Don't let the playbook overwhelm you

A lot of people avoid building a playbook because it can be an overwhelming project. To be honest, it is. If you try and write out your entire playbook right now, you won't get very far. Not only is the project fairly large, but you don't know what your processes well enough yet.

Your job right now is to get it started and then add to it every time you have a summit or find a way to do something better.

Writing and documenting processes may not be your forte. I can safely say that, because it's not the forte for most people. Don't beat yourself up over it. Take it one step at a time, and before you know it, you'll have an asset on your hands that is extremely valuable.

Think of your playbook as an intangible asset that you're building. The best kinds of assets take an upfront investment, but pay dividends for years and years to come. Just think of how much easier your business is going to be to run if you make this one project important to yourself and your company.

I have said in the past that your job as founder of the company should be to focus on strategic things and not day-to-day operational items. Building a playbook qualifies as a strategic item. Having one is a huge jump forward and will give you the edge when you need it most.

What to do if nobody is using the playbook

Over the years, if nobody is using the playbook, there is only one cause for that… You are not using the playbook. Just because the playbook is an extremely valuable asset within the business does not mean that other people will use it.

It is your job to constantly push the improvement of your playbook and make sure that it is in line with the vision that you are building for the company.

You many need to schedule regular sessions in your calendar which will require you to update and promote the playbook throughout your organization. This small bit of effort is far less stressful than having a business that doesn't know how to run itself unless it constantly bugs you.

Action work: Start your playbook

Make the decision to become the kind of entrepreneur that will build your business. Determine that you will be the kind of person that will take time on a regular basis to make the company more efficient and capable. To do that means that you will need to set aside time on a consistent basis for summits. Let's get this set up right now.

1. Open up your calendar and determine when you can take an entire day off this month to hold your first summit.
2. Create your playbook in Google Documents and share it with anyone that may be helping within the company.
3. Create a table of contents within the playbook that lists out the main business processes and job descriptions that make up your business.
4. Determine which business process you are going to improve, automate, and document at your first summit.
5. At the end of the first summit, schedule your second summit for the following month and never stop having them.

Always improve your business. Never get so caught up in the day-to-day that you forget to take time to make things better. After all, taking one day to fix something means that you'll never have to deal with it again, and that is a great feeling.

WORKSHOP 31: Automating Operations – Part 2

"The first rule of any technology used in a business is that automation applied to an efficient operation will magnify the efficiency. The second is that automation applied to an inefficient operation will magnify the inefficiency."

-Bill Gates

Automating your business can be a never ending process. That's because you can always find better and more efficient ways of getting from point A to point B. With advances in technology, there will always be new gizmos and gadgets that will promise to save you time and money. Those things are great, but they don't address the critical issues that most small businesses face in full.

With all of the advancements that today has to offer, why is it that we feel more and more overwhelmed? Why do we feel like we're spinning out of control at an ever increasing rate? It's because we haven't addressed the root of the problem when it comes to being swamped, and that's the issue of task management.

The breaking point

In any given business, there are a million things to do. You have customers to call, orders to place, books to keep, floors to sweep, and so forth. As your business grows, these tasks seem to grow in magnitude. It's for that reason that a lot of business owners decide to stop growing. They simply can't stand the thought of dealing with all the extra work that comes with expansion; in essence, they reach a breaking point.

There will come a point in your business career when you will get there too. Eventually you'll run out of steam. Your energy will cap out as your dream of running an empire wilts into ashes.

How do you get past your breaking point in style? You pull a Henry Ford. You know him as the father mass production and the assembly line.

Mr. Ford Henry took the amazingly complex process of building a car and broke it down into pieces; manageable chunks of work that anyone could do. What was the result? Let's just say that Mr. Ford sold a lot of vehicles. In fact, he's still selling a lot of vehicles and he died in 1947. Not bad if you ask me.

Every business is merely a system of grouped tasks. If you compare it to the cars that Mr. Ford built, you might say that businesses have a drive train, cooling system, electrical system, and so forth. What powers a car to move forward is nothing more than different systems put together in a fancy box with wheels.

What are the major systems in your business? Most likely you'll have the following as a starting point:

1. Sales
2. Delivery
3. Customer satisfaction
4. Finance
5. Operations
6. Vision mapping

There may be many more in your company depending on what it is that you do. However, most businesses will have the above systems.

Take a look at each of them for a moment. What could you do to streamline each system so that it operates at its most efficient level?

Do you know why most business owners reach their breaking point and stop growing? It's because they take on all of these systems themselves and do so manually. It's pretty normal to start out that way, but if you stay that way, you'll be digging your grave. Over time, you'll need to find a way to achieve three goals within each system.

Here's what each system in your business must achieve in order to be operating efficiently:

1. Someone or something (i.e. software) oversees the system to ensure that it's performing at its optimum levels.
2. There is an accountability system in place to ensure that those in charge are meeting expectations.
3. Each system is delivering a weekly dashboard to your front door so that you can get key information and make the proper decisions.

Don't try to automate each system from day one. Most likely, you'll attack one system at a time until you have the above three objectives met. When that happens, move on to the next system.

Take some time to determine which system is the most important to your organization and start there. I am assuming that it's going to be sales since every company needs new customers first and foremost. Whichever you pick, make sure that you'll get the biggest bang for your invested time to automate it.

Mapping Out Your Organization

You know those organization charts that show the president at the top of the company along with all of the people that work under him or her? I want you to create one of those today for your company. Map out the crucial positions in your company that will need to be filled in order for your business to be operating without you in it.

That means that you may have a sales manager, a delivery guy and so on. Don't add anyone unless the position is absolutely necessary and adds value to the overall company. This is a valuable exercise for several reasons. First of all, you'll be able to envision your company in its entirety when it's working properly. Secondly, you'll be able to create a map for who to hire and when. Since you will only have positions in your company that are absolutely necessary, you'll be able to say "no" when your buddy tries to get hired... Assuming that the position he wants isn't on the chart of course.

Once you get everyone listed out, do yourself a favor and list out their job title along with a brief job description. When you're done, you should have an organization chart of your company in its grandest fashion with job titles and descriptions.

Notice for now that you are probably filling all of these roles within the company. That's perfectly normal. Your goal as you grow though is to begin assigning these titles to other people or software systems.

Preparing for your first employee

Just because we have a job title and a brief description of what that person will be doing when they finally are hired, that doesn't mean that we will be ready to hire them when the time comes around.

In past workshops, we have talked about the importance of creating a playbook for your company. It's the "This is how we do it here" manual. If you'll remember, we talked about the need to put some job descriptions in there for future use.

In order to get ready for your first employee, you're going to need a full blown job description before they start. Please don't overlook this. Countless people are hired every day without a job description and what happens? They often sit around for months getting "trained". What really happens is that they try to figure out what it is that they're supposed to be doing. At the same time, the company is scratching its head saying, "Why did we hire this guy anyways?"

Hiring people without a job description is extremely expensive. Don't do it.

Mastering the job description

Every good job description has a few key parts to it that will make your life, and the life of your employees, much easier. When you create your job descriptions, make sure that they have the following information on them.

1. The title that the person will hold
2. A description of why the job position is absolutely necessary to the company
3. A list of the exact expectations and outcomes that must be achieved in order for the employee to keep the job
4. A clear description of how you will hold the person accountable for his or her work

When you're hiring someone, they're not doing you a favor by working for you. You're doing them a favor by providing them with employment. As such, they need to meet the expectations on the job description or else they are not right for the position.

Without a job description, who's to say if they are doing a good job or not?

Creating the rendezvous

A rendezvous is, in my mind, a preset time and place where you are going to meet with the employee to discuss performance.

You will need to decide when, where, why, and how the meeting is going be held. I favor a short weekly rendezvous with my employees, but some companies like to go for once a month or once a quarter. I have found that weekly keeps communication going and helps us to stay focused on our targets.

A rendezvous is not a chit chat session. As the business owner, you're responsible for achieving strategic objectives and not the day-to-day tasks. With that in mind, know that your employees are pretty busy since they're the ones that are answering phones and taking orders. So do yourself, and your employees, a favor by having an agenda for each rendezvous beforehand. Never design these meeting up on the fly.

Determine right now how often you will be holding your rendezvous and why. Create an outline for what you will talk about and what standards will be discussed.

What to expect during the Rendezvous

I want a report from each of my systems during the weekly rendezvous. Each person in charge of the system needs to come to me with a predefined status update to help me understand where we sit.

The reports should be minimal if possible. Don't expect each of your people to create some major report on a weekly basis. Doing so zaps their time. I have seen many system managers get so wrapped up in their weekly rendezvous reports that that is all they do. They spend the entire week collecting data, building forms, and forecasting numbers. At the end of the day, you end up employing a bunch of report makers who all need assistants to do the real work.

At one of my first jobs, the CFO of the company was so involved in building his weekly reports that he spent nearly all of his time doing it. When the weekly meeting rolled around, his reports were fascinating, but the company's finances were deteriorating. His first and foremost role as the CFO was to improve the financial position of the company, not report on it.

If I could go back, I would tell to him to throw everything away and start fresh with a one page report that took less than 10 minutes to fill out. The report should include the key financial metrics of the company so that we could see if we were improving or not.

I would then tell him to take the rest of his time and focus on increasing profits.

Using software instead of people

It is possible to avoid hiring an employee for certain systems. Instead, you may be able to utilize software to do the work for you. Another option would be to use a contractor to get the job done. Regardless of using software or an in-house employee, your responsibility should be the same – to create a clear and useful job description today.

That means defining what the software will need to do, how you will ensure that it's functioning properly, and what reports it will kick out to you on a weekly basis. If you know this before you venture into buying a software tool, you'll be able to avoid wasting money on the next big thing.

Action work: Map out your organization

I know that all of this seems like a lot of work, and in reality it is. Creating an organization chart along with all of the job descriptions that go along with each position takes time, but it's time well spent. Our goal is to ensure that you don't get stuck at your breaking point as a business owner. To do that, we need to have a clear understanding of who will help you in the future and why they're important.

So here is your homework for the day.

1. Map out your future organization. Start with you at the top of the company as the CEO and branch out to each job under you. Make sure that every job is absolutely necessary.
2. Make sure that each position on the organization chart has a title and a description.
3. Determine which system you will need to automate first within your business.
4. Create a job description for the person or software that will eventually run that system.
5. Determine how you will hold this person accountable and when.
6. Determine which report the can give you on a weekly basis that will update you with regards to their performance.

As you fill a position on your organizational chart with a living and breathing human being, or a super zippy and smart piece of software, you can then move on to the next system. As you do, you'll slowly work yourself out of the day-to-day operations so that you can focus on your core responsibilities as the business owner.

WORKSHOP 32: How to Not Lose Your Pants When Drop Shipping

"Whenever you see a successful business, someone once made a courageous decision."

- Peter F. Drucker

Business is full of buzzwords and cool new strategies. Drop shipping is one of those fancy ideas that seem to only be for the "in crowd". It's one of those things that you hear about in testimonials more than anything. I have run into countless testimonies online of people saying that they've made their millions by starting a drop shipping business. That may be true, but drop shipping is one of those dirty little areas of business that is fraught with disaster if you don't keep your wits about you.

Is drop shipping a viable way to make money? Absolutely. It can be a really great idea as long as you don't fall for a lot of the false promises it's rigged with.

What is drop shipping?

In past workshops, we talked about selling a product or a service. If you're selling a product, you have a major hurdle to overcome, and that's getting product to sell. How are you going to get the product? You could design your own product, get it prototyped and eventually manufactured. Doing so is a long process and will most likely cost a lot of money. That's why most businesses that follow that route usually need a substantial injection of cash up front. That means investors, loans, and writing out IOUs to your mom. It's not the ideal situation for your first business because of the large amount of risk involved.

That's where drop shipping comes into play. Let's assume that you want to sell headphones online. Knowing that you don't have the cash to design your own and go through the manufacturing and inventory process, you find a few companies that manufacture headphones that you like. When you contact them, you ask if you can sell their product and if they will drop ship it for you. This means that every time you make a sale, they pull the product off of their shelf, package it, and mail it to your customer.

This is huge for you because it means that you can ship individual orders. You don't have to invest in thousands of units. You'll never need to carry inventory, and you'll never have to make an actual purchase order to your suppliers until you've already been paid by your customers!

As good as this all sounds, you need to be aware of the inherent issues. Let's crack this bad boy open and see what's inside.

Drop shipping is a breeding ground for scammers

People start businesses every day. Given that drop shipping is so attractive, a lot of people get interested in it as a way of getting started. This means that there are plenty of people out there that are, for lack of a better word, gullible.

Scammers have found a way to cheat the honest at heart, and here is how they do it. First, understand that finding a drop shipper for your product can be difficult. Once you do find one, you then need to approach the company and qualify to be a reseller and join their drop shipping program.

Since most people don't want to go through all of that, they look for the easiest way to connect with a drop shipper. Scammers have built businesses online that promise to sell you a list of guaranteed, mind-blowing and forthcoming businesses that offer drop shipping for a nominal one-time fee. Don't trust most of them. There are hundreds if not thousands of these guys out there stealing people's money every day. Sure, many of them will deliver a list but it's garbage.

Are there companies out there that sell good lists of drop shippers? Yes. One of the better ones is at worldwidebrands.com which makes the life of a drop shipper much easier. They do a good job of linking up entrepreneurs with legitimate drop shippers. As of this writing, you pay a one-time fee of $299 and then you have life time access to their directory along with some powerful tools to evaluate drop shipping companies, the availability of products, and also the interest in products as they are selling online. Their tools are really strong and easy to understand.

The art of finding a good drop shipping relationship is in the details. You really are building a relationship with a company and you need to take your time to do it right.

A few other down sides to drop shipping

Have no fear… I'll get into the benefits in just a moment. When you do find a drop shipper to sell product through, you need to remember the following things:

- Every drop shipper charges a fee, and they all have different rates. Make sure to find a drop shipper that isn't robbing you blind with hidden or excessive fees. Know that all of them will charge you a drop ship fee to cover their time to package and sell a single unit on your behalf.

- The profits aren't huge. Since you're mainly selling one unit at a time, you don't get much of a break on pricing.

- In most instances, you can't control the packaging, since you don't control the inventory. That means that the shipping box is usually void of your brand, and you can't stick offers or coupons inside. This isn't true with all drop shippers, but many of them won't take the time to do this for you.

- Everyone is doing it. The fact that so many people are trying to start drop shipping businesses, dilutes the competitive advantage. In other words, there may be thousands of people working out of their homes drop shipping headphones. If you designed your own and manufactured them, you would be the only person with that product.

- Dealing with returns can be a little tricky. Make sure to speak with your drop shipper to understand how they deal with returns if the product is broken or doesn't meet the needs of the customer.

- Your drop shipper may run out of product. When that happens, you may have customers continuing to buy on your website and you can't fulfill their orders in time. To address the issue, you'll want to have more than one drop shipper in your back pocket.

With all of the negative things we have discussed so far, are you dissuaded from using drop shipping? You shouldn't be, if you are going into product sales. It's not the ideal solution for every startup business, but it's a great way to get started for many when there isn't a lot of cash to invest up front. With that in mind, let's look at the upside.

Drop shipping as a stepping stone to bigger things

Since we want to eliminate as much risk as possible from starting your new company, drop shipping may make a lot of sense — at least in the beginning. The goal within your business should be to control your risk and limit it as much as possible. That means that you need to avoid anything that requires a lot of cash and commitment up front.

If you are starting an online product-based company, I would suggest looking to other companies that have succeeded. Zappos is one of those companies. If you have never heard of them, just know that they sell shoes, among other things.

Zappos.com started off drop shipping shoes as a way to make money. It wasn't the only way that they generated sales, but at one point, they were doing 25% of their revenues this way.

The online shoe retailer has since grown into a giant of a company and is often used as an example in business case studies. Over time, they moved away from drop shipping so that they could control the entire buying experience of their customers. In the beginning though, drop shipping helped them to grease the wheels and make some cash.

In my mind, drop shipping is a great first stepping stone for new businesses. Think about it for a minute. You don't have to control inventory which means that you don't need a warehouse. Essentially, you could start selling almost immediately once you get a drop shipper in place. That's why drop shipping is so popular with online stores. Once the website is built and you have a shopping cart installed on the site, you could add your drop shipper's products and start selling.

As the orders come in, you don't have to deal with shipping, packaging, staff, overhead, logistics, and all of the other costs that come with carrying the product yourself.

As you get bigger, you can even make a nice transition into more profits. That's because a lot of drop shippers will offer you better deals with something called "light bulk". As your cash balances build up and you find out which products are really selling well on your website, you can purchase those products in light bulk which usually consists of orders at 500 units or less. You can start to get great discounts without having to buy 10,000 units like the big boys do.

When you move into the "light bulk" phase, you will start storing inventory, but since the quantities are small, you can usually manage it in your basement.

As you can see, drop shipping is a great way to test a product without spending thousands of dollars.

What happens when you get set up with a drop shipper?

First and foremost, you need to set up an account with a drop shipper. You can do this by contacting the drop shipper directly or by using a system like worldwidebrands.com which helps to connect you.

Once the account is set up, the drop shipper will usually send you an email with pictures of all the products along with the product description. You'll need to take that information and upload it into your online store.

Your job is to then drive people to your website and generate sales which we will talk about in the next workshop. Once the customer places an order on your site, you'll get paid immediately. At that point, you'll turn around and send an email to your drop shipper who will then package and send the item to your customer as you pay the drop shipper. In the end, you have some profit in your bank account and your customer will get his or her product.

At the end of the day, you can get your business started quickly and efficiently. Just remember to watch out for the scammers. Do your research if you're going to drop ship products, and make sure that you ask a lot of questions.

Action work: Contact your drop shippers

If you are not going to be drop shipping products, you can celebrate today because there's no homework for you! Take the day off and go sit by the pool. If you are going to be drop shipping, roll up your sleeves and let's get to work.

1. Find out which company or companies manufacture the products that you want to sell.
2. Contact the manufacturer and ask to speak with someone in the sales department.
3. Tell the sales agent that you are a retailer and that you would like to sell their product. Then ask them for a list of wholesalers in your area or region. Since you are getting the list of approved wholesalers from the manufacturer, you should be able to avoid scammers posing as wholesalers and actually work with legitimate companies.
4. Don't forget to ask if the manufacturer will drop ship directly from the factory thereby allowing you to completely skip the wholesaler. You never know!
5. Call each of the wholesalers that you got from the manufacturer. Tell them that you are a retailer and would like to begin selling the product. Then ask them if they have a drop shipping program and how you can get started.
6. Make sure that you completely understand their fee structure before you finalize the relationship.
7. If you are struggling to find wholesalers for the type of products you want to sell, consider working with a company like worldwidebrands.com to get things rolling.

This isn't as hard as it sounds, to be honest. The most important thing to remember when you are speaking with a potential drop shipper is to be completely honest. Don't fabricate your business or tell them a bunch of unnecessary information about you and your plans to take over the world. Simply tell them that you are a retailer interested in selling their products. When they ask questions, tell the truth. After all, you may end up building a business relationship with these people and the last thing you want is to start that relationship on shaky ground.

WORKSHOP 33: The Secret Sauce of Website Traffic

"Instead of one-way interruption, web marketing is about delivering USEFUL CONTENT at just the precise moment that a buyer needs it."

- David Meerman Scott

You know those famous words in business that say, "Location, location, location"? That's great advice for businesses that are going to have walk-in stores where customers have to be present in order to buy. It generally applies to retail stores and the like. The right location will mean a lot of foot traffic for the lucky entrepreneur. The wrong location spells disaster.

In the wonderful world of websites, you're going to need a lot of traffic if you're going to get sales. Traffic is a basic marketing term which refers to the number of people that are looking at your website. I want you to think for just a moment about how many websites you visit in a given day. Tons, right? How many of those websites make money off of you every day? I would venture to guess that the number is probably pretty low.

Does this mean that websites are a waste of time? Nope! You can and will make a lot of money from your website, if you understand a few things.

Here's what you need to know:

1. Not all traffic is good traffic. Most people are just browsing, which means that you need to put your website in front of a lot of people to start generating sales.
2. You need to find ways to improve the quality of your traffic over time so that your site is getting in front of people with open wallets.
3. You need to give people a reason to visit your site and an even stronger reason to come back, since most people don't buy the first time around.

Website marketing really isn't that hard. It can be a money pit, though, so don't say that I didn't warn you. I have worked with some of the best website marketers in the industry and they all approach building quality traffic the same way – they take their time, increase marketing spend over time, and test a lot.

Most people who are new to website marketing fall into the same trap, which is to throw a lot of money at it and hope that something sticks. They will throw tens of thousands of dollars towards internet marketing consultants, ads, and anything else that promises huge traffic. Those kinds of plots actually do get you a lot of traffic, but you run the risk of getting poor quality traffic.

Building the asset

Don't go into website marketing thinking that you'll be able to spend a few thousand dollars and start getting impressive sales. Instead, I want you to realize that your website is an asset that needs to be improved constantly. Over time, the site will look better, host more interesting content, and become a place where people will actually want to hear what it is that you have to say.

As you begin investing in your marketing campaign, start small and increase the budget over time as you learn what works. There is no magic pill for what we are about to talk about.

Patience really is a virtue when it comes to this stuff. With that being said, there are a few things we can do today to actually start getting traffic. It could take months or years before you start getting thousands of people to your site monthly. A lot of that has to do with what you are selling. For example, if you are an engineering firm, your traffic is going to be lower by nature that a site that sells the new trend for teenagers.

Opening the doors means squat

Know this now: When your website does go live on the internet, nobody will show up. It doesn't matter how pretty it is, it's going to be a ghost town. First of all, nobody knows it exists. Second of all, once people do know that it exists, they'll forget about it because of how busy life gets.

That's all right. Every great website starts at ground zero and earns its right to become a money maker.

Before we get started, you're going to need to set up Google Analytics, which is a free service. The idea here is that you install a piece of code within your website and then you can login to your Analytics account to see your traffic statistics. It's a powerful tool that gives every website owner a powerful look into where traffic is coming from and how to get more of it.

Since you set up your Google Apps for Business in a prior workshop, you'll be able to use your same email and password to create your Analytics account. To get this set up correctly, simply follow the video that I have posted in your downloads folder.

Finding the right keywords

If location is so important for physical retail stores, it must be a decent mantra for other types of business as well, right? Location is actually the secret sauce behind getting great website traffic. In essence, we need to put your website in different locations on the web in such a way that interested people will click on it and start buying.

There are a lot of ways to do this, and I am going to cover the big ones here today which include:

1. Writing blogs and other forms of content
2. Social media
3. Pay-per-click advertising
4. Search engine optimization

I know that there are a lot of other ways to get people to your site, but these are the most important. Before you do any of that, you need to have a list of five keywords.

Do you remember from Workshop 3 how we tested the business idea for stupidity by using the Google Keyword Tool? You'll want to head back there while we run through this workshop today. What we need to do is find five terms that we are going to use in our online marketing. You can add more later, but start with five.

Again, a keyword is a phrase that someone would type into a search engine when they're looking for more information. We need to hone in on five keywords that will drive good quality traffic to your site.

As you look for keywords, here are some guidelines:

1. Your keyword should be a phrase with no less than three words in it. Otherwise the keyword will be too broad and will drive poor traffic to your site. For example, if we were marketing a website for attorneys that specialized in divorces,

we wouldn't want "find attorney" as a keyword. If we did, we might get people landing on our site that are looking for business attorneys, estate attorneys, or even bankruptcy attorneys. Having a keyword like "Find a divorce attorney in Boston MA" would be much better.

2. Try to make the five keywords distinct from each other.

3. If you have more than one type of service, you can choose a keyword for each service, or you can choose to market one service heavily in the beginning. I would suggest the latter so that you don't spread yourself too thin.

4. Ensure that the Google Keyword Tool shows that the competition level for the keyword is no higher than medium.

5. Try to find keywords with at least 500 visitors a month. As we covered in Workshop 3, the Google Keyword Tool will tell you how many searches a particular keyword gets monthly.

6. Make sure that the keyword is a buying phrase. Think like your customer. What would they type in if they were looking to purchase your product or service?

Now that you have your five keywords, they are going to be the basis for our marketing efforts moving forward.

A final word here would be to say that each keyword should be associated with a specific page on your website. That means that I want your home page content to reference a specific keyword. Your service page or products page may focus on another keyword and so forth.

For now, it's a decent start to make sure that the keyword shows up in the content on that particular page.

If we go back to our attorney example, our keyword "Find a divorce attorney in Boston MA" may be a good keyword for the contact page which has the company's address. That way, when people type in the keyword, they will land on the contact page and see that the office is in Boston.

To set that up, you could make the header on the page say "Trying to find a divorce attorney in Boston MA?" Then you could add the keyword a few more times in the body of the content on the page.

This tells Google that that particular page has something to do with divorce attorneys in Boston.

Blogging

Don't roll your eyes. I know – most people hate having to keep up a blog. Here's the kicker, though: A good blog is actually one of the best things you can do for your website, assuming that you are writing about things that are interesting and relevant.

That's because search engines like new and fresh content. Websites that pump out such amazingness are rewarded with better search rankings.

It does take time though. Blogging is a long-term blessing that will pay off in spades.

In order to take the world by blogging storm, you'll need a strategy, and here it is:

Step #1 - Set your schedule: I would suggest writing two blog posts a week. Make each post 300 to 500 words so that it's short enough to read and remain interesting. Going shorter than 300 words is not a good idea because the search engines want a decent amount of content if they are going to share it with the world.

Step #2 - Focus on your five keywords: Each time you write a blog post, you need to pick one keyword out of your list of five as a focal point. To do that, try to get the keyword into the title of the blog post as well as into the body of the post three to four times.

Make sure that the keyword sounds natural in the writing and doesn't stick out like a sore thumb.

Step #3 - Create some hyperlinks: Highlight a keyword in the blog post and create a hyperlink. The keyword should be linked to the specific page on your website with which it correlates. On the attorney site, if we were blogging and chose to focus on the keyword, "Find a divorce attorney in Boston MA", I would highlight one of the keywords and hyperlink it to the contact page on my site.

Step #4 - Spread the word: Every time you write a blog post, tell the world about it. I like to use a service called onlywire.com which will post a link to my blog on all of my social networks with the click of a button. However you do it, make sure to get it on Facebook, LinkedIn, and any other social platform where you have connections.

Pay-Per-Click or PPC

PPC can be an instant traffic generator. It can also be expensive and time consuming without a little guidance.

When you search for something on Google, half of the websites that you see are actually ads! All of the sites on the right side of the screen as well as the first few at the top are all ads. Each of those websites are paying Google every time someone clicks on them. It's nice because you only incur marketing expenses when people actually visit your site, and yes, you can set budget limits with Google.

The PPC system is really just a big auction for marketers. The bid for your position, combined with how relevant your site is to the search, determines how close you are to the top of page one. That means that you can choose what you want to pay per click. You could bid ten cents or one hundred dollars. It's up to you. From my experience, most people are paying between $2 and $8 a click to be positioned on the first page. I have seen some businesses paying $20 a click and higher though due to competition. That's why we had you pick five keywords with lower competition.

I would recommend getting a book on PPC in order to do this right. I really like *Ultimate Guide to Google AdWords: How to Access 100 Million People in 10 Minutes* by Perry Marshall. It's easy to follow and will walk you through everything you need to know to get started with PPC.

Being successful with PPC is really based on a few basic principles:

1. Focus on specific keywords
2. Build an organized Google AdWords campaign
3. Set aside time to manage the campaign and improve it
4. Learn how to set conversion goals and improve them
5. Start with a small budget and increase it as you learn what is driving good traffic

Again, you'll get a strong grasp of those five requirements along with a lot of other good stuff in the book I mentioned.

Search Engine Marketing or SEO

You may be asking yourself how the other half of the websites show up in a Google search if they aren't ads. Google loves information. It prides itself in delivering websites that match the keyword you searched.

The websites on page one have done a good job of being relevant to the keyword so Google shows them to the world... free of charge! That's right, all of those other websites are getting free traffic while everyone else in the PPC section is paying.

Here's the catch though... Being relevant isn't easy. That's because there are going to be a lot of other websites in your industry that have been around a lot longer than you and have spent years creating content that's relevant.

That's why SEO companies popped up. An SEO company does your search engine optimization which means that they work hard to make your site more relevant to a keyword than the competing websites. Unfortunately these kinds of services usually cost an arm and a leg. As you get bigger, I would suggest hiring a company, but until then, you are going to need to make inroads yourself. Don't despair, though. There are a lot of things you can do to get this going. Due to the cost and complexity, SEO is often a long-term solution to driving traffic. So, I would suggest getting the basics of SEO going so that it pays off down the road while you do PPC today. As your SEO gets better and better through your own efforts, and eventually that of an SEO company, you can begin to peel back on the PPC if you want.

Is anyone else getting acronym sick?

Since you are tackling the basics of SEO on your own for now, here are a few pointers:

1. The blog is your best SEO weapon. Following the steps I outlined above will boost SEO ranking for your five keywords.

2. As you create great content on your blog and share it with people, you'll find that people will begin linking to your site. In the world of SEO, having other websites link to your website is vital. Those links tell Google that your content is so good that other people are willing to link to it. Google then thinks, "Hey people like this stuff. I'm going to show it more!"

3. Get a good book on how to do SEO. In all honesty, I have to defer to the *for Dummies* books on this one. You know those yellow and black books that are for Dummies? They actually came out with a pretty good SEO book that simplifies a lot of this stuff.

4. Don't lose sleep over SEO. Since it's a long-term thing, don't rack your brains over it. Just make sure that you are scheduling time to do your SEO by blogging and following the advice in your Dummies book.

Action work: Start driving traffic

In order to get started, lets walk through the homework and do things in the right order. Try not to skip ahead until you have completed the prior steps. Why? Because I don't want you spending money on marketing until you know what you're doing. Otherwise you might as well flush your cash down the toilet.

1. Since you have a live website now, go and write your first blog post following the steps I outlined earlier on in the workshop.
2. Tell your network about your blog post. If you use a lot of social networks, use onlywire.com to get the word out. I actually created an account for every social network that onlywire.com can post to which isn't a bad idea. That means that you can see my blog posts on Facebook, Digg, Bibsonomy, Google Plus, AOL Lifestream, and a host of others.
3. Set up a blogging schedule to write at least two posts a week. Don't do them on the same day either. Spread things out a bit.
4. Go out and get the book *Ultimate Guide to Google AdWords: How to Access 100 Million People in 10 Minutes* by Perry Marshall.
5. Set up your AdWords campaign and begin with a small budget.

May these tips and tricks bless you with visitors galore as your site gets bigger and bigger. Remember that building a great website takes time, but boy, is it worth it!

WORKSHOP 34: Setting Up Your Scoreboard

"I skate to where the puck is going to be, not to where it has been."

- Wayne Gretzky

Why sports are so successful

Most people like sports, and I would argue the few couldn't enjoy themselves at a live sports event. Shoot, many of you reading this may be sports addicts. The famous comedic author Erma Bombeck once said that if a man watches three football games in a row, he can be declared legally dead.

Why is it that we love sports so much? Is it because we like to see athletes perform at the top of their game? Do we like to feel like we are a part of the team? There are a lot of reasons why sports are a part of so many of our lives, but I believe the main reason we watch is because of the scoreboard. Human beings love competition. We love hanging in suspense to see if our team is going to pull through or get squashed again.

In fact, we have always loved watching competition. That same spirit is what gave way to the Roman Coliseum. It also gave birth to much of our fine arts, advances in technology, and the improvement of pretty much every aspect of our lives.

We even teach our kids to love competition from the time they are old enough to play organized games. Competition is in our blood. I'm a very competitive person. Some of you probably are as well. In business, you can focus that energy toward building a better company.

Competition is measured by the score. If you stop caring about the score, you're never going to win a game. The score is what ties everyone into the same objective. The players, fans, and coaches are all focused on the scoreboard the entire game.

Can you image what sports would be like if nobody kept score? How many people would come to the games? Not very many, that's for sure.

Business as a sport

Running a business is no different. Some companies keep score, and others don't. For the businesses that don't keep score, they tend to lose interest and vision over time and eventually putter out. The owner, employees, and customers all lose focus on the overall objective, and the business simply goes kaput.

If you run your business just like a coach would run a world class sports team, you'll have a much better result, but that means keeping score at all times.

As your company grows, you are going to need a way to know if you are winning or losing. You are going to need data to point you in the right direction.

There are different types of data that you're going to need which will include financial metrics, customer satisfaction scores, and performance indicators. Before we get into which ones are best for you, let's set up some ground rules.

I have found over the years that businesses have a hard time tracking more than five data points at a time. That's because once you track them, you need to meet with your team to improve them. If you are doing that with more than five indicators, you spread yourself too thin and never make any significant improvements.

Having less than three indicators to track is also not a good idea. It's true that things improve when they are tracked. Only tracking one or two indicators means that you're not getting enough data to make great decisions and get better daily.

Have you ever worked for a company that doesn't keep score? I sure have. It's horrible. Everyone just saunters into work on a daily basis ready to deal with whatever hits their e-mail accounts. There's no motivation to improve anything and it's about as much fun as weeding your yard in the middle of August. When a business doesn't keep score, it doesn't have soul.

On the flip side, have you ever worked in a company that does keep score? Did you notice a difference? If the score is communicated properly, a skill we'll talk about in a moment, then everyone is on the same page and working towards the same desired goal.

Your role on the team

Beyond the need to keep score, businesses are also a lot like sports in that there's a coach and a team. If you can't tell by now, you're going to be the coach on the team, and your employees will be the teammates.

A coach is vital to the success of the group. If you think about it, a coach is responsible for:

- Knowing what moves to make to improve the score
- Knowing how to utilize the team
- Communicating vision and motivation, especially when the team is losing

- Keeping the team from getting lazy when they are winning

That can actually be a lot of pressure if you think about it. That's why a lot of coaches on television look like they're about to have a heart attack. May this never happen to you.

As the coach, you need a way to keep score, inform your team of what's going on, and actually win the game.

I have walked into countless consulting meetings with businesses that aren't keeping score. As such, they don't know if they're winning or losing. My first order of business is to always set up a scoreboard and start tracking three to five key metrics or indicators.

Here's how I do it.

How to score

Before you start scoring your business, you need to know what to score. There are a lot of numbers out there that you could track, but not all of them are going to be right for your business. For example, there's no point in tracking inventory turnover if you're company doesn't hold inventory.

That's an important point to consider actually. As the coach, it's going to be up to you with regards to what metrics will be tracked. It's not good enough to simply pick three to five metrics. You need to pick metrics that are vital to your company. As you consider a metric for your scoreboard, ask yourself if the metric is a key driver in your company's success.

Let's look at an example. Pretend that you are starting a business that provides auto detailing services in your area. What kind of information would you say would be important to a business like that? The following ideas describe what the company would need in order to grow and make money:

1. Number of cars serviced each month
2. Average time to detail a car
3. Gross margin since you have to pay for labor and materials each time a car is detailed
4. Customer satisfaction rating
5. Cash on hand balance

Again, there are a lot of things we could think about when it comes to a business like this, but the five metrics I listed above are vital to the company's success.

If the company doesn't service a set number of cars monthly, they'll go out of business. It would be important to track the average time it takes to detail a car, because the longer it takes, the more it costs you. As we learned in prior workshops, gross margin tells you how profitable your company is and your job is to get that percentage as high as possible. The customer satisfaction rating would be important since your business spends so much time with the customer and their overall level of happiness will determine if they use you again. Finally, a company like this isn't likely to be sitting on mountains of cash so tracking the proper cash balances is vital.

Take some time right now to think about the three to five metrics that are the heartbeat of your company. Make sure that tracking each of your metrics will in fact help you to make more money and improve your overall operations.

Building the scoreboard

You need a place to post your scores. A scoreboard can mean a lot of different things for many businesses. In this instance, we need a place where you can post your metrics for the team to see. That's right. I personally believe that your company is going to get better when your employees know the score.

A lot of business owners are afraid to post their scores because they feel the information is sensitive. I wouldn't suggest posting people's salaries by any means, but in my opinion, most other data really is fine to share with them. Doing so will get them vested in the game.

Going back to our sporting analogy, can you imagine if only the coaches knew the scores and the players just had to play along and do their best? In the world of business, this is called closed book management. A lot of businesses practice this way. Only the top guys know what's going on and everyone else in the organization is left to wander around in the dark. Is it any wonder that there is always an expectations gap between management and employees?

The opposite of closed book management is open book management. This is where management lifts up its skirt and says, "Hey, here's how we're doing, team. Let's pull it together." I am a huge fan of open book management. When employees know the score, they can come up with ideas for improving things.

As the coach, it's your job to create a scoreboard that reflects the three to five metrics. Put that scoreboard somewhere in the office so that employees always know the score. You can have a whiteboard posting the numbers, or you can simply send out a weekly email with the new score. Either way, keep them informed of where the company is and where it needs to go.

Since you're in the startup phase right now and don't have any employees, get in the habit of creating your scoreboard, even if it's just for yourself. Doing so will keep you apprised of the score so that you can grow faster and more responsibly.

Automating the scoreboard

Most entrepreneurs love the idea of keeping a scoreboard, but few rarely do it. Do you know why? It's because keeping a scoreboard is another thing on the list of to-dos that has to get done. It takes time to dig into the data and determine the week's numbers.

If you can find a way to automate some of this work, then your scoreboards will not only be more reliable, but they'll also be in existence.

If we move along with our example above, the car detailing company could do a few different things to speed up the collection of their data. Let's take a look.

Number of cars serviced each month and the average amount of time spent detailing: Every time the company sends out an employee to detail a car, the employee could use a smart phone application to track his time. This makes it possible to not only pay him for the work that he does, but it also captures the number of cars worked on and the average amount of time spent one each car. You could then log into the app at the end of the month, and with the push of a single button have everything at your fingertips. It amazes me that a lot of companies still use paper to track this kind of stuff. Don't send your employee out into the field with a carbon copy receipt book to fill out every time he works with a customer. If you do, you'll end up with stacks of paper at the end of the month that you have to organize and manage.

Gross margin and cash on hand: These figures are going to come directly out of the company's financial statements. As the company gets bigger, it could outsource its accounting needs and have the accountant report on them weekly.

Customer Satisfaction Rating: When the employee in the field enters his time, he could also use a similar app to get the customers feedback. While he is finishing up, he could give the customer his phone and have him fill out a short survey, which is then aggregated with all the other customer's feedback.

The overall goal is that you're not bogged down with having to aggregate data and create your scoreboard each week. It may take some time to get things automated, but work toward that end, so that you can get a weekly update and lead your team.

Action work: Build your scoreboard and turn it on

After today's homework, I want you to be able to identify the three to five metrics that drive your company, have a system in place to report on them weekly, and get in the habit of focusing on those metrics to try to improve them.

Let's make it happen.

1. Define three to five key metrics that will drive your company's success.
2. Ask yourself if each one of the metrics is vital to improving how much money you make and how satisfied your customers are.
3. Create a scoreboard in your office or digitally.
4. Determine how you are going to get the data for each of the metrics. If you can automate the process with a simple tool like a smart phone app, do it.
5. Set up a weekly meeting, even if it's just with yourself right now, to review your metrics and find ways to improve them.

Remember, things bet better when they are measured. If you take the time to measure the vital statistics of your company, you're bound to get stronger as a business. Find joy in tracking performance and sharing the score. It's this one skill that will create powerful levels of motivation for yourself and your employees down the road.

WORKSHOP 35: Building a Business with a Sharp Axe

"Almost all quality improvement comes via simplification of design, manufacturing...layout, processes, and procedures."

- Tom Peters

The metaphor of the sharp axe

I want you to think of the big, burly lumberjack for a moment. He's up in the forest with his trusty axe, doing everything he can to earn a living. With every swing, he essentially earns money. He is paid to cut. Here's the problem, though: Every swing of the axe also dulls the blade a bit. It's not enough to notice from swing to swing, but over time, the lumberjack has to expend more energy and time in cutting down a single tree.

If he never stops to fix or upgrade the axe, he will eventually break the miserable thing.

A good lumberjack not only can tell when the axe is getting dull, but he has scheduled time on a periodic basis to sharpen it. He does this because he knows that taking the time to sit down, break out the sharpening stone, and grind away for a while is worth it in the end, even though he isn't making a cent when he does it.

A lot of people see this as down time. Most businesses don't sharpen their axes because doing so means that revenue isn't coming in the door. How much bigger would their operations be if they did take the time to get out their grinding stones?

Hmm… I don't know about you, but I've shopped at businesses who don't take the time to sharpen their axes and it's a painful experience. People don't know what's going on. Machines run slow. Everything is outdated and dusty. The exterior of the building is falling apart. The worst of it all is that the employees absolutely hate working there.

Here's a thought: When an entrepreneur takes the time out of his or her schedule to improve the business, what kind of message does that send to the customers and the employees who get to serve them?

It says that the business owner cares about the business. It sends the message that what we're doing here is important enough to invest in.

The improvement mindset

I'll be honest at the outset here so that no one calls me out. I'm not the best maintenance guy around. For me, if it's broken, buy a new one. On the other hand, my father-in-law knows how to fix pretty much anything.

During family parties at my house, he'll often walk around and just start fixing stuff. I'd be lying if I said I didn't love it, because I do.

My father-in-law has an improvement mindset when it comes to home maintenance. For him, when something is broken, you fix it — now. There eventually comes a point where he will opt out of maintenance mode and upgrade something. Like many people my father's age, his house doesn't look like it was from the '70s and '80s. Everything inside it is current and looks great.

Avoid over sharpening the axe and just get a new and better one

If the lumberjack kept sharpening his axe every time it got dull, he would eventually run out of metal to sharpen. There's a certain point in the life of the axe when it has lost its potential to really do a great job. It's at that point, that the lumberjack needs to invest in a new, and if possible, better axe.

In your company, you can manage things one of two ways. You can either be the business owner who buys the company assets once and then burns them into the ground, or you can be the entrepreneur who is building a machine. If you want your business to operate at optimum and be able to continually provide income to you and your family, you're going to need to be the latter.

In this workshop, we're going to talk about how to build a business that continually sharpens the axe and plans for upgrading when the time comes.

Areas of improvement

Take a moment to think about what your business is going to be doing. It's likely that you're going to start out with minimal equipment, given that we are trying to keep your startup costs low. As the company grows, you're going to need bigger and better pieces of equipment to support the additional orders, customers, and strain that your business will face.

You've heard of business owners saying, "We just tried to grow too fast" when they speak of their company's demise. It's a very real problem. Entrepreneurs often try to grow far beyond the capabilities of their companies. The end result is that customers get angry and revenues dry up.

Almost every business has a gateway to production. What I mean by that is that in order for you to produce your product or service, you usually need some machine, tool, personnel, or idea.

When you start out, you'll usually have a pretty small gateway. As you grow, your job is to be able to foresee the strain on that gateway and either repair it or make it bigger with an upgrade.

So what is the gateway of production for your company? What one area of improvement will drive the acceptable and responsible growth of your company?

Let's assume that you are manufacturing a bottled drink. As the owner of the company, you would recognize that your gateway to production is literally the machine and assembly line system that bottles and packages the drink.

Your job is to understand at what point the whole thing is going to start breaking down. Every gateway has a capacity. Your machine and assembly line in the beginning may literally be your family members in your basement filling up bottles, sticking on labels crookedly, and boxing everything up. That kind of system can't handle a thousand units an hour.

At which point does your wife threaten to leave you if you don't invest in a bottling machine?

All of this is common sense to most entrepreneurs. The problem is that many entrepreneurs don't upgrade. They stress out the current system because it saves on cash in the short term and they don't have to go through the pain of learning something new. They know how the old system works. In fact, the old system has worked will up to this point, so why shouldn't it work in the future, right? Wrong.

You need to have a plan for upgrading now before you get settled into your ways. If you and you wife both know that you'll be investing in a bottling machine as soon as you hit one hundred orders a day, she'll play along and your current system will never blow up in your face.

The 12-month plan

In business, it's hard to see past the next 30 days at times. However, I would like you to take today to single out your main production gateway and figure out how you will improve it over the next 12 months. Chances are, you may not be upgrading the entire system within this time frame. Startup businesses need to run lean, especially for the first few years so investing tons of cash into the next step may not be possible. What is possible is knowing how you will get there and planning for it.

I know there are a lot of you out there saying, "I'm starting a service-based business so I don't have a machine to upgrade." You may not have a machine to upgrade, but you still have a production gateway.

Here's a few more examples of production gateways for different types of businesses:

- A lawn mowing company has lawn mowers as well as the guys pushing them around
- A restaurant has kitchen equipment that can only produce so much food at a time
- A retail store has a purchasing agent to buy more inventory based off of what's selling
- An online store has servers, which affect the website's ability to process orders and handle large amounts of traffic
- An accounting firm has trained accountants

Once you have your production gateway figured out, take some time to determine how you will keep it oiled and maintained. You may have noticed in our little lumberjack analogy that a good lumberjack actually schedules periodic times to sit down and sharpen the axe. This is what I want you to do. Over the next 12 months, when are you going to take time to do some maintenance?

Sit down at your calendar and determine when you're going to need to take some time to keep the gateway operating smoothly. If your production gateway is a machine, schedule time to shut it down, clean it, and get it back to brand new condition.

If your production gateway is a person or group of people, schedule time to be with them, reward them, and most importantly to train them.

The five-year plan

After you've been in business for the first year, you'll probably start thinking about expansion past the capabilities of your gateway. In other words, it's time to upgrade.

I want you to have a clear picture in your head of what that means. When you upgrade, a lot of things will change including:

- How much you can output
- Your bank balance, since you have to invest money upfront to make the upgrade
- The learning curve that comes with a new piece of machinery or system
- The effect that it will have on your customers and future growth

First and foremost, if the upgrade doesn't increase your output, it's not worth it. Never upgrade something if you can't generate more money from the investment.

Again, because it will be an investment, you'll most likely have to shell out a bunch of cash to make the upgrade, which means that you need to plan for it now.

I mentioned in a previous workshop that we built our own software at Ignite Spot to help with managing our accounting system. That upgrade today has cost us approximately $15,000, which we paid in increments of $1,000 a month. Because we planned for the upgrade, we were able to build our own software, and now we have a strategic advantage over other accounting firms.

At the time, I wouldn't have been able to simply write out a $15,000 check and make everything else in the company work.

Of the items listed above, dealing with the learning curve and the effect that the upgrade will have on your customers is vital.

Learning curves can be a slow death if you don't plan for them. A lot of people make an upgrade and then expect the company and its employees to fully integrate with the upgrade immediately. The truth of the matter is that most upgrades actually slow down your company for a moment. It takes people time to get accustomed to new software, machines, staff, or any other change for the matter.

There is a lesson to be learned there. The time to upgrade isn't when your company's production level is bursting at the belt. You need to do it when your company is at 80% of its capacity. That way, you'll have some resources left to integrate the new system and learn it before any explosions occur.

Customers are the ones that ultimately feel the final product of your upgrade. How will this upgrade change their experience with you? Will it decease wait time, improve quality, or even make them feel more valued? If your upgrade doesn't improve the customer experience, it may not be a wise investment of your time and money.

Let's get back to the five-year plan. Take some time to consider your production gateway and how it's going to need to change over the next five years in order to keep up with your growth aspirations. At what point will you need to make your first upgrade and what will it look like?

What is it going to cost? How long will it take to learn? Make sure you know the answer to these questions now so that you can prepare for it when the time comes.

Action work: Map your your 1- month and 5-year plans

Make the mental switch today to be the kind of lumberjack that sharpens the axe consistently. Look at your business and do the following homework:

1. Identify your main production gateway. What is the key factor in your company that determines how much you can produce?

    _____

    _____

    _____

    _____

    _____

    _____

    _____

2. What can you do over the first 12 months of business to maintain your production gateway and keep it operating at its maximum efficiency?

    _____

    _____

    _____

    _____

    _____

    _____

    _____

3. At what point within the first five years of business will you need to upgrade your gateway and why? In other words, at which point will you be at 80% of your production and ready to start training for bigger and better?

_____
_____
_____
_____
_____
_____
_____
_____

4. What will this upgrade cost?

_____
_____
_____
_____
_____
_____
_____

5. What does the learning curve for this upgrade look like?

_____
_____
_____
_____
_____
_____
_____

6. How does this upgrade make your more money?

_____

_____

_____

_____

_____

_____

_____

7. How will this upgrade effect your customers experience with your company?

_____

_____

_____

_____

_____

_____

_____

I can distinctly remember walking into a local printing shop a few months back. The equipment was yellowed with age, the office was a disaster, and the computers were those black screens with the green type font on them. I turned around and walked out. The entire shop smelled like your grandpa's sock drawer.

Don't let this happen to you lumberjack. Get out there and start sharpening.

WORKSHOP 36: Setting Up Safety Nets

"In skating over thin ice our safety is in our speed."

- Ralph Waldo Emerson

When I was I little boy, I actually lived through one of those horrific scenes that you only see in the movies. It was potent enough to scar my memory and forever teach me a lesson that I'll never forget.

I was about nine years old at the time. My family and I decided to go on an ice fishing trip. If you've never been, the idea is to walk out on to a frozen lake, drill a hole through the ice, and do some fishing. I have never understood why someone would want to do this. You literally sit in front of a hole in the ice for hours on end and freeze to death. When you do finally catch a fish, you have pull it out of the water and get the hook out, which gets your hands wet. In normal conditions, that wouldn't be a problem, but when its freezing outside you really would prefer to keep your hands dry.

I remember distinctly thinking to myself, "Geez I'm bored!" After all, I was only nine and my ability to sit still and be quiet never lasted for more than five minutes at a time. So, I decided to get up and walk around. I was going to explore the lake while the rest of my family sat in front of the icy hole, half frozen.

I found myself probably a hundred yards out from my family at one point. They were far enough away that they looked like little ants huddled together. That's when I heard it. The Ice started cracking around me.

If you have ever been on ice when it starts to crack, you'll know that the sound is eerie enough to send shivers up your spine. The sound rippled through the cold air and I immediately stopped moving. Apparently the sound was loud enough that even my family could hear it. I could see them running towards me yelling at me to hold as still as I could... and then it happened. The ground underneath me gave way and I found myself falling into the coldest water I had ever felt. It was so cold, in fact, that my body went into instant shock and I felt like I had fallen into a bed of needles.

Luckily, my family was able to pull me out of the water and save my life. I spent the next few days in total shock and disbelief as I watched the color of my skin slowly return from blue to a pinkish hue.

If I could edit parts of my life, that event would definitely be deleted.

Our goal today is to set up a few safety nets within your business to catch you if you fall. I also want you to understand that you will most likely fall. Everyone does. We all make mistakes and poor choices and that's just part of doing business.

If you plan now for those moments ahead, you'll feel better knowing that you have a plan in place if something blows up in your face.

As you have probably guessed, setting up safety nets in business is really about ensuring that you have enough money to keep the doors open and pay the bills when something goes wrong.

Let's list some of the booby traps that may spring on you to give you an idea of why safety nets are important.

1. You may have a customer that goes bankrupt and can't pay you
2. You may get a fine or penalty from a governmental agency that you didn't foresee
3. You may get into a lawsuit

4. You may find yourself spending more money than you have, which is actually a common small business ailment
5. You may buy an expensive piece of equipment that doesn't work as planned

The list could really be endless. I tell you these things not to scare you, but to let you know that there are potholes in the road that you're traveling on now.

As long as you know they are there and you plan for them, you can get on with your journey in confidence.

Having a cash reserve of 3x operating costs

Many of today's top financial gurus help families get out of debt and get their budgets in order. One of the cardinal rules they push is to have three to five months of cash on hand.

What does this mean? It means that you need to add up your total monthly expenses, something you did in workshop 9 when you calculated your break-even point, and multiply that number by at least three. So, if it is going to cost you $5,000 a month to run your company which should include your payroll, you will need to have at least $15,000 of cash in the bank.

Obviously getting to three months of cash on hand is a big goal for almost any business, and yes, we want to avoid going into debt to get that money. The goal would be to save up that cash balance over time through current sales to customers.

This is one of those safety nets that takes time and patience. Determining how much cash you need is the first step. From there, you'll need to figure out how to set aside a little bit of money each month from your current sales. Put that money into a savings account and let it grow.

Once you do reach your goal of three months' worth of cash, you'll feel great knowing that you've reached your goal and that you have enough money to face a lot of the potholes you may encounter.

Some people ask me if they should keep saving money once they reach their goal. I would say that if you are able to pay yourself a proper wage and invest in the company to improve processes, then yes, continue saving if you have excess cash. However, if you can't pay yourself the right wage or invest in growth, start focusing your money on those areas next until they are functioning properly.

Diversifying your income streams

Who doesn't love the nest egg example? You know the one where your Uncle Joe taught you not to put all of your eggs into one basket? If possible, a great safety net in business is to try and figure out different ways to generate income within your company.

Avoid a business where you can only make money doing one thing. You'll probably remember that a key ingredient to a successful 8-Week Startup is the idea of focusing on doing something very well for a particular group of people. Am I feeding you conflicting information now? Not at all.

Let's look at an example.

Do you remember from a prior workshop when we talked about the sandwich shop down the road from my office that focuses on selling philly cheese steak sandwiches and meatballs? They do those two things really well, and as such, have a very strong fan base.

How could a company like that diversify its revenue streams without getting scatterbrained and offering a bunch of different services that would detract from what it does best?

Right now, the company makes money every time someone buys a sandwich. That's one revenue stream. Here are a few more they could consider:

- Leasing out the kitchen or other floor space during closed business hours to other entrepreneurs
- Providing a delivery service for a small fee
- Creating a partnership with local construction companies to provide their sandwich to the construction workers

Try to avoid making money through a single avenue of business. Take what you do well and figure out ways to expand upon that.

Avoiding one-off sales and focusing on recurring revenues

In Workshop 15, we discovered the art of recurring revenues. Once you figure out how to get recurring revenues, you will have created a huge safety net for yourself. Single purchases are no good by themselves. You want to try and figure out a way to get the customers coming back for more each and every month.

Once you have recurring revenues coming in, you'll better be able to forecast your cash flows and make confident decisions for your company.

Having a business with recurring revenues means that you have:

- A business that can consistently add value to your customers lives monthly, and not just once
- The ability to draft your customers' bank accounts for your fee monthly to avoid accounts receivable

If you haven't had the chance to do your homework from Workshop

15, go and do it. Taking the time to figure out how to get recurring revenues is absolutely necessary to making good money.

Avoiding unnecessary debt, but consider getting a line

Say it with me: "Debt is the black plague!" There, we've said it. I hate debt, and you should too. That doesn't mean that debt doesn't have its place in business, but it does mean that we need to treat it like the black plague.

You want to do your best to stay away from it if at all possible. Debt is contagious. Once you get a loan, you'll use it as a crutch making you lazy as a business owner.

Every time I talk to a new client at Ignite Spot, I can instantly tell if they have debt by the way that they speak to me. It's the businesses that are doing great, generating cash flow, and moving up the mountain that are debt-free. They don't have credit cards, loans, or anything else to chain them down. It's a beautiful thing. They have learned to run and grow their business in such a way that the customers finance the operations, not the bank.

At the same time, when I do speak with a business that is debt-laden, our conversations are always about how to get out of the hole and get their feet back under them. The entire tone of the discussion is different. It's miserable.

I will say, though, that getting a line of credit is a decent safety net for most companies. This is different from going out there and getting some $50,000 loan to start your business. A line of credit is when your bank gives you a limit on how much you can spend, say $5,000. When you open your line of credit, you don't have any debt with the bank until you draw on the line.

It's a beautiful safety net because when the unforeseen happens, you

370

have your line of credit as an absolute last resort to help bail you out.

A few things to note here:

1. If you do get a line of credit, know that even if you never draw any money against it, your credit report will still show that you have the ability to go into debt by the limit of the line of credit. This will have a negative effect on your credit report. However, as long as you only use the line of credit in dire emergencies and pay it back as soon as possible, your credit may actually improve from it.
2. As I said in #1, a line of credit is only for dire circumstances. Do not, I repeat, do not use it to buy office equipment or other things that your customers will pay for when they buy your product or service.
3. If you do decide to get a line of credit, know that your bank probably won't give you a very large cap at first. You may start off with an available line of $5,000. That's because your bank doesn't know how successful your business is going to be and they have been burned too many times by other entrepreneurs who use their lines of credit unwisely. As you get bigger and your relationship with your bank matures, you can increase your line's availability, if you would like.

Growing your company organically versus doing it with debt takes real skill. You have to be good with money and responsible to your goals and your business. That's one of the reasons that avoiding debt is so useful. It makes you a better entrepreneur.

The companies with debt coming out of their ears are paying interest and fees each month that are sinking their operations. If you can avoid the pothole of debt and interest expense, you'll be well ahead of the game.

As I mentioned earlier, debt does have a place in business. For some companies, they need a huge injection of cash to manufacture their product, hire a team, or whatever else it is that they are trying to accomplish. That's great for them. But remember that we are creating an 8-Week Startup, and we are building your first business to be light, profitable, and easy to start. If you want to start one of those companies that require a huge upfront capital investment, go for it as your second or third business. Just do it after your 8-Week Startup is up and profitable.

Action work: Set up some safety nets

We don't want you falling through the ice. We know that there are going to be potholes ahead. That's all right, because we are making a plan to get through them if needed. Today's homework is all about creating the safety nets that will catch you if and when you do fall.

1. Go back to Workshop 9 to remember how much cash your business is going to need each month to operate smoothly. Remember that this figure must include your monthly salary.
2. Multiply that number by three to get your three-month cash reserve.
3. Create a goal to save enough money to reach your three-month cash reserve within the first year of your business.
4. If you don't already have a savings account with your bank, create one and begin depositing your cash reserves there.
5. Return to Workshop 15 and complete the homework on setting up recurring revenues, if you haven't already done so.
6. Consider getting a line of credit with your bank.
7. Create a rule for yourself that says you will only use your line of credit for dire emergencies.

Great job today! If you got through your homework, you should have a plan in place to have a business that's protected from the boogie man. Make sure not to make this a mental exercise only. It's not enough to think that this is all a good idea and that you'll do it eventually.

It must be done today. Not tomorrow or next week. Get out there and create your safety nets now so that they will catch you when you need them.

WORKSHOP 37: How to Fire Your Boss

"Why do I want somebody to tell me what to do, tell me what I'm doing wrong? I want to be the boss."

- Bubba Watson

What it means to fire your boss

You may love your boss or you may not. I don't know. What I do know is that you do not want to work for your boss anymore. That's a fair guess on my part if you have made it all the way to the 37th workshop! Regardless of how you feel about your boss, the thought of resigning to dedicate all of your time and effort to your new-found business is literally where the rubber hits the road.

When the time comes for you to take this monumental step, you'll likely be feeling a lot of anxiety. That's because having a day job feels so much safer than being in charge of your own income. I am going to share something with you, though, and hopefully it will help ease the nerves.

One of the best parts about being an entrepreneur is that you are responsible for your success. If the ship sinks, it's because you made it sink. If it floats, you did that and nobody else. For me, and this is a reflection of my personality, I struggle with having a day job, not because I hate working for someone else, but because I'm not in control of my success. Someone else is. At any moment in time, the company could go out of business based on poor decisions that the boss makes, and who suffers? You do. Getting a raise, moving up the ladder, and crafting the lifestyle you want is largely due to how much your boss likes you and how well the company is doing. Even if the company were making millions and you were excelling in your job, you may never see the fruits of your labor if you rub your boss the wrong way.

That feels like a huge risk to me. Why spend your entire life in the hands of someone else? Aren't the rewards much bigger and more tangible if you're the key decision maker in your life?

As an entrepreneur, you get to wake up every day and be in control of how much money you make. There are very few people in this world with that kind of power. You are on the road to being one of them. It goes without saying that it takes a certain kind of person to live that kind of life. You have to be able to see positives, focus on learning and improving, and be willing to give up all of your inhibitions and step into the limelight.

Firing your boss is the first step toward saying, "I am going to be in charge of my life now. I fully accept the good and the bad that will come from this as products of my actions. If I work hard and smart, I'll be successful. If I let my fears keep me from speaking with people, selling, and getting out into the community, then I won't be."

Part of firing your boss requires you to accept such statements in their fullness. This is the point in the game where we draw a line in the sand and say, "Are you in or are you out?" You then are faced with the life-changing decision to stay where you are, or to cross that line and never look back. The best part is that it's completely up to you.

Getting your ducks in a row

Before you do fire your boss, we need to make sure that your ducks are in a row. We don't want you jumping off of a cliff without a parachute, now do we?

I would suggest creating a plan for firing your boss. To do this, you'll want to map out a few things including:

- How much your business will need to make in order to cover your bare bones salary
- How you will handle health insurance
- What loans you may need to acquire in your personal life including a mortgage, car, etc. Once you quit, it's going to be tough to get a loan for those necessities since you won't have a consistent W-2 paycheck from an established business.

Don't let these items become excuse for never starting your business. It's vital that you don't think to yourself, "Hey, we might be getting a home within the next year or two so I'll just wait until after that to get started." I'm going to be honest with you now and say that if you put off your business for a year or two, you'll probably never start.

The idea of getting your ducks in a row is all about focusing on the here and now to get life right so that you can start with less to worry about.

Many people consider moonlighting as a way to ease into their business and out of their day job. The thought here is that you go to work during the day, and you work on your company and service customers in the evening if possible. It's not a bad plan of action, but there are some serious things to consider:

1. Moonlighting is a great way to destroy your energy levels. Starting up a company is hard enough when you do it full time. To work a day job at the same time will zap your gumption.
2. Retaining the day job gives you a fall back. You end up thinking to yourself that if the business doesn't work, you always have your job. As a result, you don't put your heart and soul into your company.

3. There will eventually come a time where your new business needs you and you're going to have to quit your job. At that moment in time, you're going to have a fair amount of stress, since you'll likely be leaving in a rush. This means that you may not leave on good terms with your boss.

With all that being said, I'm not opposed to moonlighting. You just need to know the consequences. When I quit my job, I went cold turkey. I literally quit, and then began looking for clients while I was wrapping up my two weeks' notice. It was scary, but the benefit was that I had to make my business work. If I didn't, I would be able to support my family. That pressure forced me to put everything I had into my company and do whatever it took to get it going.

Whatever your personality type is, make sure that you give your business the best possible chance of succeeding by committing yourself to its growth.

Resign honestly and fairly

When the time does come for you to resign, you need to do so openly and fairly. Speak with your boss and tell him or her what's going on. It's likely that they will admire your gumption and try to offer support.

You want to be able to leave your job in good standing. The last thing that you want to do is burn this bridge. If for whatever reason your business does not work out, your boss may rehire you in the future.

As such, let him or her know that you appreciate everything that they have done for you and that you are grateful for their support.

Also, make this as easy on them as possible. Make yourself open and available to train your replacement, support the company in the transition, and provide supporting documentation. Do your very best to leave your job better than you found it.

Offer a 30 day flex plan

If it's at all possible, you may consider asking your boss if he or she will consider a 30-day plan to transition you out. The goal here would be that you would be able to have a more flexible schedule to focus on getting your business off of the ground while at the same time agreeing to do extra work in the evenings or on the weekends to help the company with the transfer. In this model, you really need to communicate how you will go above and beyond what a normal employee would do during a normal 2-week resignation period.

If your boss agrees to this, you need to realize that gift that he is giving you. He is allowing you to spend time during the day to get things rolling. That is a big sacrifice for him to make, so make it work for him.

What's the worst that could happen?

At the end of the day, what is the worst that could happen by quitting your job? I think that this is a valuable discussion to have because it actually makes taking the leap much easier.

Let's assume you quit your job and you start your business. If the planets don't align and your business tanks, you can always go back to a day job.

Sure, you'll lose some money along the way if that happens, but in the end you're going to be just fine. You're smart, hardworking, and capable. I know, because it takes that kind of person to consider doing what you are doing.

In order to make sure that you don't lose everything, I would suggest creating an "uncle" point. That's the point in the business where you yell "Uncle" if things get too painful. It's best to describe your uncle point in terms of dollars. How far depleted can you stand to see your savings account before enough is enough? However you measure it, set that point and then forget about it.

If your business does reach the uncle point, make an assessment. Does the business look like the potential is really there, or is it a total flop? If it's a total flop, exit gracefully and move on to the next chapter in your life. If it has potential and you can see how the business will be profitable, stick it out.

If you do have to return to a day job, you will walk away from all of this with accomplishment in knowing that you did it. You took a chance on yourself and you made the leap. Knowing that you were one of the few brave enough to do that is a serious accomplishment, and you should be proud.

Action work – Determine when you can fire the boss

Are you ready to let the rubber hit the road? It's time to create your boss-firing plan. Boost up your nerve and get started.

1. Recall from Workshop 9 what you calculated as your bare bones monthly salary.
2. Forecast when you believe your business will be breaking even, which includes paying your salary.
3. Can you moonlight until you reach break-even, or do you need to quit cold turkey? Describe your thinking:

_____

_____

_____

_____

_____

_____

_____

4. Describe what you will do for health insurance:

_____

_____

_____

_____

_____

_____

5. Determine your resignation date and put it on the calendar.

_____

_____

_____

_____

_____

6. Create a list of ways that you could go above and beyond in helping your current boss transition to your replacement if he will do a 30-day flex plan with you, so that you can spend time during the day to get your company rolling.

_____

_____

_____

_____

_____

Oh, to be an entrepreneur. Often the first step is the hardest. Once you take that step, you'll start running and you'll love the journey.

WORKSHOP 38: How to Get the Most from Your Grand Opening

"Look well to this day. Yesterday is but a dream and tomorrow is only a vision, but today well lived makes every yesterday a dream of happiness and every tomorrow a vision of hope. Look well therefore to this day."

- Francis Gray

What is a grand opening and what should you expect?

Not all grand openings are created equal. In fact, many grand openings aren't grand at all. Instead, they're more like subtle openings. The business owner will open the door, hang up a sign that says "Grand Opening," and then wait for the people to pour in. As you can probably guess, the crowds tend to never show up.

Why is this?

Getting a lot of people excited about your new business is challenging. That's because we are all living in our own busy little worlds, and although you have started a business, which is admirable, it's somewhat inconvenient to get away from work or our daily responsibilities to come and check it out.

Simply opening your doors and hanging up a sign will never be enough to have a great grand opening. Obviously there's more to this art of kicking off and we'll discuss a six-step plan that you can tackle to get the most out of your grand opening.

Before we do, I want to talk about expectations. It's important that you have a clear and realistic picture of what your grand opening will look like. Since we don't have hundreds of thousands of dollars to blow on hype advertising, expecting 5,000 people show up on the first day to check out your wares may be a little far-fetched.

What are your expectations for your first week in business? What would need to happen in order for you and your business to be successful? Let me give you a few examples of what I would consider to be a great grand opening.

1. The opening is supported strongly by those closest to you. Your family and friends all drop in sometime within the first week of your being open.
2. You get some decent press coverage that lets a larger group of people know about your store.
3. You get at least 100 people to become a part of your fan base. This is something we'll talk about in just a moment.
4. You generate enough sales during your one-week grand opening to cover your first month of expenses.
5. There is something unique about your grand opening that creates a draw for people and media.

If you have any other expectations, feel free to add them to the list.

Let's jump into the six-step plan on getting the most from your grand opening to see how we can accomplish all of this.

Step 1: Creating the draw

A good grand opening has a way to draw people into your store or onto your website. We need to determine what it is that you can offer that will get people to take some time out of their busy day to see what it is that you are up to.

Every time I think about creating draws, I always think of Chick-fil-A, the fast food restaurant that sells chicken sandwiches. They have created a program called "The First 100." Essentially, if you are one of the first 100 people to attend a grand opening, you win the right to get a free lunch every week for the next year.

Because of this draw, every Chick-fil-A grand opening usually has people camping out the night before. It's not uncommon to see tents and mass amounts of people hanging out in the parking lot. It creates a lot of buzz, press, and excitement for the business.

If we run the numbers, let's assume that Chick-fil-A incurs a cost of $2.5 for every meal they give away. That would mean that they would pay out a maximum of $2.5 multiplied by 52 weeks in a year equaling $130 per person. Since 100 people qualify, their total cost, spread out over a year would be approximately $13,000. That assumes that everyone will actually redeem his or her free meal every week for the entire year, which wouldn't be the case.

This draw reaps so many customers that the cost of the program is peanuts to the business. I love it.

In Workshop 2, we talked about the need to create a business that solves a specific problem for a specific group of people. I want you to remember to whom you are catering and what their problem is as you try and figure out what your draw will be at your grand opening.

What is important to these people? What one thing could you do that would make that group drop what they are doing and enter your world? Make the draw very specific and full of value to them.

This doesn't mean that you have to give away free merchandise. There are other ways to draw people into your business. Get creative and have fun with it.

Step 2: Getting the word out via friends and family

Once you know what your draw is going to be, it's up to you to invite everyone in your personal network to the grand opening. When you talk with them, get a commitment from them to come by and check out your new business.

Let me give you an example of what to say and what not to say.

This is an example of what not to say: "Bob, I just opened up a new business and we are having a grand opening this week. Why don't you stop by if you get a second?"

Here is an example of what you should say instead:

"Bob, I just opened up a new business and we are having a grand opening this week. We are doing a… (describe your draw for the people that attend the grand opening). Will you stop by this week to support us?" When he says yes, ask him if he would bring a few friends along as well. Again, these people are your family and friends, so it's all right to be bold with them. You need their help in order to have the best grand opening possible so don't be afraid to ask for it.

Step 3: Picking up some press

Approach your local newspapers and news stations to let them know about your grand opening. If your draw is interesting enough, they may do a story on you! If all you are doing is opening a store, they won't even bat their eyelashes your way.

Press comes in many forms including:

- Newspapers and television
- Blogging
- Radio

- Press releases that you write – I like prweb.com for my press releases

Step 4: Advertising the event

It's easy to blow a lot of money on advertising and get nothing out of it. Most advertising isn't targeted and, even worse, doesn't communicate a clear draw.

Since you are focused on a specific group of people and their problem, you need to determine how you can reach that group of people effectively. How do they consume information? Do they read the newspaper, spend hours a day on Facebook, blog, listen to the radio, or do they get their information from people in their networks? Where do they go and what do they do when they get there?

It is up to you to determine the best way to reach your group with as little money as possible. Set aside a budget for advertising. As we mentioned in earlier workshops, a large part of your $5,000 setup money really should be used to get customers. Set aside some of those funds to create your targeted advertising campaign.

Some options for advertising might include:

- Placing an ad in a targeted magazine that your audience reads
- Sending out direct mail to your target audience
- Adverting on Facebook to anyone that fits your target audience profile
- Posting on chat boards and forums where your audience hangs out

Avoid blanket advertising. It's expensive and has a very low response rate. A good example of this would be a billboard. Sure, tons of people see it, but it will cost you a ton of money and you won't get a huge response from it.

It may also help to consult with your mentors on this one. Ask them for ideas on advertising that will fit within your budget and reach your targeted audience.

Step 5: Having an end goal in mind

Earlier we talked about having proper expectations for your grand opening. What would you like to see come from your grand opening? After one week in business, what needs to be achieved in order for you to feel like it was a successful event?

This is actually an important step not to skip over. Visualizing what the end result will be will help you to determine what you need to do to get there.

Never open a business without a clear visualization of what you want to have happen.

Step 6: Getting ready to capture leads for your fan base

When people do visit your business or your website, what will you do to make the most of that interaction?

My suggestion is that you give them a way to become fans of your business. I would try and capture their contact information for future promotions and events. To do that, you could have each visitor sign up to become a member when they visit. In exchange for their personal information, they could be entered into whatever draw you created for your grand opening.

What to do if you don't have a physical location

You may not have a physical location for your business and that's just fine. As long as people have the ability to view a website or something similar, you can still have a virtual grand opening. If this is the case, make sure that your draw can be communicated to them without you being present.

For example, on your website, you may want to make the draw the first thing that your potential customers see. Create the offer and request that they submit their contact information in order to be a part of the draw.

Your website will also need to be strong enough to entice tire-kickers to look around and do some shopping. That's the difficult part of not having a physical location. Since you won't be present to entice them to buy, your marketing materials need to be strong enough to help out.

Action work: Hold your grand opening!

Get ready to launch your business! You have finally made it. You are nearing the end of the workshop series and you have a lot of exciting things coming up! Good for you, and good job on all of the hard work you have put into this so far.

Now, let's do a grand opening. Here is your homework.

1. What could you do as a draw during you grand opening that would be interesting and valuable to your target audience?

    _____
    _____
    _____
    _____
    _____

_____
_____
_____

2. Decide when your grand opening will be.

3. Reach out to all of your family and friends and commit them to coming during the first week of your grand opening.

4. What media outlets will you approach to try to get free press? Make sure that your draw is interesting enough to get them to send a reporter out to cover it.

_____
_____
_____
_____
_____
_____
_____
_____

5. What is the best way to communicate your grand opening and your draw through advertising to your target audience? Describe why that is so.

_____
_____
_____
_____
_____
_____
_____
_____

6. Describe your expectations for your grand opening. What you do want to get from the experience?

_____

_____

_____

_____

_____

_____

_____

7. How will you capture your visitors' contact information and add them to your fan base for future promotions and events?

_____

_____

_____

_____

_____

_____

_____

8. If you do not have a physical location, how will you ensure that your website entices them to take advantage of the draw, as well as shop with you?

_____

_____

_____

_____

_____

_____

_____

Congratulations on getting ready to open your new business! This is an exciting day for both of us. I am proud of you for getting this far in your journey. Your grand opening is an exciting event that will require a lot from you, but provide great dividends down the road. Remember that it's not enough to simply open your doors and hang up a sign that says "Grand Opening." If that's all you do, nobody will ever care.

WORKSHOP 39: What to Expect the First Year

"Accept the challenges so that you can feel the exhilaration of victory."

- General George S. Patton

The first year of your company's life is going to be a bit of a roller coaster. If I told you it was all going to be honey and roses, I would be lying. Challenges will come, but if you love your business enough, you'll be able to scale those challenges, overcome them, and become stronger for them.

What's really happening is that you are going to need time to get used to this new lifestyle. Your old life was dictated by a boss. You showed up to work and, for roughly eight hours, he or she told you what to do. There was probably little decision-making on your behalf.

Your new life however is unlimited. You can choose to go left or right, to sleep in or to get up early and make the most of your day. You can choose to discontinue a particular product, hire an employee, or change your marketing campaigns. In essence, everything has now become a choice and you are the person that has to decide yes or no. This new lifestyle takes some getting used to.

Because of all of your new-found power, you must absolutely become a master of yourself, your time, and your emotions. You must become the kind of person that elevates your game to Olympic standards. You have to become that guy or girl that would rather focus on making the business better than plopping on the couch and watching television aimlessly at night.

For some, this may require a huge shift of change in behavior. Will it always be this way? Well... Yes. Here's why. During the first year of your business, your company really needs you. You'll have a lot of late nights and you'll be fine with it, because of your excitement for where you are headed in life.

After the business is working well, you'll have the ability to choose to keep up with this lifestyle or to start watching television again. I'm willing to bet that you'll see how far you've come and what your new business has done for your life. Just looking at that will change you into a television-hating entrepreneurial mega-mind. I could be wrong, but when people experience success, they see how much fun it is and they become the kind of people that seek more achievement rather than reverting back to old habits.

I will say this... Some days are easier than others. Here's why:

Managing the emotions

You can often be your biggest enemy as a business owner. Your emotions can completely derail you if you let them. For some people, this will be a bigger challenge than others. You know yourself better than anyone else on this planet and you need to be honest when I ask you the following question.

"How do you deal with change and potential stress?"

Are you the kind of person that thrives on challenge or do you internalize it and emotionally stew on things for hours or even days? If you stew, you need to get that under control.

I remember when I had just started my accounting firm. Things were going great and then a fairly large financial blow hit the company. I immediately went into a woe-is-me mindset. However, I remember sitting up straight and saying out loud, "I don't have time to sit here and worry about it." With that, I put my head back on, and got back in the game.

Within a few days, I was able to reverse the damage and we were back on track. Had I stewed for days, I don't think I could have made it.

In business, there is no place for emotional imbalance. You really do need to pull yourself together and smile. You need to learn to get out there with your best foot forward and make it a great day even if you were just kicked in the gut.

One of the cardinal rules of business is this: Nobody, other than your family, has time to care that you had a bad day. It does you no good to wallow in the muck, because there's no money to be made down there. If you can muster up your courage, put on a smile, and have a great time doing it (even if you're just pretending, and yes, I pretend quite a bit too), you will be able to wear your entrepreneur name tag with pride. Your business will pull through because you have the passion to see it through.

Dealing with the finances

When the money goes south, don't freak out. Take a deep breath, return to the 12-month cash flow forecast that we did in Workshop 13, and adjust your income and expenses until you have a plan for getting back onto the cart. Once you understand what expenses you need to cut and how much revenue you need to generate, go and do it.

Again, you don't have time to hit the panic button. If you can keep your head together and determine what needs to be done, you'll make it happen.

Managing your time

There will be late nights. I can guarantee you that. Embrace them. You're building a business and it will be worth it. At the same time though, I don't advocate staying up until 2 a.m. just to feel like you are a dedicated entrepreneur. If you need to do that occasionally, then get it done. For me, it's more important to have a balanced day and get plenty of sleep, so that I can be effective the next day.

For many of you who have families, this one may be a little tough. I have children of my own, so I completely understand where you're coming from when you say that you want to spend time with your kids.

My response to that is that you absolutely must spend time with your family. Never sacrifice them to the needs of your business. If you do, you'll only be adding more stress to your plate.

My kids go to sleep around 8:30 in the evening. They're still pretty young. In order to make things work, here is the schedule that I tend to follow:

6:00 a.m. to 7:30 a.m. - Eat a great breakfast and go to the gym

7:30 a.m. to 8:00 a.m. – Get ready for the day

8:00 a.m. to 9:00 a.m. – Set goals for the day and read business and sales books

9:00 a.m. to 12:00 p.m. – Work on the company

12:00 p.m. to 1:00 p.m. – Lunch with the family and play time

1:00 p.m. to 5:00 p.m. – Work on the company

5:00 p.m. to 8:30 p.m. – Focus on my family

8:30 p.m. to 10:30 p.m. – Work on the company

10:30 p.m. – Go to bed

If I were you, I would get up early, exercise every day, set aside time to focus on your family, and get to bed early when possible.

Keep the communication channels open

Don't walk this road alone. You have a lot of support all around you and I suggest that you rely on it. There is never anything wrong with asking for help.

The most important people in your support group are your spouse and your mentors. Make sure to talk with them, keep them updated on what's going on, and more importantly turn to them for ideas, support, and encouragement. These are the people that truly care about you and will be your cheerleader section when you need them the most.

Entrepreneurs often paint pictures of themselves as lone wolves. They feel like they have gone out on this limb and need to fly all by themselves. They couldn't be more wrong. Relying on family and friends will keep you bolstered and smiling when the challenges come. Trust me, you don't want to face the challenges on your own.

Keeping the vision in play

The most important thing that you can do for yourself is to keep your vision in play. Never forget why you are building your company. If you remember from the first workshop, I had you write down 25 reasons why you wanted to start this business. Post that list somewhere, so that you'll always see it.

I want that list to be a constant reminder of why you need to stick with it and give it your very best.

If you lose sight of your vision, all will be lost. It's at that point that this becomes a day job, but the worst part is that you can't unload all of your problems onto your boss anymore.

With your vision clearly in mind, you'll wake up every day shaking with excitement to earn the life that you deserve.

Growing this company means freedom for you and your family. It means wealth, a sense of accomplishment, and the ability to do what you want with your life instead of always being told what to do.

Being a business owner is the greatest opportunity in the world. Don't be one of those people standing on the side of the road that lets the opportunity pass you by. Reach out and seize it with everything you've got. You'll be happy that you did.

Action work: Get ready for an amazing year!

We have talked about a lot of intangible things today. Let's leave this workshop with a good understanding of how you will meet year one head-on, with a smile.

1. Hang up the list of 25 reasons for starting this company that you created in Workshop 1.
2. Craft your daily schedule to fit your personality and needs. Ensure that you have scheduled time for your health, sleep, and the most important people in your life. The rest of the time should be dedicated to launching your company.
3. Take a hard look at yourself and determine how you will handle the emotions that you'll face. Will you be able to move on, or will you be a total mess? If you're the kind of person that doesn't do well with emotional stress, find a way to control those feelings now before they get out of check.
4. Ensure that you are keeping the communication channels open with your spouse and mentors. Find a way to keep

speaking with them about your successes, failures, emotions, and everything else that fills your entrepreneurial brain.

I just want to say that I am so proud of you for getting this far. In the last chapter, we are going to talk about The Entrepreneurs' Club in greater detail. For those of you who need additional support beyond these workshops, I would love to have you join the club and continue your growth and learning experience.

WORKSHOP 40: The Entrepreneur's Club

"Develop a passion for learning. If you do, you will never cease to grow."

- Anthony J. D'Angelo

Well, you've done it! By this point, you should have a business that is fully capable of opening its doors and generating income for you and your family.

Have we covered everything that one would need to know in order to run a business? Of course not. There's simply too much information to put into the program. Besides, you'll probably walk away from these workshops with a slew of questions that no amount of writing on my part would be able to address. That's because everyone that takes the workshops will come from different backgrounds, be starting different businesses, and have different strategies to implement.

That's why I have created The Entrepreneur's Club. My vision for doing so is to provide a place for new and growing entrepreneurs to meet with each other, myself, and other seasoned entrepreneurs to cover the material in the workshops, answer your questions, and give you that helping hand.

The Entrepreneur's Club is a Members Only space on the website dedicated to helping you succeed. If you do decide to join the club, here's what you can expect:

Weekly master classes online classes

Each week, you'll have the opportunity to attend a live class online that will cover one of the 40 workshops in detail. Each class will last 60 minutes and will be presented by me or a member of the staff. You will have the ability to ask questions as they relate to your personal business as well as interact with other class members.

Don't worry if you can't make the class. Every one of them will be recorded and available to you in the Members Only section of the website. That way, you can attend the class on your own schedule and still get those most out of your membership.

Entrepreneurs interviews

I thoroughly enjoy learning from other entrepreneurs. I love interviewing them to see what it is that they do well. As part of your membership, you'll have access to these recorded sessions with some of the best entrepreneurs I know.

Monthly footnotes

At the beginning of each month, you'll receive the Members Only Footnotes. It's our monthly newsletter summarizing new tips and tricks for growing your business, as well as information on upcoming member's only classes.

How to join The Entrepreneur's Club

If you feel like ongoing support and education will be valuable to your growing business, head over to the8weekstartup.com and upgrade to a premium monthly membership.

Well, this is it!

Every book must come to an end, and for us this is the end of the road... At least on paper. If you do decide to participate in the online forums at the8weekstartup.com or even join The Entrepreneur's Club, I would love to hear about your success!

I wish you the very best in your entrepreneurial endeavors and want to remind you that anything worth doing in this life will require the best of you, and that's how you know you're on the right track.

Create your business and build the life you deserve!

ABOUT THE AUTHOR

Eddy Hood is the CEO of Ignite Spot, a business consulting and accounting firm. He has helped hundreds of businesses owners throughout the world grow their organizations. He is also a nationwide franchisor who helps business consultants start their own practice. Eddy is also a serial entrepreneur and winner of Junto, an entrepreneurs contest held in Salt Lake City, UT.